I0128378

John Henry Newman, Lewis Edwards Gates

Selections from the Prose Writings

Ed. with notes and an introd. by Lewis E. Gates

John Henry Newman, Lewis Edwards Gates

Selections from the Prose Writings
Ed. with notes and an introd. by Lewis E. Gates

ISBN/EAN: 9783337370121

Printed in Europe, USA, Canada, Australia, Japan

Cover: Foto ©Thomas Meinert / pixelio.de

More available books at **www.hansebooks.com**

SELECTIONS

FROM THE PROSE WRITINGS OF

JOHN HENRY CARDINAL NEWMAN

Edited with
Notes and an Introduction

BY

LEWIS E. GATES
Instructor in English, Harvard University

NEW YORK
HENRY HOLT AND COMPANY
1895

PREFACE.

At just this time, when prose is apt to be either over refined and euphuistic on the one hand, or lawless and even barbarous on the other, there seems special reason for trying to make more accessible and popular the writings of Cardinal Newman. No style is more fit than Cardinal Newman's to be a model for those who are anxious to avoid all extravagance and yet to escape mediocrity. And it is with the hope of offering to the lovers of literature who are convinced of this fact a convenient means of making Newman's style better known, that the editor has put together this volume of Selections.

But there is another object which the volume has in view; the Selections are chosen for matter as well as for style. They are meant, after a few introductory passages of general interest, to give something like a connected account in Newman's own words of his theory of life and of his justification of it. There are special reasons why that theory should be known connectedly and completely to American readers. In the new world we are for the most part radical, Protestant,

iii

scientific, untraditional, and lacking in perspective and in atmosphere. Newman is intensely conservative, almost mystical, Romantic, mediæval, and everywhere alive to the imaginative splendor and power of the past. Now it is undoubtedly difficult for any one who is permeated with the modern spirit which has such free play in America, who accepts unhesitatingly its postulates, and looks at all things unquestioningly from its point of view, to comprehend how a man of real mental power, of broad and far-reaching historical knowledge, of keen intellect and piercingly certain logical method, can have held in these days of science, the ideas about religion and about life that Newman adhered to. To comprehend this is for the modern man difficult, if he has not the time to run through many volumes, and to bring into connected form the different parts of an elaborate system. The present volume aims to do this work in an unpretentious manner for the ordinary reader, and to give him, without technicalities of philosophy or theology, a fairly adequate statement, in Newman's own words, of his most characteristic ideas. With these ideas before him, the reader is left to suit himself in the matter of accepting or rejecting Newman's conclusions. The important point is that Newman's doctrine be at any rate thoroughly understood; perhaps it will have to be transcended, but it ought not to be ignorantly disregarded or put aside with a sneer.

The Introduction deals for the most part with Newman's style and rhetorical methods; the last chapter points out the relation of his work to certain character-

CONTENTS

INTRODUCTION

I.

NEWMAN's style unites in an exceptional degree the qualities of an academic style with those of the style of a man of the world. It has the accuracy, the precision of outline, and the fine conscientiousness of the scholar's style, as well as the ease, the affability, and the winning adroitness that come from much human intercourse. In its union of scholarliness and urbanity it is unique. The style of another Oxford man, whose work almost necessarily suggests itself for comparison with that of Newman, attempts very much this same combination of qualities. Matthew Arnold's ideal of good writing involves, like Newman's, a perfect union of strength and grace. But Arnold is never comparable to Newman in strictness and certainty of method; he is always so afraid of pedantry and scholasticism as to assume even greater desultoriness than is natural to him. His urbanity, too, has not quite the genuineness of Newman's; it is a somewhat costly affair. He prides himself on it too palpably. He is too consciously debonair. There is always a suspicion of self-assertion in his work that does more to detract from perfect grace of demeanor than a great deal of severity of method and strenuousness of logic would detract. In Newman's writings, even in his most personal works and in his most intimate moments, there is a curious lack of this self-assertion. Probably no book so uncompromisingly autobiographical as the *Apologia* seems from first to last so free from egotism and leaves so charming an impression of frankness and simplicity.

It is, nevertheless, not strange that among a people like the English, intensely suspicious of manner and affectedly straightforward, Newman's adroitness and grace should have exposed him to some unpleasant charges of insincerity. It is so easy for a bluff, downright man to misinterpret subtlety as duplicity, and to rebuke reticence and indirectness as deceit and hypocrisy. This is substantially what Kingsley did in his famous attack upon Newman. He had an instinctive dislike of Newman's sinuousness and suppleness, and without pausing to analyze very carefully, he spoke out fiercely against Newman's whole work as containing a special variety of ecclesiastical hypocrisy. The charge was the more plausible inasmuch as there is unquestionably a certain debased ecclesiastical manner whose cheaply insinuating suavity might, by hasty observers, be confused with Newman's bearing and style. Yet the injustice of this confusion and the unfairness of Kingsley's charges become plain after a moment's analysis.

In spite of Newman's ease and affability, you feel, throughout his writings, when you stop to consider, an underlying suggestion of uncompromising strength and unwavering conviction. You are sure that the author is really giving you himself frankly and unreservedly, notwithstanding his apparent self-effacement, and that he is imposing upon you his own conclusions, persuasively and constrainingly. Moreover, you are sure that, however adroitly he may be developing his thesis, with an eye to the skilful manipulation of your prejudices, he would at any moment give you a point-blank answer, if you put him a point-blank question. There is never any real doubt in your mind of his courage and manly English temper, or of his readiness to meet you fairly on the grounds of debate. In the last analysis, it is this fundamental sincerity of tone and this all-pervasive but unobtrusive self-assertion that preserve Newman's style from the undue flexibility and the insincerity of the debased ecclesiastical style, just as his unfailing good taste preserves him from its cheap suavity or unctuousness.

But the adroitness of Newman's methods has led to still more serious charges than those of Kingsley. In a general examination of Newman's theories, Mr. E. A. Abbott [1] has accused him of systematically doctoring or medicating the truth, and of having elaborated, though perhaps unconsciously, various ingenious methods for inveigling unsuspecting readers into the acceptance of doubtful propositions. For these methods Mr. Abbott has devised satirical names, the Art of Lubrication, the Art of Oscillation, the Art of Assimilation; he does not assert that Newman consciously palters with truth, or tries to make the worse appear the better reason. But he urges that Newman was constitutionally fonder of other things than of

[1] *Philomythus*, by E. A. Abbott, London, 1891.

truth, that he desired, with an overmastering strength, to establish certain conclusions, and that he persuaded himself of their correctness by a series of manœuvres which really involved insincere logic.

Of the details of Mr. Abbott's criticisms this is not the place to speak. But the ultimate cause of his attack on Newman seems once more to be temperamental hostility rather than anything else, an utter inability to comprehend, or, at any rate, to tolerate Newman's mental constitution and his resulting methods of conceiving of life and relating himself to its facts. Truth is to Newman a much subtler matter, a much more elusive substance, than it is to the Positivist, to the mere intellectual dealer in facts and in figures; it cannot be packed into syllogisms as pills are packed into a box; it cannot be conveyed into the human system with the simple directness which the Laputa wiseacre aimed at who was for teaching his pupils geometry by feeding them on paper duly inscribed with geometrical figures. Moreover, language is an infinitely treacherous medium; words are so "false," so capable of endless change, that he is "loath to prove reason with them." And readers, too, are widely diverse, and are susceptible to countless other appeals than that of sheer logic. For all these reasons it is doubtless the case that Newman is constantly studious of effect in his writings; that he is intensely conscious of his audience; and that he is always striving to win a way for his convictions, and aiming to insinuate them into the minds and hearts of his hearers by gently persuasive means.

But all this by no means implies any real careless-

ness of truth on Newman's part, or any trade of
truth to expediency. Truth is difficult attain-
ment, and hard to transmit; all the strenuously does Newman set himself to trace out in its
obscurity and remoteness, and to reveal in all its
intricacies. Moreover, subtle and elusive as it may
be, it is nevertheless something tangible and describ-
able and defensible; something, furthermore, of the
acquisition of which Newman can give a very definite
account; something as far as possible from mere
misty sentiment, and something, furthermore, to be
strenuously asserted and defended.

Now a fair-minded reader of Newman is always
conscious of the essential mental integrity of his
author, of his courage and readiness to be frank,
even in those passages or in those words where the
search for the subtlest shades of truth or the desire
to avoid clashing needlessly on prejudice, or the wish
to win a favorable hearing takes the author most indirectly and tortuously toward his end. It is this
underlying manliness of mind and frank readiness to
give an account of himself that prevent Newman's
prevailing subtlety, adroitness, and suavity from leaving on the mind of an unprejudiced reader any impression of timorousness or disingenuousness.

II.

IN what has been said of Newman's realization of
the elusive nature of truth and of the great difficulty
of securing a welcome for it in the minds and hearts

of the mass of men lies the key to what is most distinctive in his methods. He was a great rhetorician,
and whatever he produced shows evidence on analysis
of having been constructed with the utmost niceness
of instinct and deftness of hand. He himself frankly
admitted his rhetorical bent. Writing to Hurrell
Froude in 1836, about the management of the Tractarian agitation, he says : " You and Keble are the philosophers, and I the rhetorician." [1]   And in a somewhat
earlier letter he speaks of his aptitude for rhetoric in
even stronger terms : " I have a vivid perception of the
consequences of certain admitted principles, have a
considerable intellectual capacity of drawing them out,
have the refinement to admire them, and a rhetorical
or histrionic power to represent them." [2]

This rhetorical skill was partly natural and instinctive, and partly the result of training. From his
earliest years as a student Newman had been conspicuous for the subtlety and flexibility of his intelligence, for his readiness in assuming for speculat-
ive purposes the most diverse points of view, and
for his insight into temperaments and his comprehension of their modifying action on the white light of
truth. With this admirable equipment for effective
rhetorical work, he came directly under the influence
in Oriel College of two exceptionally great rhetoricians,
Dr. Copleston, for many years Provost of Oriel, and
Whately, one of its most influential Fellows. Copleston was a famous controversialist and dialectician
who had long been regarded as the chief champion of

---

[1] *Letters and Correspondence of J. H. Newman,* 1891, II. 156.
[2] *Ibid.,* I. 416.

the University against the attacks of outsiders. His *Advice to a young Reviewer with a Specimen of the Art*, (1807), had turned into ridicule the airs and pretensions of the young Edinburgh Reviewers and had led them into severe strictures on University methods, against which attacks, however, Dr. Copleston had vigorously defended Oxford in various publications to the satisfaction of all University men. He was the Provost of Oriel during the first year of· Newman's residence there, and suggestions of the influence of his ideas and methods are to be found throughout the early pages of the *Apologia* and the *Autobiographical Memoir*. Still more decisive, however, was the influence of a yet more famous rhetorician, Dr. Whately, whose lectures on Logic and on Rhetoric remained almost down to the present day standard text-books on those subjects. Whately was also renowned as a controversialist, and his *Historic Doubts concerning Napoleon Bonaparte* was perhaps the cleverest and most famous piece of ironical argumentation produced in England during the first quarter of the century. Newman, for several of his most impressionable years, was intimately associated with Whately. " He emphatically opened my mind," Newman says in the *Apologia,* " and taught me to think and to use my reason." [1] Under the influence of these two masters of rhetoric and redoubtable controversialists Newman's natural aptitude for rhetorical methods was encouraged and fostered, so that he became a perfect adept in all the arts of exposition and argumentation and persuasion.

[1] *Apologia*, p. 11.

Whatever work of Newman's, then, **we take** up, we may be sure that its construction will repay careful analysis. In trying to present any set of truths Newman was always consciously confronting a delicate psychological problem; he was perfectly aware of the elements that entered into the problem; he knew what special difficulties he had to face because of the special nature of the truth he was dealing with,—its abstractness, or its complexity, or its novelty. He had measured also the precise degree of resistance he must expect because of the peculiar prejudices or preoccupations of his readers. And the shape which his discussion finally took,—the particular methods that he followed,—were the result of a deliberate adaptation of means to ends; they were the methods that his trained rhetorical instinct and his insight into the truth he was handling and into the temperaments and intelligences he was to address himself to dictated as most likely to persuade.

Of course, ordinarily Newman does not explain the method he follows or comment on the difficulties of his problem. In the *Apologia*, however, he has departed from this rule. In the *Preface* to this self-justificatory piece of writing, he takes his readers into his confidence,—plainly with a purpose,—sets forth the prejudices against which he must make his way, considers the possibility of this course or that as likely to attain his end, notes the precise considerations that ultimately govern his choice, and is explicit as to the elaborate plan which underlies and controls the seeming desultoriness of the discussion.

Newman's account of the problem which in this case

confronted him will be found on pages 69–82 of the
Selections. Briefly, he had been charged by Kingsley
with teaching "lying on system." He had protested
vigorously against the charge and had obtained a
half-hearted apology. Later, however, the charge had
been reiterated more formally and with the added
taunt that as Newman recommended systematic dissimulation no one could be expected to accept his self-
exculpating word. These charges fell in precisely, as
Newman recognized, first, with the general trend of
British prejudice against Roman Catholics, and secondly
with the particular prejudice against Newman himself
that sprang from his early attempts to make the Anglican Church more Catholic, and his subsequent seces-
sion to Rome. How, then, was Newman to persuade
the public of Kingsley's injustice and his own innocence? He saw at once that to deal with each separate charge would be mere waste of time; to prove
that in a special case he had not lied or recommended
lying would carry him no whit toward his end, as
long as contemptuous distrust remained the dominant
mood of the British mind towards himself and his
party. First of all, he must conquer this mood; he
must overthrow the presumption against him, and
win for his cause at least such an unbiassed hearing as
is accorded to the ordinary man upon trial whose
record has been hitherto clean; then, he might hope
to secure for his particular denials a universal scope.
The method that he chose in order to win his readers
was admirably conceived. He would put himself
vitally and almost dramatically before them; he would
bring them within the actual sound of his voice and

2

the glance of his eye ; he would let them follow him through the long course of his years as student, tutor, preacher, and leader, and come to know him as intimately as those few friends had known him with whom he had lived most freely. Then, he would ask his readers, when he had put his personality before them in its many shifting but continuous aspects, and with all the intense persuasiveness of a dramatic portrayal, whether they were ready to believe of the man they had thus watched through the round of his duties that he was a liar. Of the peculiar power which Newman could count on exerting in thus appealing to his personal charm he was, of course, unable to speak in his *Preface.* In truth, however, he was having recourse to an influence which had always been potent whenever it had a chance to make itself felt. Throughout his life at Oxford it was true of his relations to others that "friends unasked, unhoped" had "come,"—all men who met him falling almost inevitably under the sway of his winning and commanding personality. Newman was therefore well advised when he resolved to reveal himself to the world and to trust to the conciliating effect of this self-revelation to prepare for his specific denial of Kingsley's charges.

In accordance with this purpose and plan, the *Apologia pro Vita Sua*, or History of his Religious Opinions, was written ; and for these reasons his answer to certain definite charges of equivocation and systematic and elaborate misrepresentation was so shaped as to include in its scope the story of his whole life. Of the 289 pages of the *Apologia*, only the last 15 pages are devoted to the actual refutation of Kingsley's charges ;

the preceding 274 pages are all indirectly persuasive, and simply prepare the way for the final defence. Probably in no other piece of writing is the actual demonstration so curiously small in proportion to the means that are taken to make the logic effective. Of course, it may be urged in reply to this view of the construction of the *Apologia*, that to look at the book as purely a reply to Kingsley, is to judge it from an arbitrary and artificial point of view, and hence to distort it inevitably and throw its parts out of proportion ; that the real aim of the book was simply and sincerely autobiographic, and that regarding the book as frank autobiography, the critic need find nothing strange in the proportioning of its parts. In answer to this objection, it should be noted that the last few pages of the book deal directly and argumentatively with the Kingsley episode, and thus point the purpose with which all that precedes has been written ; and that Newman himself has declared in his *Preface* that the sole reason for his self-revelations is his wish to clear away misconceptions, to win once again the confidence of that English public that had long been distrustful of him, and to make widely effective his refutation of Kingsley's charges. The book, then, is fairly to be described as an enormously elaborate and ingenious piece of special pleading to prepare the way for a few syllogisms that have now become grotesquely insignificant.

It has been worth while to lay great stress on this disproportion between persuasion and demonstration in the *Apologia*, because this disproportion illustrates, with almost the over-emphasis of caricature, certain of Newman's fundamental beliefs and resulting tricks of method. First and foremost, it illustrates the slight esteem in which he held the formal logic of the schools and syllogistic demonstrations. Not that he failed to recognize the value of analysis and logical demonstration as verifying processes; but he unhesitatingly subordinated these processes to those by which truth is originally won, and to those also by which truth is persuasively inculcated.

In a sermon on *Implicit and Explicit Reason*, he distinguishes with great elaborateness between the method by which the mind makes its way almost intuitively to the possession of a new truth or set of truths, and the subsequent analysis by which it takes account of this half-instinctive original process and renders the moments of the process self-conscious and articulate. His description of the intellect delicately and swiftly feeling its way toward truth, may well be quoted entire: "The mind ranges to and fro, and spreads out and advances forward with a quickness which has become a proverb, and a subtlety and versatility which baffle investigation. It passes on from point to point, gaining one by some indication; another on a probability; then availing itself of an association; then falling back on some received law; next seizing on testimony; then committing itself to some popular impression, or some inward instinct, or some obscure memory; and thus it makes progress not unlike a clamberer on a steep cliff, who, by quick eye, prompt hand, and firm foot, ascends, how he knows not himself, by personal endowments and by practice, rather than by rule, leaving no track behind him, and unable to teach another. It is not too much to say that the stepping by which great geniuses scale the mountain of truth is as unsafe and precarious to men in general as the ascent of a skilful mountaineer up a literal crag. It is a way which they alone can take ; and its justification lies alone in their success. And such mainly is the way in which all men, gifted or not gifted, commonly reason—not by rule, but by an inward faculty. Reasoning, then, or the exercise of reason, is a living, spontaneous energy within us, not an art." [1]

But not only is syllogistic reasoning not the original process by which truth is attained; it is in no way essential to the validity or completeness of the process. "Clearness in argument certainly is not indispensable to reasoning well. Accuracy in stating doctrines or principles is not essential to feeling and acting upon them. The exercise of analysis is not necessary to the integrity of the process analyzed. The process of reasoning is complete in itself, and independent." [2]

Finally, logical demonstration has relatively little value as a means of winning a hearing for new truth, of securing its entrance into the popular consciousness, and of giving it a place among the determining powers of life. "Logic makes but a sorry rhetoric with the multitude; first shoot round corners, and you may not despair of converting by a syllogism." [3] Men must be inveigled into the acceptance of truth ; they cannot be driven to accept it at the point of the syllogism. "The heart is commonly reached, not through

---

[1] *Oxford University Sermons*, ed. 1887, p. 257.

[2] *Ibid.*, ed. 1887, p. 259.

[3] *Selections*, p. 97.

the reason, but through the imagination, by means of
direct impressions, by the testimony of facts and
events, by history, by description. Persons influence
us, voices melt us, looks subdue us, deeds inflame
us." [1]

The application of all this,—particularly of what
Newman says touching the persuasiveness of a personal
appeal,—to the whole method of the *Apologia*, hardly
needs pointing out. The work is, from first to last,
intensely personal in its tone and matter, pursuasive
because of its concreteness, its dramatic vividness, the
modulations of the speaker's voice, the sincerity and
dignity of his look and bearing. Logic, of course,
gives coherence to the discussions. The processes of
thought by which Newman moved from point to point
in his theological development, are consistently set
forth; but the convincing quality of the book comes
from its embodiment of a life, not from its systemat-
ization of a theory.

In accordance with this general character of the
book is its tone throughout; its style is the perfection
of informality and easy colloquialism. Now and then, in
describing his ideas on specially complicated questions,
Newman makes use of numbered propositions, and
proceeds for the time being with the precaution and
precision of the dialectician. But for the most part he
is as unconstrained and apparently fortuitous in his
presentation of ideas as if he were merely emulating
Montaigne in confidential self-revelation, and had no
ulterior controversial purpose in view. Perhaps no

---

[1] *Selections*, p. 96.

writer has surpassed, or even equalled, Newman in combining apparent desultoriness of treatment with real definiteness of purpose and clairvoyance of method.

III.

ANOTHER admirable example of Newman's least formal, and perhaps most characteristic method, may be found in his series of papers on the *Rise and Progress of Universities*. Here again there is apparent desultoriness, or at most a careless following of historical sequence. One after another, with what seems like a hap-hazard choice, Newman describes a half-dozen of the most famous Universities of the past, explains popularly their organization, methods, and aims, entertaining the reader meanwhile with such superlative pieces of rhetoric as the description of Attica and Athens (*Selections*, p. 3) and with such dramatic episodes as that of Abelard. Yet underneath this apparent caprice runs the controlling purpose of putting the reader in possession, through concrete illustrations, of the complete idea of a typically effective University. Each special school that Newman describes illustrates some essential attribute of the ideal school; and incidentally, as it were, the reader who is all the time beguiled, from chapter to chapter, by Newman's picturesque detail, takes into his mind the various features, and ultimately the complete image, of the perfect type.

In the series of *Discourses on the Idea of a University* Newman's method is more formal and his tone more controversial. The purpose of the *Discourses* will be found explained in the *Notes* of the present volume p. 198. Newman was addressing a distinctly scholarly audience, and was treating of a series of abstract topics, on which he was called to pronounce in his character of probable vice-chancellor of the proposed University. Accordingly, throughout these *Discourses* he is consistently academic in tone and manner and formal and elaborate in method. He lays out his work with somewhat mechanical precision; he sketches his plan strictly beforehand; he defines terms and refines upon possible meanings, and guards at each step against misinterpretations; he pauses often to come to an understanding with his hearers about the progress already made, and to consider what line of advance severe logical method next dictates. In all these ways he is deliberate, explicit, and demonstrative. Yet despite this strenuous regard for system and method, not even here does Newman become crabbedly scholastic or pedantically over-formal; the result of his strenuousness is, rather, a finely conscientious circumspection of demeanor and an academic dignity of bearing. There is something irresistibly impressive in the perfect poise with which he moves through the intricacies of the many abstractions that his subject involves. He exhibits each aspect of his subject in just the right perspective and with just the requisite minuteness of detail; he leads us unerringly from each point of view to that which most naturally follows; he keeps us always aware of the relation of each aspect to the total sum of truth he is trying to help us to grasp; and so, little by little, he secures for us that perfect command of an intellectual region, in its concrete facts and in its abstract relations, which exposition aims to make possible. These *Discourses* are as fine an example as exists in English of the union of strict method with charm of style in the treatment of an abstract topic.

In the *Development of Christian Doctrine* and the *Grammar of Assent* the severity of Newman's method is somewhat greater, as is but natural in strictly scientific treatises. Yet even in these abstract discussions his style retains an inalienable charm due to the luminousness of the atmosphere, the wide-ranging command of illustrations, the unobtrusively tropical phrasing, and the steady harmonious sweep of the periods. Few books on equally abstract topics are as easy reading.

While Newman's method is under consideration a word or two about his *Present Position of Catholics* will be in place. The book is controversial throughout, and contains some of Newman's most ingenious and caustic irony. But it is specially interesting because it illustrates once more his consummate skill in adapting his method to the matter in hand. His purpose in this case is to right the Roman Catholic Church with the English nation, to exhibit the Romanists as he knows them really to be, a conscientious, honorable, patriotic body of men, and to put an end once for all, if possible, to the long tradition of calumny that has persecuted them. Such is his problem. He sets about its solution characteristically. He does not undertake to demonstrate the truth of Roman doctrines, or by direct evidence and argument to refute the wild charges of hypocrisy and corruption which

Protestants are habitually making against Romanists. <u>His methods are much subtler than these and also much more comprehensive and final.</u> He sets himself to analyse Protestant prejudice, and to destroy it by resolving it into its elements. He takes it up historically, and exhibits its origin in an atmosphere of intense partisan conflict, and its development in the midst of peculiarly favorable intellectual and moral conditions ; he shows that it is political in its origin and has been inwrought into the very fibre of English national life :—
" English Protestantism is the religion of the throne : it is represented, realized, taught, transmitted in the succession of monarchs and an hereditary aristocracy. It is religion grafted upon loyalty ; and its strength is not in argument, not in fact, not in the unanswerable controversialist, not in an apostolical succession, not in sanction of Scripture—but in a royal road to faith, in backing up a King whom men see, against a Pope whom they do not see. The devolution of its crown is the tradition of its creed ; and to doubt its truth is to be disloyal towards its Sovereign. Kings are Englishmen's saints and doctors ; he likes somebody or something at which he can cry, ' huzzah,' and throw up his hat." [1]

To hate a Romanist, then, is as natural for John Bull as to hate a Frenchman, and to libel him is a matter of patriotism. The Englishman's romantic imagination has for generations long been spinning myths of Catholic misdoing to satisfy these deep instinctive animosities. Moreover, besides loyalty and

[1] *Selections*, p. 62.

patriotism, many other typical English qualities have contributed to foster and develop this Protestant prejudice. Such are the controlling practical interests of the English, their content with compromise-working schemes, and their contempt for abstractions and subtleties; their shuddering dislike of innovation; their well-meaning obstinacy in ignorance, and their heroic adherence to familiar though undeniable error; their insularity; their hatred of foreigners in general, and their frenzied fear of the Pope in particular. With unfailing adroitness of suggestion, Newman makes clear how these national traits, and many others closely related to them, have co-operated to originate and develop Protestant hatred of Roman Catholicism. His mastery of the details of social life and of motives of action is in this discussion of English history and contemporary life specially conspicuous. Every phase of peculiarly English thought and feeling is present to him; every intricacy of the curiously subterranean British national temperament is traced out. And the result is that prejudice is explained out of existence. The intense hostility that seems so primitive an instinct as to justify itself like the belief in God or in an outer world, is resolved into the expression of a vast mass of petty and often discreditable instincts, and so loses all its validity in losing its apparent primitiveness and mystery.

Such is the general plan and scope of Newman's attack on Protestant prejudice; in carrying out the plan and making his attack brilliantly effective, he shows inexhaustible ingenuity and unwearied invention. He uses fables, allegories, and elaborate pieces of irony;

he develops an unending series of picturesque illustrations of Protestant prejudice, drawn from all sources, past and present; he sets curious traps for this prejudice, catches it at unawares and shows it up to his readers in guises they can hardly defend; he plays skilfully upon the instincts that lie at its root, and by clever manipulation makes them declare themselves in a twinkling in favor of some aspect of Romanism. In short, he uses all the rhetorical devices of which he is master to win a hearing from the half-hostile, to beguile the unwilling, to amuse the half-captious, and finally to insinuate into the minds of his readers an all-permeating mood of contempt for Protestant narrowness and bigotry, and of open-minded appreciation of the merits of Roman Catholics.

IV.

For still another reason the lectures on the *Present Position of Catholics* are specially interesting to a student of Newman's methods; they illustrate exceptionally well his skill in the use of irony. To the genuine rhetorician there is something specially attractive in the duplicity of irony, because of the opportunity it offers him of playing with points of view, of juggling with phrases, of showing his virtuosity in the manipulation of both thoughts and words. Newman was too much of a rhetorician not to feel this fascination. Moreover, he had learned from his study of Copleston and Whately the possibilities of irony as a controversial weapon. Copleston's *Advice to a Young Reviewer*, and Whately's *Historic Doubts Concerning Napoleon Buonaparte* were typical specimens of academic irony, where with impressive dignity and suavity and the most plausible simplicity and candor the writers, while seemingly advocating a certain policy or theory or set of conclusions, were really sneering throughout at a somewhat similar policy or theory—that of their opponents—and laying it open helplessly to ridicule.

One of the most noteworthy characteristics of Newman's irony—and in this point his irony resembled that of his masters—was its positive argumentative value. Often an elaborate piece of irony is chiefly destructive ; it turns cleverly into ridicule the general attitude of mind of the writer's opponents, but makes no attempt to supply a substitute for the faith it destroys. Swift's irony, for example, is usually of this character. It is intensely ill-natured and savage, and so extravagant that it sometimes defeats its own end as argument. Its hauteur and bitterness produce a reaction in the mind of the reader, and force him to distrust the judgment and sanity of a man who can be so inveterately and fiercely insolent. Its indictment is so sweeping and its mood so cynical, that the reader, though he is bullied out of any regard for the ideas that Swift attacks, is repelled from Swift himself, and made to hate his notions as much as he despises those of Swift's opponents. Moreover, full of duplicity and innuendo as it is, its innuendoes often are merely disguised sneers, and not suggestions of genuinely valid reasons why the opinions or prejudices which the writer is assailing should be abandoned. In the *Mod-*

est Proposal and the *Argument against Abolishing Christianity*, for example, the irony reduces to one long sneer at the prejudice, the selfishness, and the cruelty of Yahoo human nature; there is very little positive argument in behalf of the oppressed Irish on the one hand, or in favor of Christianity on the other.

Newman's irony, on the contrary, is always subtle, intellectual, and suggestive. It is positive in its insinuation of actual reasons for abandoning prejudice against Romanists; it is tirelessly adroit, and adjusts itself delicately to every part of the opposing argument; it is suggestive of new ideas, and not only makes the reader see the absurdity of some time-worn prejudice, but hints at its explanation and insinuates a new opinion to take its place. In tone, too, it is very different from Swift's irony; it is not enraged and blindly savage, but more like the best French irony—self-possessed, suave, and insinuating. Newman addresses himself with unfailing skill to the prejudices of those whom he is trying to move, and carries his readers with him in a way that Swift was too contemptuous to aim at. Newman's irony wins the wavering, while it routs the hostile. This is the double task that it always proposes to itself.

An example of his irony at its best may be found in the amusing piece of declamation against the British Constitution and John Bullism which Newman puts into the mouth of a Russian Count. The passage occurs in a lecture on the *Present Position of Catholics*, which was delivered just before the war with Russia, when English jealousy of Russia and contempt for Russian prejudice and ignorance were most intense. It was, of course, on these feelings of jealousy and contempt that Newman skilfully played when he represented the Russian Count as grotesquely misinterpreting the British Constitution and *Blackstone's Commentaries*, and as charging them with irreligion and blasphemy. His satirical portrayal of the Russian and the clever manipulation by which he forces the Count to exhibit all his stores of ungentle dullness and all his stock of malignant prejudice delighted every ordinary British reader, and threw him into a pleasant glow of self-satisfaction, and of sympathy with the author ; now this was the very mood, as Newman was well aware, in which, if ever, the anti-Catholic reader might be led to question with himself whether after all he was perfectly informed about Roman Catholicism, or whether he did not, like the Russian Count, take most of his knowledge at second-hand and inherit most of his prejudice. Throughout this passage the ingenuity is conspicuous with which Newman makes use of English dislike of Russia and blind loyalty to Queen and Constitution ; the passage everywhere exemplifies the adroitness, the flexibility, the persuasiveness, and the far-reaching calculation of Newman's irony.

Indeed, this elaborateness and self-consciousness, and deliberateness of aim, are perhaps, at times, limitations on the success of his irony; it is a bit too cleverly planned and a trifle over-elaborate. In these respects it contrasts disadvantageously with French irony, which at its best, is so delightfully by the way, so airily unexpected, so accidental, and yet so dextrously fatal. It would be an instructive study in literary method to compare Newman's ironical defence of Roman Catholicism in the passage already referred to with Montesquieu's ironical attack upon the same system in the *Lettres Persanes.*

––––––

V.

WHEN we turn from Newman's methods to his style in the narrower meaning of the term, we still find careful elaboration and ingenious calculation of effect, although here again the conscientious workmanship becomes evident only on reflection, and the general impression is that of easy and instinctive mastery. Nevertheless, Newman wrought out all that he wrote, with much patient recasting and revising. "It is simply the fact," he tells a friend in one of his letters, "that I have been obliged to take great pains with everything I have written, and I often write chapters over and over again, besides innumerable corrections and interlinear additions. . . . . I think I have never written for writing's sake ; but my one and single desire and aim has been to do what is so difficult—viz., to express clearly and exactly my meaning ; this has been the motive principle of all my corrections and re-writings." [1]

It is perhaps this sincerity of aim and this sacrifice of the decorative impulse in the strenuous search for adequacy of expression that keep out of Newman's writing every trace of artificiality. Sophisticated as is

––––––

[1] *Letters,* II. 476.

his style it is never mannered. There is no pretence, no flourish, no exhibition of rhetorical resources for their own sake. The most impressive and the most richly imaginative passages in his prose come in because he is betrayed into them in his conscientious pursuit of all the aspects of the truth he is illustrating. Moreover, they are ·curiously congruous in tone with the most colloquial parts of his writing. There is no sudden jar perceptible when in the midst of his ordinary discourse, one chances upon these passages of essential beauty; perfect continuity of texture is characteristic of his work. This perfect continuity of texture illustrates both the all-pervasive fineness and nobleness of Newman's temper which constantly holds the elements of· moral and spiritual beauty in solution, and which imprints a certain distinction upon even the commonplace, and also the flexibility and elasticity of his style, which enables him with such perfect gradation of effect to change imperceptibly from the lofty to the common. At least, two admirable examples of this exquisite gradation of values or of this continuity of texture will be found in the *Selections,*—one in the description of Athens, pages 1–7, the other in the passage on *Theology*, pages 106–113. In the former passage a style almost easily colloquial is made subservient to the production of really gorgeous descriptive effects; yet despite the splendor of the scene that Newman calls up in the paragraphs on pages 4–7, there is no jar when he returns suddenly to simple exposition. Similarly, in the passage on *Theology*, the change from a scientific explanation of the duties of the theologian to the almost impassioned eloquence of the ascription of goodness and might to the Deity is effected with no shock or sense of discontinuity.

In its freedom from artificiality and in it sperfect sincerity, Newman's style contrasts noticeably with the style of a great rhetorician from whom he nevertheless took many hints—De Quincey. Of his careful study of De Quincey's style there can be no question. In the passage on the Deity, pages 109–111, to which reference has just been made, there are unmistakable reminiscences of De Quincey in the iteration of emphasis on an important word, in the frequent use of inversions. in the rise and fall of the periods, and indeed in the subtle rhythmic effects throughout. The piece of writing, however, where the likeness to De Quincey and the imitation of his manner and music are most obtrusive, is the sermon on the *Fitness of the Glories of Mary*,—that piece of Newman's prose, it should be noted, which is least defensible against the charge of artificiality and undue ornateness. A passage near the close of the sermon best illustrates the points in question : "And therefore she died in private. It became Him, who died for the world, to die in the world's sight; it became the Great Sacrifice to be lifted up on high, as a light that could not be hid. But she, the Lily of Eden, who had always dwelt out of the sight of man, fittingly did she die in the garden's shade, and amid the sweet flowers in which she had lived. Her departure made no noise in the world. The Church went about her common duties, preaching, converting, suffering. There were persecutions, there was fleeing from place to place, there were martyrs, there were triumphs. At length the rumour spread abroad that the Mother of God was no longer upon earth. Pilgrims went to and fro; they sought for her relics, but they found them not; did she die at Ephesus? or did she die at Jerusalem? reports varied; but her tomb could not be pointed out, or if it was found, it was open; and instead of her pure and fragrant body, there was a growth of lilies from the earth which she had touched. So inquirers went home marvelling, and waiting for further light." [1]

Though the cadences of Newman's prose are rarely as marked as here, a subtle musical beauty runs elusively through it all. Not that there is any of the singsong of pseudo-poetic prose. The cadences are always wide-ranging and delicately shifting, with none of the halting iteration and feeble sameness of half-metrical work. Moreover, the rhythms, subtly pervasive as they are, and even symbolic of the mood of the passage as they often prove to be, never compel direct recognition, but act merely as a mass of undistinguished under-and over-tones like those which give to a human voice depth and tenderness and suggestiveness.

Newman understood perfectly the symbolic value of rhythm and the possibility of imposing upon a series of simple words, by delicately sensitive adjustment, a power over the feelings and the imagination like that of an incantation. Several of the passages already quoted or referred to illustrate his instinctive adaptation of cadence to meaning and tone; another remarkable passage of this kind is that on p. 161 of the *Selections* which describes the apparent moral chaos in

---

[1] *Discourses to Mixed Congregations*, ed. 1892, p. 373.

human history. For subtlety of modulation, however, and symbolic suggestiveness, perhaps the tender leave-taking with which the *Apologia* closes is the most beautiful piece of prose that Newman has written: " I have closed this history of myself with St. Philip's name upon St. Philip's feast-day; and having done so, to whom can I more suitably offer it, as a memorial of affection and gratitude, than to St. Philip's sons, my dearest brothers of this House, the Priests of the Birmingham Oratory, AMBROSE ST. JOHN, HENRY AUSTIN MILLS, HENRY BITTLESTON, EDWARD CASWALL, WILLIAM PAINE NEVILLE, and HENRY IGNATIUS DUDLEY RIDER, who have been so faithful to me; who have been so sensitive of my needs; who have been so indulgent to my failings; who have carried me through so many trials; who have grudged no sacrifice, if I have asked for it; who have been so cheerful under discouragements of my causing; who have done so many good works, and let me have the credit of them;—with whom I have lived so long, with whom I hope to die.

"And to you especially, dear AMBROSE ST. JOHN whom God gave me, when He took every one else away; who are the link between my old life and my new; who have now for twenty-one years been so devoted to me, so patient, so zealous, so tender; who have let me lean so hard upon you; who have watched me so narrowly; who have never thought of yourself, if I was in question.

"And in you I gather up and bear in memory those familiar affectionate companions and counsellors, who in Oxford were given to me, one after another, to be my daily solace and relief; and all those others, of

great name and high example, who were my thorough
friends, and showed me true attachment in times long
past; and also those many younger men, whether I
knew them or not, who have never been disloyal to me
by word or deed; and of all these, thus various in their
relations to me, those more especially who have since
joined the Catholic Church.

"And I earnestly pray for this whole company, with a
hope against hope, that all of us, who once were so
united, and so happy in our union, may even now be
brought at length, by the Power of the Divine Will,
into One Fold and under One Shepherd."

VI.

THE careful gradation of values in Newman's style
and the far-reaching sweep of his periods connect
themselves closely with another of his noteworthy
characteristics,—his breadth of handling. He mani-
pulates with perfect ease and precision vast masses of
facts and makes them all contribute with unerring co-
operation to the production of a single effect. However minute his detail,—and his liking for concreteness
which will be presently illustrated often incites him to
great minuteness,—he never confuses his composition,
destroys the perspective, or loses sight of total effect.
The largeness of his manner and the certainty of his
handling place him at once among really great constructive artists.

Against this assertion it will be urged that in his fiction it is just this breadth of effect and constructive skill that are most noticeably lacking; that each of his novels, whatever its merits in places, is unsuccessful as a whole, and leaves a blurred impression. This must at once be granted. But after all it is in his theoretical or moral or historical work that the real Newman is to be found; in such work he is much more himself, much more thoroughly alive and efficient than in his stories, which, though cleverly turned out, were after all things by the way, were amateurish in execution, and never completely called forth his strength. Moreover, even in his novels, we find occasionally the integrating power of his imagination remarkably illustrated. The description in *Callista* of the invading and ravaging locusts is admirably sure in its treatment of detail and even and impressive in tone; the episode of Gurta's madness is powerfully conceived, is swift and sure in its action, and is developed with admirable subordination and coloring of detail and regard to climax.

On the whole, however, it must be granted that in his fiction Newman's sense of total effect and constructive skill are least conspicuous. In his abstract discussions they never fail him. First and foremost, they shew themselves in the plan of each work as a whole. The treatment is invariably symmetrical and exhaustive; part answers to part with the precision and the delicacy of adjustment of a work of art. Each part is conscious of the whole and has a vitally loyal relation to it, so that the needs and purposes of the whole organism seem present as controlling and centralizing instincts in every chapter, and paragraph, and sentence.

In his use of elaborate illustrations for the sake of securing concreteness and sensuous beauty, Newman shows this same integrating power of imagination. In the long illustrations which often take almost the proportions of episodes in the epical progress of his argument or exposition, the reader never has a sense of bewilderment or uncertainty of aim; the strength of Newman's mind and purpose subdues perfectly all his endlessly diverse material, and compels it into artistic coherence and vital unity; all details are colored in harmony with the dominant tone of the piece, and re-enforce a predetermined mood. When a reader commits himself to one of Newman's discussions he must resign himself to him body and soul, and be prepared to live and move and have his being in the medium of Newman's thought, and, moreover, in the special range of thought, and the special mood that this particular discussion provokes. Perhaps this omnipresence of Newman in the minutest details of each discussion becomes ultimately to the careful student of his writing the most convincing proof of the largeness of his mind, of the intensity of his conception, and of the vigor and vitality of his imagination.

It may be urged that the copiousness of Newman at times becomes wearisome; that he is over-liberal of both explanation and illustration; and that his style, though never exuberant in ornament, is sometimes annoyingly luminous, and blinds with excess of light. This is probably the point in which Newman's style is

most open to attack. It is a cloyingly explicit, rather
than a stimulatingly suggestive, style; it does almost
too much for the reader, and is almost inconsiderately
generous. " To really strenuous minds there is a
pleasurable stimulus in the challenge for a continuous
effort on their part, to be rewarded by securer and more
intimate grasp of the author's sense. Self-restraint, a
skilful economy of means, *ascêsis*, that too has a beauty
of its own." [1] Whether in much of his work Newman
has not neglected the ideal which these sentences of
Mr. Pater inculcate, may fairly be questioned, yet it
should be noted that Mr. Pater himself, very soon
after setting up this standard of style, instances Newman's *Idea of a University* as an example of " the perfect handling of a theory."

One characteristic of the purely suggestive style is
certainly to be found in Newman's writing,—great
beauty and vigor of phrase. This fact is the more
noteworthy because a writer who, like Newman,
is impressive in the mass, and excels in securing
breadth of effect, very often lacks the ability to strike
out memorable epigrams. A few quotations, brought
together at random, will show what point and terseness
Newman could command when he chose. " Ten thousand difficulties do not make a doubt." [2] " Great
things are done by devotion to one idea." [3] " Calculation never made a hero." [4] " All aberrations are
founded on, and have their life in, some truth or

---

[1] Pater's *Appreciations*, ed. 1890, p. 14.
[2] *Apologia*, p. 239. [3] *Hist. Sketches*, ed. 1891, III. p. 197.
[4] *Development of Christian Doctrine*, ed. 1891, p. 328.

other." [1] "Great acts take time." [2] "A book after all cannot make a stand against the wild living intellect of man." [3] "To be converted in partnership." [4] "It is not at all easy (humanly speaking) to wind up an Englishman to a dogmatic level." [5] "Paper logic." [6] "One is not at all pleased when poetry, or eloquence, or devotion is considered as if chiefly intended to feed syllogisms." [7] "Here below to live is to change, and to be perfect is to have changed often." [8] In terseness and sententiousness these utterances could hardly be surpassed by the most acrimonious searcher after epigram, though of course they have not the glitter of paradox to which modern coiners of phrases aspire.

Of wit there is very little to be found in Newman's writings; it is not the natural expression of his temperament. Wit is too dryly intellectual, too external and formal, too little vital to suit Newman's mental habit. To the appeal of humour he was distinctly more open. It is from the humorous incongruities of imaginary situations that his irony secures its most persuasive effects. Moreover, whenever he is not necessarily preoccupied with the tragically serious aspects of life and of history, or forced by his subject-matter, and audience, into a formally restrained manner and method, he has, in treating any topic, that urbanity and half-playful kindliness that come from a large-minded and almost tolerant recognition of the essential imperfections of

---

[1] *Apologia*, p. 188.   [2] *Ibid.* p. 169.   [3] *Ibid.*, p. 245.   [4] *Ibid.* 219.
[5] *Ibid.* 204.   [6] *Ibid.* 169.   [7] *Ibid.* p. 170.
[8] *Devel. of Christian Doctrine*, ed. 1891, p. 40.

life and human nature. The mood of the man of the
world, sweetened and ennobled, and enriched by profound knowledge and deep feeling and spiritual seriousness, gives to much of Newman's work its most
distinctive note. When he is able to be thoroughly
colloquial, this mood and this tone can assert themselves most freely, and the result is a style through
which a gracious kindliness which is never quite
humor, and which yet possesses all its elements,
diffuses itself pervasively and persuasively. Throughout the whole of the *Rise and Progress of Universities*
this tone is traceable, and, to take a specific example,
it is largely to its influence that the description of
Athens, quoted on pages 3–7, owes its peculiar charm.
What can be more deliciously incongruous than a commercial traveller, or "drummer," and the Acropolis?
or more curiously ill-adjusted than his standards of
valuation to the qualities of the Grecian landscape?
Yet how little malicious is Newman's use of this
incongruity or disproportion, and how unsuspiciously
the "agent of a London Company" ministers to the
quiet amusement of the reader, and also helps to
heighten, by contrast, the effect of beauty and romance
and mystery that Newman is aiming at.

Several allusions have already been made to Newman's liking for concreteness. And in an earlier paragraph his distrust of the abstract was described and
illustrated at length. These predilections of his have
left their unmistakable mark everywhere on his style
in ways more technical than those that have thus far
been noted. His vocabulary is, for a scholar, exceptionally idiomatic and unliterary; the most ordinary

and unparsable turns of every-day speech are inwrought into the texture of his style. In the *Apologia* he speaks of himself in one place as having had "a lounging free-and-easy way of carrying things on," [1] and the phrase both defines and illustrates one characteristic of his style. Idioms that have the crude force of popular speech, the vitality without the vulgarity of slang, abound in his writings. Of his increasingly clear recognition, in 1839, of the weakness of the Anglican position, he says: "The Via Media was an impossible idea; it was what I had called 'standing on one leg.'" [2]. His loss of control over his party in 1840 he describes as follows: "I never had a strong wrist, but at the very time when it was most needed, the reins had broken in my hands." [3] Of the ineradicableness of evil in human nature he exclaims: "You do but play a sort of 'hunt the slipper,' with the fault of our nature, till you go to Christianity." [4] Illustrations of this idiomatic and homely phrasing might be endlessly multiplied. Moreover, to the concreteness of colloquial phrasing Newman adds the concreteness of the specific word. Other things being equal, he prefers the name of the species to that of the genus, and the name of the class to that of the species; he is always urged forward toward the individual and the actual; his mind does not lag in the region of abstractions and formulas, but presses past the general term or abstraction or law, to the image or the example, and into the tangible, glowing, sensible world of fact. His imagery, though never

---

[1] *Apologia*, p. 59. [2] *Ibid.*, p. 149. [3] *Ibid.*, p. 128,
[4] *Dis. and Arg.*, p. 274

obtrusive, is almost lavishly present, and though never purely decorative, is often very beautiful. It is so inevitable, however, springs so organically from the thought and the mood of the moment, that the reader accepts it unmindfully, and is conscious only of grasping easily and securely the writer's meaning. He must first look back through the sentences and study the style in detail before he will come to realize its continual but decisive divergence from the literal and commonplace, and its essential freshness and distinction.

On occasion, of course, Newman uses elaborate figures; but always for purposes of exposition or persuasion. In such cases the reader should note the thoroughness with which the figure adjusts itself to every turn and phase of the thought, and the surprising omnipresence and suggestiveness of the tropical phrasing. These qualities of Newman's style are well illustrated in the following passage from the *Development of Christian Doctrine :—*

"Whatever be the risk of corruption from intercourse with the world around, such a risk must be encountered if a great idea is duly to be understood, and much more if it is to be fully exhibited. It is elicited and expanded by trial, and battles into perfection and supremacy. Nor does it escape the collision of opinion even in its earlier years, nor does it remain truer to itself, and with a better claim to be considered one and the same, though externally protected from vicissitude and change. It is indeed sometimes said that the stream is clearest near the spring. Whatever use may fairly be made of this image, it does not apply to the history of a philosophy or belief, which on the contrary is more equable, and purer, and stronger, when its bed has become deep, and broad, and full. It necessarily rises out of an existing state of things, and for a time savors of the soil. Its vital element needs disengaging from what is foreign and temporary, and is employed in efforts after freedom which become more vigorous and hopeful as its years increase. Its beginnings are no measure of its capabilities, nor of its scope. At first no one knows what it is, or what it is worth. It remains perhaps for a time quiescent; it tries, as it were, its limbs, and proves the ground under it, and feels its way. From time to time, it makes essays which fail, and are in consequence abandoned. It seems in suspense which way to go; it wavers, and at length strikes out in one definite direction. In time it enters upon strange territory; points of controversy alter their bearing; parties rise and fall around it; dangers and hopes appear in new relations; and old principles reappear under new forms. It changes with them in order to remain the same. In a higher world it is otherwise, but here below to live is to change, and to be perfect is to have changed often.[1] " The image of the river pervades this passage throughout and yet is never obtrusive and never determines or even constrains the progress of the thought. The imagery simply seems to insinuate the ideas into the reader's mind with a certain novelty of appeal and half-sensuous persuasiveness. Another passage of much this kind has already been quoted on page xx, where Newman describes the adventurous investigator scaling the crags of truth.

[1] *Development of Christian Doctrine*, ed. 1891, pp. 39-49.

Closely akin to this use of figures is Newman's generous use of examples and illustrations. Whatever be the principle he is discussing, he is never content till he has realized it for the reader in tangible, visible form, until he has given it the cogency and intensity of appeal that only sensations or images possess. In all these ways, then, by his idiomatic and colloquial phrasing, by his specific vocabulary, by his delicately adroit use of metaphors, by his carefully elaborated imagery, and by his wealth of examples and illustrations, Newman keeps resolutely close to the concrete, and imparts everywhere to his style warmth, vividness, color, convincing actuality.

VII.

It remains to suggest briefly Newman's relation to what was most characteristic in the thought and feeling of his times. This is not the place for a discussion of his theological position, or for a technical account of the great religious movements which he partly originated and largely guided and determined. But without an attempt at any such special analysis of his doctrine or determination of the processes of his thought, it will be possible to connect him, by virtue of certain temperamental characteristics, and certain prevailing modes of conceiving life, with what was most distinctive in the literature of the early part of the century.

Perhaps the most general formula for the work of

English literature during the first quarter of the present century is the rediscovery and vindication of the concrete. The special task of the eighteenth century had been to order, and to systematize, and to name ; its favorite methods had been analysis and generalization. It asked for no new experience ; it sought only to master and reduce to formulas, and to find convenient labels for what experience it already possessed. It was perpetually in search of standards and canons ; it was conventional through and through ; and its men felt secure from the ills of time only when sheltered under some ingenious artificial construction of rule and precedent. Whatever lay beyond the scope of their analysis and defied their laws, they disliked and dreaded ; the outlying regions of mystery which hem life in on every side, are inaccessible to the intellect and irreducible in terms of its laws, were strangely repellent to them, and from such shadowy vistas they resolutely turned their eyes and fastened them on the solid ground at their feet. The familiar bustle of the town, the thronging streets of the city, the gay life of the drawing-room and coffee-house and play-house ; or the more exalted life of Parliament and Court. the intrigues of State-chambers, the manœuvres of the battle-field ; the aspects of human activity, wherever collective man in his social capacity goes through the orderly and comprehensible changes of his ceaseless pursuit of worldly happiness and worldly success ; these were the subjects that for the men of the eighteenth century had absorbing charm, and in seeking to master this intricate play of forces, to fathom the motives below it, to tabulate its experiences, to set up

standards to guide the individual successfully through
the intricacies of this commonplace every-day world,
they spent their utmost energy, and to these tasks they
instinctively limited themselves.   In poetry it was a
generalized view of life that they aimed at, a semi-phil-
osophical representation of man's nature and actions.
Pope, the typical poet of the century, " stooped to truth
and moralized his song."   Dr. Johnson, the most
authoritative critic of the century, taught that the poet
should " remark general properties and large appear-
ances . . . . and must neglect the minuter discrimi-
nations, which one may have remarked, and another
have neglected, or those characteristics which are alike
obvious to vigilance and carelessness."   In prose the
same moralizing and generalizing tendencies prevailed
and found their most adequate and thorough-going expression in the abstract and pretentiously Latinized
style of Dr. Johnson.

Everywhere thought gave the law ; the senses and
the imagination were kept jealously in subordination.
The abstract, the typical, the general—these were everywhere exalted at the expense of the image, the specific experience, the vital fact.   In religion the same tendencies showed themselves.   Orthodoxy and Deism
alike were mechanical in their conception of Nature
and of God.   Free-thinkers and Apologists alike tried
to systematize religious experience, and to rationalize
theology.   In the pursuit of historical evidences and
of logical demonstrations of the truth or falsity of religion, genuine religious emotion was almost neglected
or was actually condemned.   Enthusiasm was dis-
trusted or abhorred ; an enthusiast was a madman.   In-

tense feeling of all kinds was regarded askance, and avoided as irrational, unsettling, prone to disarrange systems and to overturn standards and burst the bonds of formulas.

Now it was to this limited manner of living life and of conceiving of life that the great movement which, for lack of a better name, may be called the Romantic Movement, was to put an end. The Romanticists sought to enrich life with new emotions, to conquer new fields of experience, to come into imaginative touch with far distant times, to give its due to the encompassing world of darkness and mystery, and even to pierce through the darkness in the hope of finding, at the heart of the mystery, a transcendental world of infinite beauty and eternal truth. A keener sense of the value of life penetrated them and stirred them into imaginative sympathy with much that had left the men of the eighteenth century unmoved. They found in the naïve life of nature and animals and children a picturesqueness and grace that was wanting in the sophisticated life of the "town;" they delighted in the mysterious chiaroscuro of the middle ages, in its rich blazonry of passion, and its ever-changing spectacular magnificence; they looked forward with ardor into the future, and dreamed dreams of the progress of man; they opened their hearts to the influences of the spiritual world, and religion became to them something more than respectability and morality. In every way they endeavored to give some new zest to life, to impart to it some fine novel flavor, to attain to some exquisite new experience. They sought this new experience imaginatively in the past, with Scott and

4

Southey; they sought it with fierce insistence in foreign lands, following Byron, and in the wild exploitation of individual fancy and caprice; they sought it with Coleridge and Wordsworth through the revived sensitiveness of the spirit and its intuitions of a transcendental world of absolute reality; they sought it with Shelley in the regions of the vast inane.

Now it was in the midst of these restless conditions and under the influence of all this new striving and aspiration that Newman's youth and most impressionable years of development were spent, and he took color and tone from his epoch to a degree that has often been overlooked. His work, despite its reactionary character, indeed, partly because of it, is a genuine expression of the Romantic spirit, and can be understood only when thus interpreted and brought into relation with the great tendencies of thought and feeling of the early part of our century. Of his direct indebtedness to Scott, Wordsworth, and Coleridge, he has himself made record in the *Apologia* [1] and in his *Autobiographical Sketch*. [2] But far more important than the influence of any single man was the penetrating and determining action upon him of the romantic atmosphere, overcharged as it was with intense feeling, and tingling with new thought. The results of this action may be traced throughout his temperament and in all his work.

Mediævalism, as we have seen, was a distinctive note of the Romantic spirit, and, certainly, Newman was intensely alive to the beauty and the poetic charm of the life of the Middle Ages. One is sometimes

---

[1] *Apologia*, p. 96.　　[2] *Letters and Correspondence*, I. 18.

tempted to describe him as a great mediæval ecclesiastic astray in the nineteenth century and heroically striving to remodel modern life in harmony with his temperamental needs. His imagination was possessed with the romantic vision of the greatness of the Mediæval Church,—of its splendor and pomp and dignity, and of its power over the hearts and lives of its members; and the Oxford movement was in its essence an attempt to reconstruct the English Church in harmony with this romantic ideal, to rouse the Church to a vital realization of its own great traditions, and to restore to it the prestige and the dominating position it had had in the past. As Scott's imagination was fascinated with the picturesque paraphernalia of feudalism,—with its jousts, and courts of love, and its coats of mail and buff-jerkins,[1]—so Newman's imagination was captivated by the gorgeous ritual and ceremonial, the art and architecture of mediæval Christianity, and found in them the symbols of the spirit of mystery and awe which was for him the essentially religious spirit, and of the mystical truths of which revealed religion was made up. The Church, as Newman found it, was Erastian and worldly; it was apt to regard itself as merely an ally of the State for the maintenance of order and spread of morality; it was coldly rational in belief and theology, and prosaic in its conception of religious truth and of its own position and functions. Newman sought to revive in the Church a mediæval faith in its own divine mission and the intense spiritual consciousness of the Middle Ages; he aimed to restore to religion its mystical character, to exalt the sacra-

---

[1] Leslie Stephen, *Hour in a Library.*

mental system as the divinely appointed means for the salvation of souls, and to impose once more on men's imaginations the mighty spell of a hierarchical organization, the direct representative of God in the world's affairs. Such was the mediæval ideal to which he devoted himself. Both he and Scott substantially ruined themselves through their mediævalism. Scott's luckless attempt was to place his private and family life upon a feudal basis and to give it mediæval color and beauty; Newman undertook a much nobler and more heroic but more intrinsically hopeless task,—that of re-creating the whole English Church in harmony with mediæval conceptions.

Before Newman, Keble had already conceived of the English Church in this imaginative spirit. In the passage quoted in the *Selections*, pp. 55–58, Newman describes how Keble had made the Church " poetical," had " kindled hearts towards it," and by " his happy magic " had thrown upon its ritual, offices, and servants a glamour and beauty of which they had for many generations been devoid. It was to the continuance and the furtherance of this process of regeneration and transfiguration that Newman devoted the Oxford movement.

But the essentially Romantic character of the new movement comes out in other ways than in its idealization of the Church. The relation of Newman and of his friends to Nature was precisely like that of the Romanticists. Newman, like Wordsworth, Coleridge, and Shelley, found Nature mysteriously beautiful and instinct with strange significance, a divinely elaborated language whereby God speaks through symbols to the human soul. Keble's *Christian Year* is full of this interpretation of natural sights and sounds as images of spiritual truth, and with this mystical conception of Nature Newman was in perfect sympathy. Nature was for him as rich in its spiritual suggestiveness, as for Wordsworth or Shelley, and was as truly for him as for Carlyle or Goethe the visible garment of God. But in interpreting the emotional value of Nature Newman has recourse to a symbolism drawn ready-made from Christianity. The mystical beauty of Nature, instead of calling up in his imagination a Platonic ideal world as with Shelley, or adumbrating the world of eternal verity of German transcendentalism as with Wordsworth and Coleridge, suggested to Newman the presence and power of seraphs and angels. Of the angels he says, " Every breath of air and ray of light and heat, every beautiful prospect, is, as it were, the skirts of their garments, the waving of the robes of those whose faces see God." Again, he asks, " What would be the thoughts of a man who, when examining a flower, or a herb, or a pebble, or a ray of light, which he treats as something so beneath him in the scale of existence, suddenly discovered that he was in the presence of some powerful being who was hidden behind the visible things he was inspecting, —who, though concealing his wise hand, was giving them their beauty, grace, and perfection, as being God's instrument for the purpose,—nay, whose robe and ornaments those objects were, which he was so eager to analyze?" [1]

Despite the somewhat conventional symbolism that

[1] *Apologia*, p. 28.

pervades these passages, the mystical mood in the
contemplation of Nature that underlies and suggests
them is substantially the same that expresses itself
through other imagery in the Romantic poets. In his
intense sensitiveness, then, to the emotional value of
the visible Universe, and in his interpretation of the
beauty of hill and valley and mountain and stream in
terms of subjective emotion, Newman may justly be
said to have shared in the Romantic Return to Nature.

But in a still more important way Newman's work
was expressive of the Return to Nature. Under this
term is to be included not merely the fresh delight that
the Romanticists felt in the splendor of the firmament
and the tender beauty or the sublimity of sea and land,
but also their eager recognition of the value of the
instinctive, the spontaneous, the *natural* in life, as
opposed to the artificial, the self-conscious, the systematic, and the conventional. This recognition pervades all the literature of the first quarter of our century, and, in fact, in one form or another, is the characteristic note of what is most novel in the thought and
the life of the time. In this Return to Nature Newman
shared. For him, as for all the Romanticists, life
itself is more than what we think about life, experience
is infinitely more significant than our formulas for
summing it up, and transcends them incalculably.
General terms are but the makeshifts of logic and can
never cope with the multiplicity and the intensity of
sensation and feeling. Newman's elaborate justification of this indictment of logic is wrought out in the
Grammar of Assent and in his Sermon on *Implicit and
Explicit Reason.*

Throughout these discourses he pleads for those vital processes of thought and feeling and intuition which every man goes through for himself in his acquisition of concrete truth, and which he can perhaps describe in but a stammering and inconsequent fashion in the terms of the schoolman's logic. It is by these direct, spontaneous processes, Newman urges, that most men reach truth in whatever concrete matter they apply themselves to, and the truth that they reach is none the less true because they have not the knack of setting forth syllogistically their reasons for accepting it. In his rejection, then, of formal demonstration as the sole method for attaining truth, in his recognition of the limitations of logic, and in his deep conviction of the surpassing importance of the spontaneous and instinctive in life, Newman was at one with the Romanticists, and in all these particulars he shared in their Return to Nature.

This insistence of Newman's on the vital character of truth is a point the importance of which cannot be exaggerated when the attempt is being made to grasp what is essential in his psychology and his ways of conceiving of life and of human nature. For him truth does not exist primarily as for the formalist in the formulas or the theorems of text-books, but in the minds and the hearts of living men. In these minds and hearts truth grows and spreads in countless subtle ways. Its appeal is through numberless other channels than those of the mind. Man is for Newman primarily an agent,—an acting creature,—not an intellect with merely accidental relations to an outer world. First and foremost he is a doer, a bringer about of results, a realizer of hopes and ambitions and ideals. He is a mass of instincts and impulses, of prejudices and passions; and it is in response to these mighty and ceaselessly operating springs of action that he makes his way through the world and subdues it to himself. Truth, then, to commend itself to such a being, must come not merely by way of the brain but also by that of the heart; it must not be a collection of abstract formulas, but must be concrete and vital. If it be religious truth, it must not take the form of logical demonstrations, but must be beautifully enshrined in the symbols of an elaborate ritual, illustrated in the lives of saints and doctors, authoritative and venerable in the creeds and liturgies of a hierarchical organization, irresistibly cogent as inculcated by the divinely appointed representatives of the Source of all Truth. In these forms religious truth may be able to impose itself upon individuals, to take complete possession of them, to master their minds and hearts, and to rule their lives.

But what shall be the test of such truth? How shall the individual be sure of its claims? How shall he choose between rival systems? Here again Newman refuses to be content with the formal and the abstract, and goes straight to life itself. In the search for a criterion of truth he rejects purely intellectual tests, and has recourse to tests which call into activity the whole of a man's nature. It is the Illative Sense that detects and distinguishes truth, and the Illative Sense is simply the entire mind of the individual vigorously grasping concrete facts with all their implications for the heart and for the imagination and for conduct and extracting from them their peculiar significance. This process, by which the individual searches for and attains truth in concrete matters, is admirably described in the passage quoted in the *Introduction*, p. xx. The formal logic of the schools can never thus reach truth; it always falls short of life; its symbols are general terms, colorless abstractions, from which all the palpitating warmth and persuasiveness of real life have been carefully drained. Propositions fashioned out of these colorless general terms cannot by any process of syllogistic jugglery be made to comprehend the whole truth of a religious system. They leave out inevitably what is most vital, and what is therefore most intimate in its appeal to the individual,— to his heart and practical instincts, and his imagination. " We proceed as far indeed as we can, by the logic of language, but we are obliged to supplement it by the more subtle and elastic logic of thought ; for forms by themselves prove nothing." [1] " It is to the living mind that we must look for the means of using correctly principles of whatever kind." [2] " In all of these separate actions of the intellect, the individual is supreme and responsible to himself, nay, under circumstances, may be justified in opposing himself to the judgment of the whole world ; though he uses rules to his great advantage, as far as they go, and is in consequence bound to use them." [1] Absolute " proof can never be furnished to us by the logic of words, for as certitude is of the mind, so is the act of inference which leads to it. Every one who reasons is his own

---

[1] *Grammar of Assent*, ed. 1889, p. 359.   [2] *Ibid.*, p. 360.
[3] *Ibid.* ed., 1889, p. 353.

centre."[1] The progress of the individual "is a living growth, not a mechanism; and its instruments
are mental acts, not the formulas and contrivances of language."[2]

The foregoing analysis has tended to illustrate the
facts that Newman aimed to make religion an intensely concrete personal experience, and to fill out
the spiritual life with widely-varying and richly-beauti-
ful feeling; and that he also set himself everywhere
consciously and directly against the eighteenth century
ideal, according to which reason was the sole dis-
coverer and arbiter of truth and regulator of conduct.
In these respects Newman's work was in perfect harmony with that of the Romanticists. Like them he
was pleading for the spontaneous, for the emotions
and the imagination, for what is most vital in life, in
opposition to the formalists, the systematizers, and
the devotees of logic.

In the following points, then, Newman's kinship with
the Romanticists is recognizable: in his imaginative
sympathy with the past, in the range and perspective
of his historical consciousness, and in his devotion
to an ideal framed largely in accordance with a loving
reverence for mediæval life. His vein of mysticism,
his imaginative sympathy with nature, his interpretation of nature as symbolic of spiritual truth, his rejection of reason as the guide of life, and his recognition
of the inadequacy of generalizations and formulas to
the wealth of actual life and to the intensity and variety

[1] *Grammar of Assent,* p. 345.
[2] *Ibid.,* ed. 1889, p. 350.

of personal experience, are also characteristics that mark his relation to the men of his period.

These are a few of the considerations which make it possible to bring Newman's temperament and work into intelligible connection with the conditions of thought and feeling most characteristic of his time, and which help to render comprehensible the Oxford movement and the Roman Catholic revival as expressions of tendencies widely operative throughout English life and literature. It will perhaps be urged that, after all, what is individual to a man or a movement is far more significant than what the man or movement shares with others, and that therefore to study wherein Newman differed from his contemporaries would have been far more profitable than by a curious blurring of traits to try to reduce Newman's form and face to somewhat the same pattern with those of various men quite unrelated to him in actual life. This contention would be perfectly just if appreciation were the sole end in the study of literature. But if the search for causes be also part of the task of criticism, and if a piece of literature is thoroughly grasped only when it is comprehended in its relations to the general conditions of thought and feeling in the midst of which the author lived and wrought, then the justification for such an analysis of an author's work as that which has just been attempted, becomes apparent. It has been with a view to helping students to a broader and at the same time more penetrating comprehension of Newman's character and work and of the qualities of his style, that these closing suggestions have been made.

BIBLIOGRAPHY.

Abbott, Edwin A. Philomythus. London, 1891.

Arnold, Matthew. Culture and Anarchy. Ed. 1883. Pp. 29–30.

Birrell, Augustine. Res Judicatæ. London, 1892.

Brodrick, George C. A History of the University of Oxford. London, 1886.

Bulwer-Lytton. England and the English. London, 1833. Bk. III, chaps. 4 and 5; bk. IV, chap. 9.

Church, R. W. The Life and Letters of Dean Church. Edited by his daughter. London, 1894.

Church, R. W. The Oxford Movement: twelve years, 1833–1845. London, 1891.

Couch, L. Quiller, *editor*. Reminiscences of Oxford by Oxford men. 1559–1850. Oxford, 1892.

Froude, J. A. The Oxford Counter-reformation. Short Studies on Great Subjects. 4tn series. London, 1883. pp. 151–235.

Froude, J. A. The Revival of Romanism. Short Studies, 3d series.

Hore, A. H. Eighteen Centuries of the Church in England. London, 1881.

Hutton, Richard Holt. Cardinal Newman. Boston, 1890.

Hutton, R. H. Essays on Some of the Modern Guides of English Thought in Matters of Faith. London, 1887.

Kingsley, Charles. "What, then, does Dr. Newman mean?" London, 1864.

Liddon, Henry Parry. Life of E. B. Pusey. London, 1894. 3 vols.

Liddon, Henry Parry. Thoughts on Present Church Troubles. London, 1882.

Martineau, James. Essays. London, 1866. pp. 329–406: Personal Influences on Present Theology.

Meynell, Wilfrid. Cardinal Newman: a Monograph. By John Oldcastle [pseudonym]. London. [1890.] *Portraits.*

Molesworth, William Nassau. History of the Church of England from 1660. London, 1882.

Mozley, Anne. Letters and Correspondence of John Henry Newman. London, 1891. 2 vols.

Mozley, J. B. Letters. London, 1885.

Mozley, Thomas. Reminiscences chiefly of Oriel College and the Oxford Movement. Boston, 1882. 2 vols.

Newman, Francis W. Contributions chiefly to the early history of Cardinal Newman; with comments. 2d ed. London, 1891.

Palmer, *Sir* William, *Bart.* A Narrative of Events connected with the Tracts of the Times. London, 1883.

Pattison, Mark. Memoirs. London, 1885.

Pfleiderer, Otto von. Die Entwicklung der Protestantischen Theologie. Freiburg, 1891.

Shairp, J. C. Aspects of Poetry. London, 1881. pp. 438-464.

Stephen, Leslie. An Agnostic's Apology. London, 1893. (Newman's theory of belief.)

Tulloch, John. Movements of Religious Thought, etc. London, 1885.

Ward, Wilfrid. William George Ward and the Oxford Movement. London, 1889.

Ward, Wilfrid. William George Ward and the Catholic Revival. London, 1893.

Ward, Wilfrid. Witnesses to the Unseen, and other Essays. London, 1893.

Wilberforce, Samuel, *Bishop.* Essays. London, 1874. 2 vols. I. pp. 334-93.

Williams, Isaac. Autobiography. London, 1892.

Wordsworth, Charles (*Bishop of St. Andrews*). Annals of my Early Life: 1806-1846. 2d ed. London, 1891. (Appendix on the Oxford Movement.)

Wordsworth, Charles. Annals of my Life: 1847-1856. London, 1893.

SELECTIONS

Site of a University.

IF we would know what a University is, considered
in its elementary idea, we must betake ourselves to the
first and most celebrated home of European literature
and source of European civilization, to the bright and
beautiful Athens,—Athens, whose schools drew to her
bosom, and then sent back again to the business of life,
the youth of the Western World for a long thousand
years. Seated on the verge of the continent, the city
seemed hardly suited for the duties of a central metropolis of knowledge; yet, what it lost in convenience
of approach, it gained in its neighbourhood to the
traditions of the mysterious East, and in the loveliness
of the region in which it lay. Hither, then, as to a
sort of ideal land, where all archetypes of the great and
the fair were found in substantial being, and all departments of truth explored, and all diversities of intellectual power exhibited, where taste and philosophy
were majestically enthroned as in a royal court, where
there was no sovereignty but that of mind, and no no-
bility but that of genius, where professors were rulers,

I

and princes did homage, hither flocked continually from the very corners of the *orbis terrarum*, the many-tongued generation, just rising, or just risen into man hood, in order to gain wisdom.

Pisistratus had in an early age discovered and nursed the infant genius of his people, and Cimon, after the Persian war, had given it a home. That war had established the naval supremacy of Athens; she had become an imperial state; and the Ionians, bound to her by the double chain of kindred and of subjection, were importing into her both their merchandise and their civilization. The arts and philosophy of the Asiatic coast were easily carried across the sea, and there was Cimon, as I have said, with his ample fortune, ready to receive them with due ·honours. Not content with patronizing their professors, he built the first of those noble porticos, of which we hear so much in Athens, and he formed the groves, which in process of time became the celebrated Academy. Planting is one of the most graceful, as in Athens it was one of the most beneficent, of employments. Cimon took in hand the wild wood, pruned and dressed it, and laid it out with handsome walks and welcome fountains. Nor, while hospitable to the authors of the city's civilization, was he ungrateful to the instruments of her prosperity. His trees extended their cool, umbrageous branches over the merchants, who assembled in the Agora, for many generations.

Those merchants certainly had deserved that act of bounty; for all the while their ships had been carrying forth the intellectual fame of Athens to the western world. Then commenced what may be called her

University existence. Pericles, who succeeded Cimon both in the government and in the patronage of art, is said by Plutarch to have entertained the idea of making Athens the capital of federated Greece : in this he failed, but his encouragement of such men as Phidias and Anaxagoras led the way to her acquiring a far more lasting sovereignty over a far wider empire. Little understanding the sources of her own greatness, Athens would go to war : peace is the interest of a seat of commerce and the arts ; but to war she went ; yet to her, whether peace or war, it mattered not. The political power of Athens waned and disappeared ; kingdoms rose and fell ; centuries rolled away,—they did but bring fresh triumphs to the city of the poet and the sage. There at length the swarthy Moor and Spaniard were seen to meet the blue-eyed Gaul ; and the Cappadocian, late subject of Mithridates, gazed without alarm at the haughty conquering Roman. Revolution after revolution passed over the face of Europe, as well as of Greece, but still she was there,—Athens, the city of mind,—as radiant, as splendid, as delicate, as young, as ever she had been.

Many a more fruitful coast or isle is washed by the blue Ægean, many a spot is there more beautiful or sublime to see, many a territory more ample ; but there was one charm in Attica, which, in the same perfection, was nowhere else. The deep pastures of Arcadia, the plain, Argos, the Thessalian vale, these had not the gift; Bœotia, which lay to its immediate north, was notorious for its very want of it. The heavy atmosphere of that Bœotia might be good for vegetation, but it was associated in popular belief with the dulness of the Bœotian intellect : on the contrary, the special purity, elasticity, clearness, and salubrity of the air of Attica, fit concomitant and emblem of its genius, did that for it which earth did not :—it brought out every bright hue and tender shade of the landscape over which it was spread, and would have illuminated the face of even a more bare and rugged country.

A confined triangle, perhaps fifty miles its greatest length, and thirty its greatest breadth ; two elevated rocky barriers, meeting at an angle ; three prominent mountains, commanding the plain,—Parnes, Penteli-cus, and Hymettus ; an unsatisfactory soil ; some streams, not always full ;—such is about the report which the <u>agent of a London company</u> would have made of Attica. He would report that the climate was mild ; the hills were limestone ; there was plenty of good marble ; more pasture land than at first survey might have been expected, sufficient certainly for sheep and goats ; fisheries productive ; silver mines once, but long since worked out ; figs fair ; oil first-rate ; olives in profusion. But what he would not think of noting down, was, that that olive tree was so choice in nature and so noble in shape that it excited a relig-ious veneration ; and that it took so kindly to the light soil, as to expand into woods upon the open plain, and to climb up and fringe the hills. He would not think of writing word to his employers, how that clear air, of which I have spoken, brought out, yet blended and subdued, the colours on the marble, till they had a softness and harmony, for all their richness, which in a picture looks exaggerated, yet is after all within the truth. He would not tell, how that same delicate and

brilliant atmosphere freshened up the pale olive, till
the olive forgot its monotony, and its cheek glowed like
the arbutus or beech of the Umbrian hills. He would
say nothing of the thyme and the thousand fragrant
herbs which carpeted Hymettus; he would hear nothing of the hum of its bees; nor take much account of
the rare flavour of its honey, since Gozo and Minorca
were sufficient for the English demand. He would
look over the Ægean from the height he had ascended; he would follow with his eye the chain of
islands, which, starting from the Sunian headland,
seemed to offer the fabled divinities of Attica, when
they would visit their Ionian cousins, a sort of viaduct
thereto across the sea: but that fancy would not occur
to him, nor any admiration of the dark violet billows
with their white edges down below; nor of those graceful, fan-like jets of silver upon the rocks, which slowly
rise aloft like water spirits from the deep, then shiver,
and break, and spread, and shroud themselves, and
disappear in a soft mist of foam; nor of the gentle, in-
cessant heaving and panting of the whole liquid plain;
nor of the long waves, keeping steady time, like a line
of soldiery as they resound upon the hollow shore, he
would not deign to notice that restless living element at
all except to bless his stars that he was not upon it.
Nor the distinct details, nor the refined colouring, nor
the graceful outline and roseate golden hue of the jut-
ting crags, nor the bold shadows cast from Otus or
Laurium by the declining sun;—our agent of a mer-
cantile firm would not value these matters even at a
low figure. Rather we must turn for the sympathy we
seek to yon pilgrim student, come from a semi-barba-

rous land to that small corner of the earth, as to a
shrine, where he might take his fill of gazing on those
emblems and coruscations of invisible unoriginate
perfection.   It was the stranger from a remote
province, from Britain or from Mauritania, who in a
scene so different from that of his chilly, woody
swamps, or of his fiery, choking sands, learned at once
what a real University must be, by coming to understand the sort of country which was its suitable home.

Nor was this all that a University required, and
found in Athens.   No one, even there, could live on
poetry.   If the students at that famous place had nothing better than bright hues and soothing sounds, they
would not have been able or disposed to turn their
residence there to much account.   Of course they
must have the means of living, nay, in a certain sense,
of enjoyment, if Athens was to be an Alma Mater at
the time, or to remain afterwards a pleasant thought in
their memory.   And so they had : be it recollected
Athens was a port, and a mart of trade, perhaps the
first in Greece ; and this was very much to the point,
when a number of strangers were ever flocking to it,
whose combat was to be with intellectual, not physical
difficulties, and who claimed to have their bodily wants
supplied, that they might be at leisure to set about
furnishing their minds.   Now, barren as was the soil
of Attica, and bare the face of the country, yet it had
only too many resources for an elegant, nay, luxurious
abode there.   So abundant were the imports of the
place, that it was a common saying, that the productions, which were found singly elsewhere, were brought
all together in Athens.   Corn and wine, the staple of

subsistence in such a climate, came from the isles of
the Ægean; fine wool and carpeting from Asia Minor;
slaves, as now, from the Euxine, and timber too; and
iron and brass from the coasts of the Mediterranean.
The Athenian did not condescend to manufactures himself, but encouraged them in others; and a population
of foreigners caught at the lucrative occupation both for
home consumption and for exportation. Their cloth,
and other textures for dress and furniture, and their
hardware—for instance, armour—were in great request.
Labour was cheap; stone and marble in plenty; and
the taste and skill, which at first were devoted to public
buildings, as temples and porticos, were in the course
of time applied to the mansions of public men. If
nature did much for Athens, it is undeniable that art
did much more.

Here some one will interrupt me with the remark:
"By the by, where are we, and whither are we going?
—what has all this to do with a University? at least
what has it to do with education? It is instructive
doubtless; but still how much has it to do with your
subject?" Now I beg to assure the reader that I am
most conscientiously employed upon my subject; and
I should have thought every one would have seen this:
however, since the objection is made, I may be allowed
to pause awhile, and show distinctly the drift of what I
have been saying, before I go farther. *What* has this
to do with my subject! why, the question of the *site* is
the very first that comes into consideration, when a
Studium Generale is contemplated; for that site should
be a liberal and noble one; who will deny it? All
authorities agree in this, and very little reflection will

be sufficient to make it clear. I recollect a conversation I once had on this very subject with a very eminent man. I was a youth of eighteen, and was leaving my University for the Long Vacation, when I found myself in company in a public conveyance with a middle-aged person, whose face was strange to me. However, it was the great academical luminary of the day, whom afterwards I knew very well. Luckily for me, I did not suspect it; and luckily too, it was a fancy of his, as his friends knew, to make himself on easy terms especially with stage-coach companions. So, what with my flippancy and his condescension, I managed to hear many things which were novel to me at the time; and one point which he was strong upon, and was evidently fond of urging, was the material pomp and circumstance which should environ a great seat of learning. He considered it was worth the consideration of the government, whether Oxford should not stand in a domain of its own. An ample range, say four miles in diameter, should be turned into wood and meadow, and the University should be approached on all sides by a magnificent park, with fine trees in groups and groves and avenues, and with glimpses and views of the fair city, as the traveller drew near it. There is nothing surely absurd in the idea, though it would cost a round sum to realize it. What has a better claim to the purest and fairest possessions of nature, than the seat of wisdom? So thought my coach companion; and he did but express the tradition of ages and the instinct of mankind.

For instance, take the great University of Paris. That famous school engrossed as its territory the whole south bank of the Seine, and occupied one half, and that the pleasanter half, of the city. King Louis had the island pretty well as his own,—it was scarcely more than a fortification; and the north of the river was given over to the nobles and citizens to do what they could with its marshes; but the eligible south, rising from the stream, which swept around its base, to the fair summit of St. Genevieve, with its broad meadows, its vineyards and its gardens, and with the sacred elevation of Montmartre confronting it, all this was the inheritance of the University. There was that pleasant Pratum, stretching along the river's bank, in which the students for centuries took their recreation, which Alcuin seems to mention in his farewell verses to Paris, and which has given a name to the great Abbey of St. Germain-des-Prés. For long years it was devoted to the purposes of innocent and healthy enjoyment; but evil times came on the University; disorder arose within its precincts, and the fair meadow became the scene of party brawls; heresy stalked through Europe, and Germany and England no longer sending their contingent of students, a heavy debt was the consequence to the academical body. To let their land was the only resource left to them: buildings rose upon it, and spread along the green sod, and the country at length became town. Great was the grief and indignation of the doctors and masters, when this catastrophe occurred. "A wretched sight," said the Proctor of the German nation, "a wretched sight, to witness the sale of that ancient manor, whither the Muses were wont to wander for retirement and pleasure. Whither shall

the youthful student now betake himself, what relief
will he find for his eyes, wearied with intense reading,
now that the pleasant stream is taken from him?"
Two centuries and more have passed since this com-
plaint was uttered; and time has shown that the
outward calamity, which it recorded, was but the emblem of the great moral revolution, which was to
follow; till the institution itself has followed its green
meadows, into the region of things which once were
and now are not.—*Historical Sketches*, ed. 1891, vol. iii.,
pp. 18–26 (1854).

To-day I have confined myself to saying that that training of the intellect, which is best for the individual himself, best enables him to discharge his duties to society. The Philosopher, indeed, and the man of the world differ in their very notion, but the methods, by which they are respectively formed, are pretty much the same. The Philosopher has the same command of matters of thought, which the true citizen and gentleman has of matters of business and conduct. If then a practical end must be assigned to a University course, I say it is that of training good members of society. Its art is the art of social life, and its end is fitness for the world. It neither confines its views to particular professions on the one hand, nor creates heroes or inspires genius on the other. Works indeed of genius fall under no art; heroic minds come under no rule; a University is not a birthplace of poets or of immortal authors, of founders of schools, leaders of colonies, or conquerors of nations. It does not promise a generation of Aristotles or Newtons, of Napoleons or Washingtons, of Raphaels or Shakespeares, though such miracles of nature it has before now contained within its precincts. Nor is it content on the other hand with forming the critic or the experimentalist, the economist or the engineer, though

11

such too it includes within its scope. But a University training is the great ordinary means to a great but ordinary end ; it aims at raising the intellectual tone of society, at cultivating the public mind, at purifying the national taste, at supplying true principles to popular enthusiasm and fixed aims to popular aspiration, at giving enlargement and sobriety to the ideas of the age, at facilitating the exercise of political power, and refining the intercourse of private life. It is the education which gives a man a clear conscious view of his own opinions and judgments, a truth in developing them, an eloquence in expressing them, and a force in urging them. It teaches him to see things as they are, to go right to the point, to disentangle a skein of thought, to detect what is sophistical, and to discard what is irrelevant. It prepares him to fill any post with credit, and to master any subject with facility. It shows him how to accommodate himself to others, how to throw himself into their state of mind, how to bring before them his own, how to influence them, how to come to an understanding with them, how to bear with them. He is at home in any society, he has common ground with every class ; he knows when to speak and when to be silent ; he is able to converse, he is able to listen ; he can ask a question pertinently, and gain a lesson seasonably, when he has nothing to impart himself ; he is ever ready, yet never in the way ; he is a pleasant companion, and a comrade you can depend upon ; he knows when to be serious and when to trifle, and he has a sure tact which enables him to trifle with gracefulness and to be serious with effect. He has the repose of a mind which lives in itself, while it lives in the world, and which has resources for its happiness at home when it cannot go abroad. He has a gift which serves him in public, and supports him in retirement, without which good fortune is but vulgar, and with which failure and disappointment have a charm. The art which tends to make a man all this, is in the object which it pursues as useful as the art of wealth or the art of health, though it is less susceptible of method, and less tangible, less certain, less complete, in its result.—*Idea of a University*, ed. 1891, pp. 177-178 (1852).

PRIDE, under such training, instead of running to waste in the education of the mind, is turned to account; it gets a new name; it is called self-respect; and ceases to be the disagreeable, uncompanionable quality which it is in itself. Though it be the motive principle of the soul, it seldom comes to view; and when it shows itself, then delicacy and gentleness are its attire, and good sense and sense of honour direct its motions. It is no longer a restless agent, without definite aim; it has a large field of exertion assigned to it, and it subserves those social interests which it would naturally trouble. It is directed into the channel of industry, frugality, honesty, and obedience; and it becomes the very staple of the religion and morality held in honour in a day like our own. It becomes the safeguard of chastity, the guarantee of veracity, in high and low; it is the very household god of society, as at present constituted, inspiring neatness and decency in the servant girl, propriety of carriage and refined manners in her mistress, uprightness, manliness, and generosity in the head of the family. It diffuses a light over town and country; it covers the soil with handsome edifices and smiling gardens; it tills the field, it stocks and embellishes the shop. It is the stimulating principle of providence on the one hand, and of free expenditure on the other; of an honourable ambition, and of elegant enjoyment. It breathes upon the face of the community, and the hollow sepulchre is forthwith beautiful to look upon.

Refined by the civilization which has brought it into activity, this self-respect infuses into the mind an intense horror of exposure, and a keen sensitiveness of notoriety and ridicule. It becomes the enemy of extravagances of any kind; it shrinks from what are called scenes; it has no mercy on the mock-heroic, on pretence or egotism, on verbosity in language, or what is called prosiness in conversation. It detests gross adulation; not that it tends at all to the eradication of the appetite to which the flatterer ministers, but it sees the absurdity of indulging it, it understands the annoyance thereby given to others, and if a tribute must be paid to the wealthy or the powerful, it demands greater subtlety and art in the preparation. Thus vanity is changed into a more dangerous self-conceit, as being checked in its natural eruption. It teaches men to suppress their feelings, and to control their tempers, and to mitigate both the severity and the tone of their judgments. As Lord Shaftesbury would desire, it prefers playful wit and satire in putting down what is objectionable, as a more refined and good-natured, as well as a more effectual method, than the expedient which is natural to uneducated minds. It is from this impatience of the tragic and the bombastic that it is now quietly but energetically opposing itself to the unchristian practice of duelling, which it brands as simply out of taste, and as the remnant of a barbarous age; and certainly it seems likely to effect what Religion has aimed at abolishing in vain.

Hence it is that it is almost a definition of a gentleman to say he is one who never inflicts pain. This description is both refined and, as far as it goes, accurate. He is mainly occupied in merely removing the obstacles which hinder the free and unembarrassed action of those about him; and he concurs with their movements rather than takes the initiative himself. His benefits may be considered as parallel to what are called comforts or conveniences in arrangements of a personal nature: like an easy-chair or a good fire, which do their part in dispelling cold and fatigue, though nature provides both means of rest and animal heat without them. The true gentleman in like manner carefully avoids whatever may cause a jar or a jolt in the minds of those with whom he is cast;—all clashing of opinion, or collision of feeling, all restraint, or suspicion, or gloom, or resentment; his great concern being to make every one at their ease and at home. He has his eyes on all his company; he is tender towards the bashful, gentle towards the distant, and merciful towards the absurd; he can recollect to whom he is speaking; he guards against unseasonable allusions, or topics which may irritate; he is seldom prominent in conversation, and never wearisome. He makes light of favours while he does them, and seems to be receiving when he is conferring. He never speaks of himself except when compelled, never defends himself by a mere retort, he has no ears for slander or gossip, is scrupulous in imputing motives to those who interfere with him, and interprets every-thing for the best. He is never mean or little in his disputes, never takes unfair advantage, never mistakes personalities or sharp sayings for arguments, or insinuates evil which he dare not say out. From a long-sighted prudence, he observes the maxim of the ancient sage, that we should ever conduct ourselves towards our enemy as if he were one day to be our friend. He has too much good sense to be affronted at insults, he is too well employed to remember injuries, and too indolent to bear malice. He is patient, forbearing, and resigned, on philosophical principles ; he submits to pain, because it is inevitable, to bereavement, because it is irreparable, and to death, because it is his destiny. If he engages in controversy of any kind, his disciplined intellect preserves him from the blundering discourtesy of better, perhaps, but less educated minds ; who, like blunt weapons, tear and hack instead of cutting clean, who mistake the point in argument, waste their strength on trifles, misconceive their adversary, and leave the question more involved than they find it. He may be right or wrong in his opinion, but he is too clear-headed to be unjust ; he is as simple as he is forcible, and as brief as he is decisive. Nowhere shall we find greater candor, consideration, indulgence : he throws himself into the minds of his opponents, he accounts for their mistakes. He knows the weakness of human reason as well as its strength, its province and its limits. If he be an unbeliever, he will be too profound and large-minded to ridicule religion or to act against it ; he is too wise to be a dogmatist or fanatic in his in-

2

fidelity.   He respects piety and devotion ; he even
supports institutions as venerable, beautiful, or useful,
to which he does not assent ; he honours the ministers
of religion, and it contents him to decline its mysteries
without assailing or denouncing them.   He is a friend
of religious toleration, and that, not only because his
philosophy has taught him to look on all forms of
faith with an impartial eye, but also from the gentleness and effeminacy of feeling, which is the attendant
on civilization.

Not that he may not hold a religion too, in his own
way, even when he is not a Christian.   In that case
his religion is one of imagination and sentiment ; it is
the embodiment   of   those   ideas   of   the   sublime,
majestic, and beautiful, without which there can be no
large philosophy.   Sometimes he acknowledges the
being of God, sometimes he invests an unknown
principle or quality with the attributes of perfection.
And this deduction of his reason, or creation of his
fancy, he makes the occasion of such excellent
thoughts, and the starting-point of so varied and systematic a teaching, that he even seems like a disciple
of Christianity itself.   From the very accuracy and
steadiness of his logical powers, he is able to see
what sentiments are consistent in those who hold any
religious doctrine at all, and he appears to others to
feel and to hold a whole circle of theological truths,
which exist in his mind no otherwise than as a number
of deductions.—*Idea of a University*, ed. 1891, pp.
207–211, (1852).

It were well if the English, like the Greek language, possessed some definite word to express, simply and generally, intellectual proficiency or perfection, such as " health," as used with reference to the animal frame, and " virtue," with reference to our moral nature. I am not able to find such a term;—talent, ability, genius, belong distinctly to the raw material, which is the subject-matter, not to that excellence which is the result of exercise and training. When we turn, indeed, to the particular kinds of intellectual perfection, words are forthcoming for our purpose, as, for instance, judgment, taste, and skill; yet even these belong, for the most part, to powers or habits bearing upon practice or upon art, and not to any perfect condition of the intellect, considered in itself. Wisdom, again, is certainly a more comprehensive word than any other, but it has a direct relation to conduct, and to human life. Knowledge, indeed, and Science express purely intellectual ideas, but still not a state or quality of the intellect; for knowledge, in its ordinary sense, is but one of its circumstances, denoting a possession or a habit; and science has been appropriated to the subject-matter of the intellect, instead of belonging in English, as it ought to do, to the intellect itself. The consequence is that, on an occasion like this, many

19

words are necessary, in order, first, to bring out and convey what surely is no difficult idea in itself,—that of the cultivation of the intellect as an end; next, in order to recommend what surely is no unreasonable object; and lastly, to describe and make the mind realize the particular perfection in which that object consists. Every one knows practically what are the constituents of health or of virtue; and every one recognizes health and virtue as ends to be pursued; it is otherwise with intellectual excellence, and this must be my excuse, if I seem to any one to be bestowing a good deal of labour on a preliminary matter.

In default of a recognized term, I have called the perfection or virtue of the intellect by the name of philosophy, philosophical knowledge, enlargement of mind, or illumination; terms which are not uncommonly given to it by writers of this day : but, whatever name we bestow on it, it is, I believe, as a matter of history, the business of a University to make this intellectual culture its direct scope, or to employ itself in the education of the intellect,—just as the work of a Hospital lies in healing the sick or wounded, of a Riding or Fencing School, or of a Gymnasium, in exercising the limbs, of an Almshouse, in aiding and solacing the old, of an Orphanage, in protecting innocence, of a Penitentiary, in restoring the guilty. I say, a University, taken in its bare idea, and before we view it as an instrument of the Church, has this object and this mission; it contemplates neither moral impression nor mechanical production; it professes to exercise the mind neither in art nor in duty; its function is intellectual culture; here it may leave its scholars, and it has done its work when it has done as much as this. It educates the intellect to reason well in all matters, to reach out towards truth, and to grasp it.

This, I said in my foregoing Discourse, was the object of a University, viewed in itself, and apart from the Catholic Church, or from the State, or from any other power which may use it; and I illustrated this in various ways. I said that the intellect must have an excellence of its own, for there was nothing which had not its specific good; that the word "educate" would not be used of intellectual culture, as it is used, had not the intellect had an end of its own; that, had it not such an end, there would be no meaning in calling certain intellectual exercises "liberal," in contrast with "useful," as is commonly done; that the very notion of a philosophical temper implied it, for it threw us back upon research and system as ends in themselves, distinct from effects and works of any kind; that a philosophical scheme of knowledge, or system of sciences, could not, from the nature of the case, issue in any one definite art or pursuit, as its end; and that, on the other hand, the discovery and contemplation of truth, to which research and systematizing led, were surely sufficient ends, though nothing beyond them were added, and that they had ever been accounted sufficient by mankind.

Here then I take up the subject; and, having determined that the cultivation of the intellect is an end distinct and sufficient in itself, and that, so far as words go, it is an enlargement or illumination, I proceed to inquire what this mental breadth, or power, or light, or philosophy consits in. A Hospital heals a broken limb or cures a fever : what does an Institution effect, which professes the health, not of the body, not of the soul, but of the intellect ? What is this good, which in former times, as well as our own, has been found worth the notice, the appropriation, of the Catholic Church ?

I have then to investigate, in the Discourses which follow, those qualities and characteristics of the intellect in which its cultivation issues or rather consists ; and, with a view of assisting myself in this undertaking, I shall recur to certain questions which have already been touched upon. These questions are three : viz. the relation of intellectual culture, first, to *mere* knowledge ; secondly, to *professional* knowledge ; and thirdly, to *religious* knowledge. In other words, are *acquirements* and *attainments* the scope of a University Education ? or *expertnesss in particular arts* and *pursuits ?* or *moral and religious proficiency ?* or something besides these three ? These questions I shall examine in succession, with the purpose I have mentioned ; and I hope to be excused, if, in this anxious undertaking, I am led to repeat what, either in these Discourses or elsewhere, I have already put upon paper. And first, of *Mere Knowledge,* or Learning, and its connection with intellectual illumination or Philosophy.

I suppose the *prima-facie* view which the public at large would take of a University, considering it as a place of Education, is nothing more or less than a place for acquiring a great deal of knowledge on a great many subjects. Memory is one of the first developed of the mental faculties ; a boy's business when he goes to school is to learn, that is, to store up things in his memory. For some years his intellect is little more than an instrument for taking in facts, or a receptacle for storing them ; he welcomes them as fast as they come to him ; he lives on what is without ; he has his eyes ever about him ; he has a lively susceptibility of impressions ; he imbibes information of every kind ; and little does he make his own in a true sense of the word, living rather upon his neighbours all around him. He has opinions, religious, political and literary, and, for a boy, is very positive in them and sure about them ; but he gets them from his schoolfellows, or his masters, or his parents, as the case may be. Such as he is in his other relations, such also is he in his school exercises ; his mind is observant, sharp, ready, retentive ; he is almost passive in the acquisition of knowledge. I say this in no disparagement of the idea of a clever boy. Geography, chronology, history, language, natural history, he heaps up the matter of these studies as treasures for a future day. It is the seven years of plenty with him : he gathers in by handfuls, like the Egyptians, without counting ; and though, as time goes on, there is exercise for his argumentative powers in the Elements of Mathematics, and for his taste in the Poets and Orators, still, while at school, or at least, till quite the last years of his time, he acquires, and little more ; and when he is leaving for the University, he is mainly the creature of foreign influences and circumstances, and made up of accidents, homogeneous or not, as the case may be. More-

over, the moral habits, which are a boy's praise, encourage and assist this result; that is, diligence,
assiduity, regularity, despatch, persevering application; for these are the direct conditions of acquisition,
and naturally lead to it. Acquirements, again, are
emphatically producible, and at a moment; they are a
something to show, both for master and scholar; an
audience, even though ignorant themselves of the
subject of an examination, can comprehend when
questions are answered and when they are not. Here
again is a reason why mental culture is in the minds
of men identified with the acquisition of knowledge.

The same notion possesses the public mind, when it
passes on from the thought of a school to that of a
University: and with the best of reasons so far as this,
that there is no true culture without acquirements, and
that philosophy presupposes knowledge. It requires a
great deal of reading, or a wide range of information,
to warrant us in putting forth our opinions on any serious subject; and without such learning the most original mind may be able indeed to dazzle, to amuse, to
refute, to perplex, but not to come to any useful result
or any trustworthy conclusion. There are indeed persons who profess a different view of the matter, and
even act upon it. Every now and then you will find a
person of vigorous or fertile mind, who relies upon his
own resources, despises all former authors, and gives
the world, with the utmost fearlessness, his views upon
religion, or history, or any other popular subject. And
his works may sell for a while; he may get a name in
his day; but this will be all. His readers are sure to
find on the long run that his doctrines are mere

theories, and not the expression of facts, that they are chaff instead of bread, and then his popularity drops as suddenly as it rose.

Knowledge then is the indispensable condition of expansion of mind, and the instrument of attaining to it; this cannot be denied, it is ever to be insisted on; I begin with it as a first principle; however, the very truth of it carries men too far, and confirms to them the notion that it is the whole of the matter. A narrow mind is thought to be that which contains little knowledge; and an enlarged mind, that which holds a great deal; and what seems to put the matter beyond dispute is, the fact of the great number of studies which are pursued in a University, by its very profession. Lectures are given on every kind of subject; examinations are held; prizes awarded. There are moral, metaphysical, physical Professors; Professors of languages, of history, of mathematics, of experimental science. Lists of questions are published, wonderful for their range and depth, variety and difficulty; treatises are written, which carry upon their very face the evidence of extensive reading or multifarious information; what then is wanting for mental culture to a person of large reading and scientific attainments? what is grasp of mind but acquirement? where shall philosophical repose be found, but in the consciousness and enjoyment of large intellectual possessions?

And yet this notion is, I conceive, a mistake, and my present business is to show that it is one, and that the end of a Liberal Education is not mere knowledge, or knowledge considered in its *matter;* and I shall best attain my object, by actually setting down some cases, which will be generally granted to be instances of the process of enlightenment or enlargement of mind, and others which are not, and thus, by the comparison, you will be able to judge for yourselves, Gentlemen, whether Knowledge, that is, acquirement, is after all the real principle of the enlargement, or whether that principle is not rather something beyond it.

For instance,* let a person, whose experience has hitherto been confined to the more calm and unpretending scenery of these islands, whether here or in England, go for the first time into parts where physical nature puts on her wilder and more awful forms, whether at home or abroad, as into mountainous districts ; or let one, who has ever lived in a quiet village, go for the first time to a great metropolis,—then I suppose he will have a sensation which perhaps he never had before. He has a feeling not in addition or increase of former feelings, but of something different in its nature. He will perhaps be borne forward, and find for a time that he has lost his bearings. He has made a certain progress, and he has a consciousness of mental enlargement; he does not stand where he did, he has a new centre, and a range of thoughts to which he was before a stranger.

Again, the view of the heavens which the telescope opens upon us, if allowed to fill and possess the mind, may almost whirl it round and make it dizzy. It

---

* The pages which follow are taken almost *verbatim* from the author's 14th (Oxford) University Sermon, which, at the time of writing this Discourse, he did not expect ever to reprint.

brings in a flood of ideas, and is rightly called an intellectual enlargement, whatever is meant by the term.

And so again, the sight of beasts of prey and other foreign animals, their strangeness, the originality (if I may use the term) of their forms and gestures and habits, and their variety and independence of each other, throw us out of ourselves into another creation, and as if under another Creator, if I may so express the temptation which may come on the mind. We seem to have new faculties, or a new exercise for our faculties, by this addition to our knowledge ; like a prisoner, who, having been accustomed to wear manacles or fetters, suddenly finds his arms and legs free.

Hence Physical Science generally, in all its departments, as bringing before us the exuberant riches and resources, yet the orderly course, of the Universe, elevates and excites the student, and at first, I may say, almost takes away his breath, while in time it exercises a tranquillizing influence upon him.

Again, the study of history is said to enlarge and enlighten the mind, and why ? because, as I conceive, it gives it a power of judging of passing events, and of all events, and a conscious superiority over them, which before it did not possess.

And in like manner, what is called seeing the world, entering into active life, going into society, travelling, gaining acquaintance with the various classes of the community, coming into contact with the principles and modes of thought of various parties, interests, and races, their views, aims, habits and manners, their religious creeds and forms of worship,—gaining experience how various yet how alike men are, how low-minded, how bad, how opposed, yet how confident in their opinions; all this exerts a perceptible influence upon the mind, which it is impossible to mistake, be it good or be it bad, and is popularly called its enlargement.

And then again, the first time the mind comes across the arguments and speculations of unbelievers, and feels what a novel light they cast upon what he has hitherto accounted sacred; and still more, if it gives in to them and embraces them, and throws off as so much prejudice what it has hitherto held, and, as if waking from a dream, begins to realize to its imagination that there is now no such thing as law and the transgression of law, that sin is a phantom, and punishment a bugbear, that it is free to sin, free to enjoy the world and the flesh; and still further, when it does enjoy them, and reflects that it may think and hold just what it will, that " the world is all before it where to choose," and what system to build up as its own private persuasion; when this torrent of wilful thoughts rushes over and inundates it, who will deny that the fruit of the tree of knowledge, or what the mind takes for knowledge, has made it one of the gods, with a sense of expansion and elevation,—an intoxication in reality, still, so far as the subjective state of the mind goes, an illumination? Hence the fanaticism of individuals or nations, who suddenly cast off their Maker. Their eyes are opened; and, like the judgment-stricken king in the Tragedy, they see two suns, and a magic universe, out of which they look back upon their former state of faith and innocence with a sort of contempt and indignation, as if they were then but fools, and the dupes of imposture.

On the other hand, Religion has its own enlargement, and an enlargement, not of tumult, but of peace. It is often remarked of uneducated persons, who have hitherto thought little of the unseen world, that, on their turning to God, looking into themselves, regulating their hearts, reforming their conduct, and meditating on death and judgment, heaven and hell, they seem to become, in point of intellect, different beings from what they were. Before, they took things as they came, and thought no more of one thing than another. But now every event has a meaning; they have their own estimate of whatever happens to them ; they are mindful of times and seasons, and compare the present with the past ; and the world, no longer dull, monotonous, unprofitable, and hopeless, is a various and complicated drama, with parts and an object, and an awful moral.

Now from these instances, to which many more might be added, it is plain, first, that the communication of knowledge certainly is either a condition or the means of that sense of enlargement, or enlightenment of which at this day we hear so much in certain quarters : this cannot be denied ; but next, it is equally plain, that such communication is not the whole of the process. The enlargement consists, not merely in the passive reception into the mind of a number of ideas hitherto unknown to it, but in the mind's energetic and simultaneous action upon and towards and among those new ideas, which are rushing in upon it. It is the action of a formative power, reducing to order and meaning the matter of our acquirements; it is a making the objects of our knowledge subjectively our own, or, to use a familiar word, it is a digestion of what we receive, into the substance of our previous state of thought; and without this no enlargement is said to follow. There is no enlargement, unless there be a comparison of ideas one with another, as they come before the mind, and a systematizing of them. We feel our minds to be growing and expanding *then*, when we not only learn, but refer what we learn to what we know already. It is not the mere addition to our knowledge that is the illumination; but the locomotion, the movement onwards, of that mental centre, to which both what we know, and what we are learning, the accumulating mass of our acquirements, gravitates. And therefore a truly great intellect, and recognized to be such by the common opinion of mankind, such as the intellect of Aristotle, or of St. Thomas, or of Newton, or of Goethe (I purposely take instances within and without the Catholic pale, when I would speak of the intellect as such), is one which takes a connected view of old and new, past and present, far and near, and which has an insight into the influence of all these one on another; without which there is no whole, and no centre. It possesses the knowledge, not only of things, but also of their mutual and true relations; knowledge, not merely considered as acquirement but as philosophy.

Accordingly, when this analytical, distributive, harmonizing process is away, the mind experiences no enlargement, and is not reckoned as enlightened or comprehensive, whatever it may add to its knowledge. For instance, a great memory, as I have already said, does not make a philosopher, any more than a dictionary can be called a grammar. There are men who embrace in their minds a vast multitude of ideas, but with little sensibility about their real relations towards each other. These may be antiquarians, annalists, naturalists; they may be learned in the law; they may be versed in statistics; they are most useful in their own place; I should shrink from speaking disrespectfully of them; still, there is nothing in such attainments to guarantee the absence of narrowness of mind. If they are nothing more than well-read men, or men of information, they have not what specially deserves the name of culture of mind, or fulfils the type of Liberal Education.

In like manner, we sometimes fall in with persons who have seen much of the world, and of the men who, in their day, have played a conspicuous part in it, but who generalize nothing, and have no observation, in the true sense of the word. They abound in information in detail, curious and entertaining, about men and things; and, having lived under the influence of no very clear or settled principles, religious or political, they speak of every one and every thing, only as so many phenomena, which are complete in themselves, and lead to nothing, not discussing them, or teaching any truth, or instructing the hearer, but simply talking. No one would say that these persons, well informed as they are, had attained to any great culture of intellect or to philosophy.

The case is the same still more strikingly where the

persons in question are beyond dispute men of inferior powers and deficient education. Perhaps they have been much in foreign countries, and they receive, in a passive, otiose, unfruitful way, the various facts which are forced upon them there. Seafaring men, for example, range from one end of the earth to the other; but the multiplicity of external objects, which they have encountered, forms no symmetrical and consistent picture upon their imagination ; they see the tapestry of human life, as it were on the wrong side, and it tells no story. They sleep, and they rise up, and they find themselves, now in Europe, now in Asia ; they see visions of great cities and wild regions ; they are in the marts of commerce, or amid the islands of the South ; they gaze on Pompey's Pillar, or on the Andes ; and nothing which meets them carries them forward or backward, to any idea beyond itself. Nothing has a drift or relation ; nothing has a history or a promise. Every thing stands by itself, and comes and goes in its turn, like the shifting scenes of a show, which leave the spectator where he was. Perhaps you are near such a man on a particular occasion, and expect him to be shocked or perplexed at something which occurs ; but one thing is much the same to him as another, or, if he is perplexed, it is as not knowing what to say, whether it is right to admire, or to ridicule, or to disapprove, while conscious that some expression of opinion is expected from him ; for in fact he has no standard of judgment at all, and no landmarks to guide him to a conclusion. Such is mere acquisition, and, I repeat, no one would dream of calling it philosophy.

Instances, such as these, confirm, by the contrast, the conclusion I have already drawn from those which preceded them. That only is true enlargement of mind which is the power of viewing many things at once as one whole, of referring them severally to their true place in the universal system, of understanding their respective values, and determining their mutual dependence. Thus is that form of Universal Knowledge, of which I have on a former occasion spoken, set up in the individual intellect, and constitutes its perfection. Possessed of this real illumination, the mind never views any part of the extended subject-matter of Knowledge without recollecting that it is but a part, or without the associations which spring from this recollection. It makes everything in some sort lead to everything else; it would communicate the image of the whole to every separate portion, till that whole becomes in imagination like a spirit, everywhere pervading and penetrating its component parts, and giving them one definite meaning. Just as our bodily organs, when mentioned, recall their function in the body, as the word "creation" suggests the Creator, and "subjects" a sovereign, so, in the mind of the Philosopher, as we are abstractedly conceiving of him, the elements of the physical and moral world, sciences, arts, pursuits, ranks, offices, events, opinions, individualities, are all viewed as one, with correlative functions, and as gradually by successive combinations converging, one and all, to the true centre.

To have even a portion of this illuminative reason and true philosophy is the highest state to which nature can aspire, in the way of intellect; it puts the

3

mind above the influences of chance and necessity, above anxiety, suspense, unsettlement, and superstition, which is the lot of the many. Men, whose minds are possessed with some one object, take exaggerated views of its importance, are feverish in the pursuit of it, make it the measure of things which are utterly foreign to it, and are startled and despond if it happens to fail them. They are ever in alarm or in transport. Those on the other hand who have no object or principle whatever to hold by, lose their way every step they take. They are thrown out, and do not know what to think or say, at every fresh juncture; they have no view of persons, or occurrences, or facts, which come suddenly upon them, and they hang upon the opinion of others for want of internal resources. But the intellect, which has been disciplined to the perfection of its powers, which knows, and thinks while it knows, which has learned to leaven the dense mass of facts and events with the elastic force of reason, such an intellect cannot be partial, cannot be exclusive, cannot be impetuous, cannot be at a loss, cannot but be patient, collected, and majestically calm, because it discerns the end in every beginning, the origin in every end, the law in every interruption, the limit in each delay; because it ever knows where it stands, and how its path lies from one point to another. It is the τετράγωνος of the Peripatetic, and has the "nil admirari" of the Stoic,—

Felix qui potuit rerum cognoscere causas,
Atque metus omnes, et inexorabile fatum
Subjecit pedibus, strepitumque Acherontis avari.

There are men who, when in difficulties, originate at the moment vast ideas or dazzling projects; who, under the influence of excitement, are able to cast a light, almost as if from inspiration, on a subject or course of action which comes before them; who have a sudden presence of mind equal to any emergency, rising with the occasion, and an undaunted magnanimous bearing, and an energy and keenness which is but made intense by opposition. This is genius, this is heroism; it is the exhibition of a natural gift, which no culture can teach, at which no Institution can aim: here, on the contrary, we are concerned, not with mere nature, but with training and teaching. That perfection of the Intellect, which is the result of Education, and its *beau ideal*, to be imparted to individuals in their respective measures, is the clear, calm, accurate vision and comprehension of all things, as far as the finite mind can embrace them, each in its place, and with its own characteristics upon it. It is almost prophetic from its knowledge of history; it is almost heart-searching from its knowledge of human nature; it has almost supernatural charity from its freedom from littleness and prejudice; it has almost the repose of faith, because nothing can startle it; it has almost the beauty and harmony of heavenly contemplation, so intimate is it with the eternal order of things and the music of the spheres.

And now, if I may take for granted that the true and adequate end of intellectual training and of a University is not Learning or Acquirement, but rather, is Thought or Reason. exercised upon Knowledge, or

what may be called Philosophy, I shall be in a
position to explain the various mistakes which at the
present day beset the subject of University Education.

*   *   *   *   *   *   *

I will tell you, Gentlemen, what has been the practical
error of the last twenty years,—not to load the memory
of the student with a mass of undigested knowledge,
but to force upon him so much that he has rejected all.
It has been the error of distracting and enfeebling
the mind by an unmeaning profusion of subjects ; of
implying that a smattering in a dozen branches of
study is not shallowness, which it really is, but enlargement, which it is not; of considering an acquaintance
with the learned names of things and persons, and
the possession of clever duodecimos, and attendance
on eloquent lecturers, and membership with scientific
institutions, and the sight of the experiments of a
platform and the specimens of a museum, that all this
was not dissipation of mind, but progress. All things
now are to be learned at once, not first one thing,
then another, not one well, but many badly. Learning
is to be without exertion, without attention, without
toil ; without grounding, without advance, without
finishing. There is to be nothing individual in it ; and
this, forsooth, is the wonder of the age. What the
steam engine does with matter, the printing-press is
to do with mind ; it is to act mechanically, and the
population is to be passively, almost unconsciously
enlightened, by the mere multiplication and dissemina-
tion of volumes. Whether it be the school-boy, or
the school-girl, or the youth at college, or the mechanic
in the town, or the politician in the senate, all have

been the victims in one way or other of this most preposterous and pernicious of delusions. Wise men have lifted up their voices in vain ; and at length, lest their own institutions should be outshone and should disappear in the folly of the hour, they have been obliged, as far as they could with a good conscience, to humour a spirit which they could not withstand, and make temporizing concessions at which they could not but inwardly smile.

* * * * * * *

I protest to you, Gentlemen, that if I had to choose between a so-called University, which dispensed with residence and tutorial superintendence, and gave its degrees to any person who passed an examination in a wide range of subjects, and a University which had no professors or examinations at all, but merely brought a number of young men together for three or four years, and then sent them away as the University of Oxford is said to have done some sixty years since, if I were asked which of these two methods was the better discipline of the intellect,—mind, I do not say which is *morally* the better, for it is plain that compulsory study must be a good and idleness an intolerable mischief,—but if I must determine which of the two courses was the more successful in training, moulding, enlarging the mind, which sent out men the more fitted for their secular duties, which produced better public men, men of the world, men whose names would descend to posterity, I have no hesitation in giving the preference to that University which did nothing, over that which exacted of its members an acquaintance with every science under the sun. And, paradox

as this may seem, still if results be the test of systems,
the influence of the public schools and colleges of
England, in the course of the last century, at least will
bear out one side of the contrast as I have drawn
it. What would come, on the other hand, of the ideal
systems of education which have fascinated the imagination of this age, could they ever take effect,
and whether they would not produce a generation
frivolous, narrow-minded, and resourceless, intellect-
ually considered, is a fair subject for debate; but so
far is certain, that the Universities and scholastic
establishments, to which I refer, and which did little
more than bring together first boys and then youths in
large numbers, these institutions, with miserable de-
formities on the side of morals, with a hollow profession of Christianity, and a heathen code of ethics,—I
say, at least they can boast of a succession of heroes
and statesmen, of literary men and philosophers, of
men conspicuous for great natural virtues, for habits
of business, for knowledge of life, for practical judgment, for cultivated tastes, for accomplishments, who
have made England what it is,—able to subdue the
earth, able to domineer over Catholics.

How is this to be explained? I suppose as follows:
When a multitude of young men, keen, open-hearted,
sympathetic, and observant, as young men are, come
together and freely mix with each other, they are sure
to learn one from another, even if there be no one to
teach them; the conversation of all is a series of
lectures to each, and they gain for themselves new
ideas and views, fresh matter of thought, and distinct
principles for judging and acting, day by day. An

infant has to learn the meaning of the information
which its senses convey to it, and this seems to be its
employment. It fancies all that the eye presents to it
to be close to it, till it actually learns the contrary, and
thus by practice does it ascertain the relations and
uses of those first elements of knowledge which are
necessary for its animal existence. A parallel teaching is necessary for our social being, and it is secured
by a large school or a college ; and this effect may be
fairly called in its own department an enlargement of
mind. It is seeing the world on a small field with
little trouble ; for the pupils or students come from
very different places, and with widely different notions, and there is much to generalize, much to adjust,
much to eliminate, there are inter-relations to be
defined, and conventional rules to be established,
in the process, by which the whole assemblage is
moulded together, and gains one tone and one character.

Let it be clearly understood, I repeat it, that I am
not taking into account moral or religious considerations ; I am but saying that that youthful community
will constitute a whole, it will embody a specific idea,
it will represent a doctrine, it will administer a code of
conduct, and it will furnish principles of thought and
action. It will give birth to a living teaching, which in
course of time will take the shape of a self-perpetuat-
ing tradition, or a *genius loci*, as it is sometimes called ;
which haunts the home where it has been born, and
which imbues and forms, more or less, and one by one,
every individual who is successively brought under its
shadow. Thus it is that, independent of direct in-

struction on the part of Superiors, there is a sort of self-education in the academic institutions of Protestant England; a characteristic tone of thought, a recognized standard of judgment is found in them, which as developed in the individual who is submitted to it, becomes a twofold source of strength to him, both from the distinct stamp it impresses on his mind, and from the bond of union which it creates between him and others,—effects which are shared by the authorities of the place, for they themselves have been educated in it, and at all times are exposed to the influence of its ethical atmosphere. Here then is a real teaching, whatever be its standards and principles, true or false; and it at least tends towards cultivation of the intellect; it at least recognizes that knowledge is something more than a sort of passive reception of scraps and details; it is a something, and it does a something, which never will issue from the most strenuous efforts of a set of teachers, with no mutual sympathies and no intercommunion, of a set of examiners with no opinions which they dare profess, and with no common principles, who are teaching or questioning a set of youths who do not know them, and do not know each other, on a large number of subjects, different in kind, and connected by no wide philosophy, three times a week, or three times a year, or once in three years, in chill lecture-rooms or on a pompous anniversary.—*Idea of a University*, ed. 1891, pp. 124–148 (1852).

Lord Bacon.

BETTER, far better, to make no professions, you will say, than to cheat others with what we are not, and to scandalize them with what we are. The sensualist, or the man of the world, at any rate is not the victim of fine words, but pursues a reality and gains it. The Philosophy of Utility, you will say, Gentlemen, has at least done its work ; and I grant it,—it aimed low, but it has fulfilled its aim. If that man of great intellect who has been its Prophet in the conduct of life played false to his own professions, he was not bound by his philosophy to be true to his friend or faithful in his trust. Moral virtue was not the line in which he undertook to instruct men ; and though, as the poet calls him, he were the " meanest " of mankind, he was so in what may be called his private capacity and without any prejudice to the theory of induction. He had a right to be so, if he chose, for any thing that the Idols of the den or the theatre had to say to the contrary. His mission was the increase of physical enjoyment and social comfort ; * and most wonderfully, most awfully has he fulfilled his conception and his design. Almost day by day have we fresh and

* It will be seen that on the whole I agree with Lord Macaulay in his Essay on Bacon's Philosophy. I do not know whether he would agree with me.

fresh shoots, and buds, and blossoms, which are to
ripen into fruit, on that magical tree of Knowledge
which he planted, and to which none of us perhaps,
except the very poor, but owes, if not his present life,
at least his daily food, his health, and general well-
being. He was the divinely provided minister of temporal benefits to all of us so great, that, whatever I
am forced to think of him as a man, I have not the
heart, from mere gratitude, to speak of him severely.
And, in spite of the tendencies of his philosophy,
which are, as we see at this day, to depreciate, or to
trample on Theology, he has himself, in his writings,
gone out of his way, as if with a prophetic misgiving
of those tendencies, to insist on it as the instrument of
that beneficent Father,* who, when He came on earth
in visible form, took on Him first and most prom-
inently the office of assuaging the bodily wounds of
human nature. And truly, like the old mediciner in
the tale, "he sat diligently at his work, and hummed,
with cheerful countenance, a pious song ; " and then
in turn " went out singing into the meadows so gaily,
that those who had seen him from afar might well
have thought it was a youth gathering flowers for his

---

* De Augment. iv. 2, vid. Macaulay's Essay ; vid. also " In
principio operis, ad Deum Patrem, Deum Verbum, Deum Spiri-
tum, preces fundimus humillimas et ardentissimas, ut humani
generis ærumnarum memores et peregrinationis istius vitæ in
quâ dies paucos et malos terimus, *novis suis eleemosynis, per manus
nostras,* familiam humanam dotare dignentur. Atque illud insuper
supplices rogamus, ne *humana divinis officiant,* neve *ex resera-
tione viarum sensûs* et accensione majore luminis naturalis *aliquid
incredulitatis* et noctis animis nostris erga divina mysteria obori-
atur:" etc. *Præf.* Instaur. Magn.

beloved, instead of an old physician gathering healing herbs in the morning dew." *

Alas, that men, in the action of life or in their heart of hearts, are not what they seem to be in their moments of excitement, or in their trances or intoxications of genius,—so good, so noble, so serene ! Alas, that Bacon too in his own way should after all be but the fellow of those heathen philosophers who in their disadvantages had some excuse for their inconsistency, and who surprise us rather in what they did say than in what they did not do ! Alas, that he too, like Socrates or Seneca, must be stripped of his holy-day coat, which looks so fair, and should be but a mockery amid his most majestic gravity of phrase ; and, for all his vast abilities, should, in the littleness of his own moral being, but typify the intellectual narrowness of his school ! However, granting all this, heroism after all was not his philosophy :—I cannot deny he has abundantly achieved what he proposed. His is simply a Method whereby bodily discomforts and temporal wants are to be most effectually removed from the greatest number ; and already, before it has shown any signs of exhaustion, the gifts of nature, in their most artificial shapes and luxurious profusion and diversity, from all quarters of the earth, are, it is undeniable, by its means brought even to our doors, and we rejoice in them.—*Idea of a University*, ed. 1891, pp. 117-119 (1852).

* Fouqué's Unknown Patient.

HERE then, I say, you are involved in a difficulty greater than that which besets the cultivation of Science; for, if Physical Science be dangerous, as I have said, it is dangerous, because it necessarily ignores the idea of moral evil; but Literature is open to the more grievous imputation of recognizing and understanding it too well. Some one will say to me perhaps: " Our youth shall not be corrupted. We will dispense with all general or national Literature whatever, if it be so exceptionable; we will have a Christian Literature of our own, as pure, as true, as the Jewish." You cannot have it :—I do not say you cannot form a select literature for the young, nay, even for the middle or lower classes; this is another matter altogether : I am speaking of University Education, which implies an extended range of reading, which has to deal with standard works of genius, or what are called the *classics* of language : and I say, from the nature of the case, if Literature is to be made a study of human nature, you cannot have a Christian Literature. It is a contradiction in terms to attempt a sinless Literature of sinful man. You may gather together something very great and high, something higher than any Literature ever was; and when you have done so, you will find that it is not Literature at all. You will have

44

simply left the delineation of man, as such, and have
substituted for it, as far as you have had anything to
substitute, that of man, as he is or might be, under
certain special advantages. Give up the study of man,
as such, if so it must be ; but say you do so. Do not
say you are studying him, his history, his mind and
his heart, when you are studying something else.
Man is a being of genius, passion, intellect, conscience, ˗
power. He exercises these various gifts in various
ways, in great deeds, in great thoughts, in heroic acts,
in hateful crimes. He founds states, he fights battles,
he builds cities, he ploughs the forest, he subdues the
elements, he rules his kind. He creates vast ideas,
and influences many generations. He takes a thousand shapes, and undergoes a thousand fortunes.
Literature records them all to the life.

> Quicquid agunt homines, votum, timor, ira, voluptas,
> Gaudia, discursus.

He pours out his fervid soul in poetry ; he sways to
and fro, he soars, he dives, in his restless speculations ; his lips drop eloquence ; he touches the canvas,
and it glows with beauty ; he sweeps the strings, and
they thrill with an ecstatic meaning. He looks back
into himself, and he reads his own thoughts, and notes
them down ; he looks out into the universe, and tells
over and celebrates the elements and principles of
which it is the product.

Such is man : put him aside, keep him before you ;
but, whatever you do, do not take him for what he is
not, for something more divine and sacred, for man re-
generate. Nay, beware of showing God's grace and

its work at such disadvantage as to make the few whom
it has thoroughly influenced compete in intellect with
the vast multitude who either have it not, or use it ill.
The elect are few to choose out of, and the world is
inexhaustible.   From the first, Jabel and Tubal cain,
Nimrod " the stout hunter," the learning of the
Pharaohs, and the wisdom of the East country, are of
the world.   Every now and then they are rivalled by a
Solomon or a Beseleel, but the *habitat* of natural gifts
is the natural man.   The Church may use them, she
cannot at her will originate them.   Not till the whole
human race is made new will its literature be pure and
true.   Possible of course it is in idea, for nature,
inspired by heavenly grace, to exhibit itself on a large
scale, in an originality of thought or action, even far
beyond what the world's literature has recorded or
exemplified ; but, if you would in fact have a literature
of saints, first of all have a nation of them.

What is a clearer proof of the truth of all this than
the structure of the Inspired Word itself ?   It is un-
deniably *not* the reflection or picture of the many,
but of the few; it is no picture of life, but an anticipation of death and judgment.   Human literature is
about all things, grave or gay, painful or pleasant;
but the Inspired Word views them only in one aspect,
and as they tend to one scope.   It gives us little insight into the fertile developments of mind ; it has no
terms in its vocabulary to express with exactness the
intellect and its separate faculties : it knows nothing
of genius, fancy, wit, invention, presence of mind,
resource.   It does not discourse of empire, commerce,
enterprise, learning, philosophy, or the fine arts.

Slightly too does it touch on the more simple and innocent courses of nature and their reward. Little
does it say* of those temporal blessings which rest
upon our worldly occupations, and make them
easy; of the blessings which we derive from the
sunshine day and the serene night, from the succession of the seasons, and the produce of the
earth. Little about our recreations and our daily
domestic comforts; little about the ordinary occa-
sions of festivity and mirth, which sweeten human
life; and nothing at all about various pursuits or
amusements, which it would be going too much into
detail to mention. We read indeed of the feast when
Isaac was weaned, and of Jacob's courtship, and of
the religious merry-makings of holy Job; but excep-
tions, such as these, do but remind us what might be
in Scripture, and is not. If then by Literature is
meant the manifestation of human nature in human
language, you will seek for it in vain except in the
world. Put up with it, as it is, or do not pretend to
cultivate it; take things as they are, not as you could
wish them.

Nay, I am obliged to go further still; even if we
could, still we should be shrinking from our plain
duty, Gentlemen, did we leave out Literature from Education. For why do we educate, except to prepare
for the world? Why do we cultivate the intellect of
the many beyond the first elements of knowledge,
except for this world? Will it be much matter in the

---

*Vide the Author's Parochial Sermons, vol. i. 25.

world to come whether our bodily health or whether
our intellectual strength was more or less, except of
course as this world is in all its circumstances a trial for
the next ?   If then a University is a direct preparation
for this world, let it be what it professes.   It is not a
Convent, it is not a Seminary ; it is a place to fit men
of the world for the world.   We cannot possibly keep
them from plunging into the world, with all its ways
and principles and maxims, when their time comes ;
but we can prepare them against what is inevitable ;
and it is not the way to learn to swim in troubled
waters, never to have gone into them.   Proscribe (I
do not merely say particular authors, particular works,
particular passages) but Secular Literature as such ;
cut out from your class books all broad manifestations
of the natural man ; and those manifestations are
waiting for your pupil's benefit at the very doors of
your lecture room in living and breathing substance.
They will meet him there in all the charm of novelty, and all the fascination of genius or of amiable-
ness.   To-day a pupil, to-morrow a member of the
great world :   to-day confined to the Lives of the
Saints, to-morrow thrown upon Babel ;—thrown on
Babel, without the honest indulgence of wit and humour and imagination having ever been permitted to
him, without any fastidiousness of taste wrought into
him, without any rule given him for discriminating
" the precious from the vile," beauty from sin, the
truth from the sophistry of nature, what is innocent
from what is poison.   You have refused him the
masters of human thought, who would in some sense
have educated him, because of their incidental cor-

ruption : you have shut up from him those whose thoughts strike home to our hearts, whose words are proverbs, whose names are indigenous to all the world, who are the standard of their mother tongue, and the pride and boast of their countrymen, Homer. Ariosto, Cervantes, Shakespeare, because the old Adam smelt rank in them ; and for what have you reserved him ? You have given him "a liberty unto" the multitudinous blasphemy of his day ; you have made him free of its newspapers, its reviews, its magazines, its novels, its controversial pamphlets, of its Parliamentary debates, its law proceedings, its platform speeches, its songs, its drama, its theatre, of its enveloping, stifling atmosphere of death. You have succeeded but in this,— in making the world his University.

Difficult then as the question may be, and much as it may try the judgments and even divide the opinions of zealous and religious Catholics, I cannot feel any doubt myself, Gentlemen, that the Church's true policy is not to aim at the exclusion of Literature from Secular Schools, but at her own admission into them. Let her do for Literature in one way what she does for Science in another ; each has its imperfection, and she has her remedy for each. She fears no knowledge, but she purifies all ; she represses no element of our nature, but cultivates the whole. Science is grave, methodical, logical ; with Science then she argues, and opposes reason to reason. Literature does not argue, but declaims and insinuates ; it is multiform and versatile : it persuades instead of convincing, it seduces, it carries captive ; it appeals to the sense of honour, or to the imagination, or to the stimulus of curiosity ; it

4

makes its way by means of gaiety, satire, romance, the beautiful, the pleasurable. Is it wonderful that with an agent like this the Church should claim to deal with a vigour corresponding to its restlessness, to interfere in its proceedings with a higher hand, and to wield an authority in the choice of its studies and of its books which would be tyrannical, if reason and fact were the only instruments of its conclusions? But anyhow, her principle is one and the same throughout ; not to prohibit truth of any kind, but to see that no doctrines pass under the name of Truth but those which claim it rightfully.—*Idea of a University*, ed. 1891, pp. 229–234 (1852).

Such at least is the lesson which I am taught by all the thought which I have been able to bestow upon the subject; such is the lesson which I have gained from the history of my own special Father and Patron, St. Philip Neri. He lived in an age as traitorous to the interests of Catholicism as any that preceded it, or can follow it. He lived at a time when pride mounted high, and the senses held rule; a time when kings and nobles never had more of state and homage, and never less of personal responsibility and peril; when mediæval winter was receding, and the summer sun of civilization was bringing into leaf and flower a thousand forms of luxurious enjoyment; when a new world of thought and beauty had opened upon the human mind, in the discovery of the treasures of classic literature and art. He saw the great and the gifted, dazzled by the Enchantress, and drinking in the magic of her song; he saw the high and the wise, the student and the artist, painting, and poetry, and sculpture, and music, and architecture, drawn within her range, and circling round the abyss: he saw heathen forms mounting thence, and forming in the thick air:—all this he saw, and he perceived that the mischief was to be met, not with argument, not with science, not with protests and warnings, not by the recluse or the preacher, but by means of the great counter fascination of purity and truth. He was raised up to do a work almost peculiar in the Church,—not to be a Jerome Savonarola, though Philip had a true devotion towards him and a tender memory of his Florentine house; not to be a St. Charles, though in his beaming countenance Philip had recognized the aureole of a saint; not to be a St. Ignatius, wrestling with the foe, though Philip was termed the Society's bell of call, so many subjects did he send to it; not to be a St. Francis Xavier, though Philip had longed to shed his blood for Christ in India with him; not to be a St. Caietan, or hunter of souls, for Philip preferred, as he expressed it, tranquilly to cast in his net to gain them; he preferred to yield to the stream, and direct the current, which he could not stop, of science, literature, art, and fashion, and to sweeten and to sanctify what God had made very good and man had spoilt.

And so he contemplated as the idea of his mission, not the propagation of the faith, nor the exposition of doctrine, nor the catechetical schools; whatever was exact and systematic pleased him not; he put from him monastic rule and authoritative speech, as David refused the armour of his king. No; he would be but an ordinary individual priest as others : and his weapons should be but unaffected humility and unpretending love. All He did was to be done by the light, and fervour, and convincing eloquence of his personal character and his easy conversation. He came to the Eternal City and he sat himself down there, and his home and his family gradually grew up around him, by the spontaneous accession of materials from without. He did not so much seek his own as

draw them to him. He sat in his small room, and
they in their gay worldly dresses, the rich and the
wellborn, as well as the simple and the illiterate,
crowded into it. In the mid-heats of summer, in the
frosts of winter, still was he in that low and narrow
cell at San Girolamo, reading the hearts of those who
came to him, and curing their souls' maladies by the
very touch of his hand. It was a vision of the Magi
worshipping the infant Saviour, so pure and innocent,
so sweet and beautiful was he ; and so loyal and so dear
to the gracious Virgin Mother. And they who came
remained gazing and listening, till at length, first one
and then another threw off their bravery, and took
his poor cassock and girdle instead : or, if they kept
it, it was to put haircloth under it, or to take on them
a rule of life, while to the world they looked as before.

In the words of his biographer, " he was all things
to all men. He suited himself to noble and ignoble,
young and old, subjects and prelates, learned and
ignorant; and received those who were strangers to
him with singular benignity, and embraced them with
as much love and charity as if he had been a long
while expecting them. When he was called upon to
be merry he was so ; if there was a demand upon his
sympathy he was equally ready. He gave the same
welcome to all : caressing the poor equally with the
rich, and wearying himself to assist all to the utmost
limits of his power. In consequence of his being so
accessible and willing to receive all comers, many
went to him every day, and some continued for the
space of thirty, nay forty years, to visit him very often
both morning and evening, so that his room went by

the agreeable nickname of the Home of Christian mirth. Nay, people came to him, not only from all parts of Italy, but from France, Spain, Germany, and all Christendom ; and even the infidels and Jews, who had ever any communication with him, revered him as a holy man."* The first families of Rome, the Massimi, the Aldobrandini, the Colonnas, the Altieri, the Vitelleschi, were his friends and his penitents. Nobles of Poland, Grandees of Spain, Knights of Malta, could not leave Rome without coming to him. Cardinals, Archbishops, and Bishops were his intimates ; Federigo Borromeo haunted his room and got the name of " Father Philip's soul." The Cardinal-Archbishops of Verona and Bologna wrote books in his honour. Pope Pius the Fourth died in his arms. Lawyers, painters, musicians, physicians, it was the same too with them. Baronius, Zazzara, and Ricci, left the law at his bidding, and joined his congregation, to do its work, to write the annals of the Church, and to die in the odour of sanctity. Palestrina had Father Philip's ministrations in his last moments. Animuccia hung about him during life, sent him a message after death, and was · conducted by him through Purgatory to Heaven. And who was he, I say, all the while, but an humble priest, a stranger in Rome, with no distinction of family or letters, no claim of station or of office, great simply in the attraction with which a Divine Power had gifted him ? and yet thus humble, thus un-ennobled, thus empty-handed, he has achieved the glorious title of Apostle of Rome.—*Idea of a University*, ed. 1891, pp. 234–238 (1852).

* Bacci, vol. i., p. 192, ii., p. 98.

John Keble.

Such was the gift of the author of the Christian Year, and he used it in attaching the minds of the rising generation to the Church of his predecessors, Ken and Herbert. He did that for the Church of England which none but a poet could do : he made it poetical. It is sometimes asked whether poets are not more commonly found external to the Church than among her children ; and it would not surprise us to find the question answered in the affirmative. Poetry is the refuge of those who have not the Catholic Church to flee to and repose upon, for the Church herself is the most sacred and august of poets. Poetry, as Mr. Keble lays it down in his University Lectures on the subject, is a method of relieving the over-burdened mind ; it is a channel through which emotion finds expression, and that a safe, regulated expression. Now what is the Catholic Church, viewed in her human aspect, but a discipline of the affections and passions ? What are her ordinances and practices but the regulated expression of keen, or deep, or turbid feeling, and thus a "cleansing," as Aristotle would word it, of the sick soul ? She is the poet of her children ; full of music to soothe the sad and control the wayward,— wonderful in story for the imagination of the romantic ; rich in symbol and imagery, so that gentle and delicate

feelings, which will not bear words, may in silence intimate their presence or commune with themselves.
Her very being is poetry; every psalm, every petition,
every collect, every versicle, the cross, the mitre, the
thurible, is a fulfilment of some dream of childhood or
aspiration of youth/ Such poets as are born under her
shadow, she takes into her service; she sets them to
write hymns, or to compose chants, or to embellish
shrines, or to determine ceremonies, or to marshal pro-
cessions; nay, she can even make schoolmen of them,
as she made St. Thomas, till logic becomes poetical.
Now the author of the Christian Year found the Anglican system all but destitute of this divine element,
which is an essential property of Catholicism;—a
ritual dashed upon the ground, trodden on, and broken
piece-meal;—prayers, clipped, pieced, torn, shuffled
about at pleasure, until the meaning of the composition perished, and offices which had been poetry were
no longer even good prose;—antiphones, hymns, ben-
edictions, invocations, shovelled away;—Scripture lessons turned into chapters;—heaviness, feebleness, un-
wieldiness, where the Catholic rites had had the light-
ness and airiness of a spirit;—vestments chucked off,
lights quenched, jewels stolen, the pomp and circumstances of worship annihilated; a dreariness which
could be felt, and which seemed the token of an incip-
ient Socinianism, forcing itself upon the eye, the ear,
the nostrils of the worshipper; a smell of dust and
damp, not of incense; a sound of ministers preaching
Catholic prayers, and parish clerks droning out Catholic canticles; the royal arms for the crucifix; huge ugly
boxes of wood, sacred to preachers, frowning on the

congregation in the place of the mysterious altar; and
long cathedral aisles unused, railed off, like the tombs
(as they were,) of what had been and was not; and for
orthodoxy, a frigid, unelastic, inconsistent, dull, help-
less dogmatic, which could give no just account of
itself, yet was intolerant of all teaching which contained a doctrine more or a doctrine less, and resented
every attempt to give it a meaning,—such was the
religion of which this gifted author was,—not the judge
and denouncer (a deep spirit of reverence hindered
it,)—but the renovator, as far as it has been reno-
vated. Clear as was his perception of the degeneracy
of his times, he attributed nothing of it to his Church,
over which he threw the poetry of his own mind and
the memory of better days.

His happy magic made the Anglican Church seem
what Catholicism was and is. The established system
found to its surprise that it had been all its life talking
not prose, but poetry.

"Miraturque novas frondes et non sua poma."

Beneficed clergymen used to go to rest as usual on
Christmas Eve, and leave to ringers, or sometimes to
carollers, the observance which was paid, not without
creature comforts, to the sacred night; but now they
suddenly found themselves, to their great surprise, to
be "wakeful shepherds;" and "still as the day came
round," "in music and in light," the new-born Saviour
"dawned upon their prayer." Anglican bishops had
not only lost the habit of blessing, but had sometimes
been startled and vexed when asked to do so; but now
they were told of their "gracious arm stretched out to

bless ; " moreover, what they had never dreamed when
they were gazetted or did homage, they were taught
that each of them was " an Apostle true, a crowned
and robed seer." The parish church had been shut
up, except for vestry meetings and occasional services,
all days of the year but Sundays, and one or two other
sacred days; but church-goers were now assured that
" Martyrs and Saints " " dawned on their way," that
the absolution in the Common Prayer Book was " the
Golden Key each morn and eve ; " and informed, moreover, at a time too when the Real Presence was all but
utterly forgotten or denied, of " the dear feast of Jesus
dying, upon that altar ever lying, while Angels pros-
trate fall." They learned, besides, that what their
pastors had spoken of, and churchwardens had used
at vestry meetings, as a mere table, was " the dread
altar ; " and that " holy lamps were blazing; " " per-
fumed embers quivering bright," with " stoled priests
ministering at them," while the " floor was by knees of
sinners worn."

Such doctrine coming from one who had such claims
on his readers from the weight of his name, the depth
of his devotional and ethical tone, and the special gift
of consolation, of which his poems themselves were
the evidence, wrought a great work on the Establishment. The Catholic Church speaks for itself, the Anglican needs external assistance ; his poems became a
sort of comment upon its formularies and ordinances,
and almost elevated them into the dignity of a religious system. It kindled hearts towards his Church ; it
gave a something for the gentle and forlorn to cling
to ; and it raised up advocates for it among those, who

otherwise, if God and their good Angel had suffered
it, might have wandered away into some sort of philosophy, and acknowledged no Church at all. Such
was the influence of his Christian Year; and doubtless his friends hail his Lyra Innocentium, as being
likely to do a similar work in a more critical time.
And it is to be expected that for a while something of
a similar effect may follow its publication. That so
revered, so loved a name as the author's, a name
known by Oxford men for thirty years and more,—that
one who has been " a hermit spirit " unlike the world
all his days, who even in his youth caused the eyes of
younger men to turn keenly towards him, if he was
pointed out to them in public schools or college
garden, who by the mere first touch of his hand has
made them feel pierced through, so that they could
have sunk into the earth for shame, and who, when removed from his loved University, was still an unseen
silent influence moving hearts at his will,—that a
" whisper " from such a man, " with no faint and erring
voice," will for the time retain certain persons in the
English Church, who otherwise, to say the least, would
have contemplated a return to that true Mother whose
baptism they bear, the one sole Ark of salvation, of
this we make no question at all. But there is another
point, of which we entertain just as little doubt, or
rather are a great deal more confident,—that as far as
the Volume has influence, that influence will, on the
long run, tell in favor of the Catholic Church ; and
will do what the author does not, nay, from his position, alas ! cannot, may not contemplate,—will in
God's good time bring in a blessed harvest into the

granaries of Christ. And being sure of this, much as
the immediate effects of its publication may pain the
hearts of those who are sighing and praying for the
souls of others, we can bear to wait, we can afford to
be patient, and awfully to watch the slow march of the
divine providences towards this poor country.—*Essays
Critical and Historical*, ed. 1885, Vol. ii., pp. 442–446
(1846).

Keble was young in years, when he became a University celebrity, and younger in mind. He had the
purity and simplicity of a child. He had few sympathies with the intellectual party, who sincerely
welcomed him as a brilliant specimen of young Oxford.
He instinctively shut up before literary display, and
pomp and donnishness of manner, faults which always
will beset academical notabilities. He did not respond
to their advances. His collision with them (if it may
be so called) was thus described by Hurrell Froude in
his own way. "Poor Keble!" he used gravely to say,
"he was asked to join the aristocracy of talent, but he
soon found his level." He went into the country, but
his instance serves to prove that men need not, in the
event, lose that influence which is rightly theirs, because they happen to be thwarted in the use of the
channels natural and proper to its exercise. He did
not lose his place in the minds of men because he was
out of their sight.

Keble was a man who guided himself and formed
his judgments, not by processes of reason, by inquiry
or by argument, but, to use the word in a broad sense,

by authority. Conscience is an authority; the Bible is an authority; such is the Church; such is Antiquity; such are the words of the wise; such are hereditary lessons; such are ethical truths; such are historical memories, such are legal saws and state maxims; such are proverbs; such are sentiments, presages, and prepossessions. It seemed to me as if he ever felt happier, when he could speak or act under some such primary or external sanction ; and could use argument mainly as a means of recommending or explaining what had claims on his reception prior to proof. He even felt a tenderness, I think, in spite of Bacon, for the Idols of the Tribe and the Den, of the Market and the Theatre. What he hated instinctively was heresy, insubordination, resistance to things established, claims of independence, disloyalty, innovation, a critical, censorious spirit. And such was the main principle of the school which in the course of years was formed around him ; nor is it easy to set limits to its influence in its day ; for multitudes of men, who did not profess its teaching, or accept its peculiar doctrines, were willing nevertheless, or found it to their purpose, to act in company with it.

Indeed for a time it was practically the champion and advocate of the political doctrines of the great clerical interest through the country, who found in Mr. Keble and his friends an intellectual, as well as moral support to their cause, which they looked for in vain elsewhere. His weak point, in their eyes, was his consistency; for he carried his love of authority and old times so far, as to be more than gentle towards the Catholic Religion, with which the Toryism

of Oxford and of the Church of England had no
sympathy.   Accordingly, if my memory be correct, he
never could get himself to throw his heart into the
opposition made to Catholic Emancipation, strongly
as he revolted from the politics and the instruments by
means of which that Emancipation was won.   I fancy
he would have had no difficulty in accepting Dr. Johnson's saying about "the first Whig;" and it grieved
and offended him that the "Via prima salutis" should
be opened to the Catholic body from the Whig quarter.
In spite of his reverence for the Old Religion, I conceive that on the whole he would rather have kept its
professors beyond the pale of the Constitution with
the Tories, than admit them on the principles of the
Whigs.   Moreover, if the Revolution of 1688 was too
lax in principle for him and his friends, much less, as
is very plain, could they endure to subscribe to the
revolutionary doctrines of 1776 and 1789, which they
felt to be absolutely and entirely out of keeping with
theological truth.—*Apologia,* ed. 1890, pp. 289–291
(1864).

EVERY year brings changes and reforms. We do not know what is the state of Oxley Church now; it may have rood-loft, piscina, sedilia, all new; or it may be reformed backwards, the seats on principle turning from the Communion-table, and the pulpit planted in the middle of the aisle; but at the time when these two young men walked through the churchyard, there was nothing very good or very bad to attract them within the building; and they were passing on, when they observed, coming out of the church, what Sheffield called an elderly don, a fellow of a college whom Charles knew. He was a man of family, and had some little property of his own, had been a contemporary of his father's at the University, and had from time to time been a guest at the parsonage. Charles had, in consequence, known him from a boy; and now, since he came into residence, he had, as was natural, received many small attentions from him. Once, when he was late for his own hall, he had given him his dinner in his rooms; he had taken him out on a fishing expedition towards Faringdon; and had promised him some tickets for some ladies, lionesses of his, who were coming up to the Commemoration. He was a shrewd, easy-tempered, free-spoken man, of small desires and no ambition; of no very keen sensi-

63

bilities or romantic delicacies, and very little religious pretension; that is, though unexceptionable in his deportment, he hated the show of religion, and was impatient with those who affected it. He had known the University for thirty years, and formed a right estimate of most things in it. He had come out to Oxley to take a funeral for a friend, and was now returning home. He hallooed to Charles, who, though feeling at first awkward on finding himself with two such different friends and in two such different relations, was, after a time, partially restored to himself by the unconcern of Mr. Malcolm; and the three walked home together. Yet, even to the last, he did not quite know how and where to walk, and how to carry himself; particularly when they got near Oxford, and he fell in with various parties who greeted him in passing.

Charles, by way of remark, said they had been looking in at a pretty little chapel on the common, which was now in the course of repair. Mr. Malcolm laughed. "So, Charles," he said, "*you're* bit with the new fashion."

Charles coloured, and asked, "What fashion?" adding, that a friend, by accident, had taken them in.

"You ask what fashion," said Mr. Malcolm; "why, the newest, latest fashion. This is a place of fashions; there have been many fashions in my time. The greater part of the residents, that is, the boys, change once in three years; the fellows and tutors, perhaps, in half a dozen; and every generation has its own fashion. There is no principle of stability in Oxford, except the Heads, and they are always the same and always will be the same to the end of the chapter.

What is in now," he asked, "among you youngsters—drinking or cigars ? "

Charles laughed modestly, and said he hoped drinking had gone out everywhere.

"Worse things may come in," said Mr. Malcolm; "but there are fashions everywhere. There once was a spouting club, perhaps it is in favor still; before it was the music-room. Once geology was all the rage; now it is theology; soon it will be architecture, or mediæval antiquities, or editions and codices. Each wears out in its turn; all depends on one or two active men; but the secretary takes a wife, or the professor gets a stall; and then the meetings are called irregularly, and nothing is done in them, and so gradually the affair dwindles and dies."

Sheffield asked whether the present movement had not spread too widely through the country for such a termination; he did not know much about it himself, but the papers were full of it, and it was the talk of every neighbourhood; it was not confined to Oxford.

"I don't know about the country," said Malcolm, "that is a large question; but it has not the elements of stability here. These gentlemen will take livings and marry, and that will be the end of the business. I am not speaking against them; they are, I believe, very respectable men; but they are riding on the springtide of a fashion."

Charles said it was a nuisance to see the party-spirit it introduced. Oxford ought to be a place of quiet and study; peace and the Muses always went together; whereas there was talk, talk, in every quarter. A man could not go about his duties in a

5

natural way, and take every one as he came, but was obliged to take part in questions, and to consider points which he might wish to put from him, and must sport an opinion when he really had none to give.

Mr. Malcolm assented in a half-absent way, looking at the view before him, and seemingly enjoying it. "People call this country ugly," said he, "and perhaps it is ; but whether I am used to it or no, I always am pleased with it. The lights are always new ; and thus the landscape, if it deserves the name, is always presented in a new dress. I have known Shotover there take the most opposite hues, sometimes purple, sometimes a bright saffron or tawny orange." Here he stopped : " Yes, you speak of party-spirit ; very true, there's a good deal of it. . . No, I don't think there's much," he continued, rousing ; " certainly there is more division just at this minute in Oxford, but there always is division, always rivalry. The separate societies have their own interests and honour to maintain, and quarrel, as the orders do in the Church of Rome. No, that's too grand a comparison ; rather, Oxford is like an almshouse for clergymen's widows. Self-importance, jealousy, tittle-tattle are the order of the day. It has always been so in my time. The two great ladies, Mrs. Vice-Chancellor and Mrs. Divinity-Professor, can't agree, and have followings respectively : or Vice-Chancellor himself, being a new broom, sweeps all the young Masters clean out of Convocation House, to their great indignation : or Mr. Slaney, Dean of St. Peter's, does not scruple to say in a stage-coach that Mr. Wood is no scholar ; on which the said Wood calls him in return ' slanderous Slaney ; '

or the elderly Mr. Barge, late Senior Fellow of St. Michael's, thinks that his pretty bride has not been received with due honours ; or Dr. Crotchet is for years kept out of his destined bishopric by a sinister influence ; or Mr. Professor Carraway has been infamously shown up, in the *Edinburgh*, by an idle fellow whom he plucked in the schools ; or (*majora movemus*) three colleges interchange a mortal vow of opposition to a fourth ; or the young working Masters conspire against the Heads. Now, however, we are improving ; if we must quarrel, let it be the rivalry of intellect and conscience, rather than of interest or temper ; let us contend for things, not for shadows."

Sheffield was pleased at this, and ventured to say the present state of things was more real, and therefore more healthy. Mr. Malcolm did not seem to hear him, for he did not reply ; and, as they were now approaching the bridge again, the conversation stopped. Sheffield looked slily at Charles, as Mr. Malcolm proceeded with them up High Street ; and both of them had the triumph and the amusement of being convoyed safely past a proctor, who was patrolling it, under the protection of a Master.—*Loss and Gain*, ed. 1893, chap. 5, pp. 29-33 (1848).

Mr. Kingsley begins then by exclaiming,—"O the chicanery, the wholesale fraud, the vile hypocrisy, the conscience-killing tyranny of Rome! We have not far to seek for an evidence of it! There's Father Newman to wit: one living specimen is worth a hundred dead ones. He, a Priest, writing of Priests, tells us that lying is never any harm."

I interpose: "You are taking a most extraordinary liberty with my name. If I have said this, tell me when and where."

Mr. Kingsley replies: "You said it, Reverend Sir, in a sermon which you preached, when a Protestant, as Vicar of St. Mary's, and published in 1844; and I could read you a very salutary lecture on the effects which that Sermon had at the time on my own opinion of you."

I make answer: "Oh. . . *Not*, it seems, as a priest speaking of priests; but let us have the passage."

Mr. Kingsley relaxes: "Do you know I like your *tone*. From your *tone*, I rejoice, greatly rejoice, to be able to believe that you did not mean what you said."

I rejoin: "*Mean* it! I maintain I never *said* it, whether as a Protestant or as a Catholic."

Mr. Kingsley replies: " I waive that point."

I object: "Is it possible? What? waive the main
68

question ! I either said it or I didn't. You have made a monstrous charge against me ; direct, distinct, public. You are bound to prove it as directly, as distinctly, as publicly ;—or to own you can't !"

"Well," says Mr. Kingsley, "if you are quite sure you did not say it, I'll take your word for it; I really will."

My *word !* I am dumb. Somehow I thought that it was my *word* that happened to be on trial. The *word* of a Professor of lying, that he does not lie !

But Mr. Kingsley reassures me : "We are both gentlemen," he says : " I have done as much as one English gentleman can expect from another."

I begin to see : he thought me a gentleman at the very time that he said I taught lying on system. After all, it is not I, but it is Mr. Kingsley who did not mean what he said. " Habemus confitentem reum." So we have confessedly come round to this, preaching without practising ; the common theme of satirists from Juvenal to Walter Scott !—*Apologia*, ed. 1865, pp. 17–18 (1864).

I cannot be sorry to have forced my Accuser to bring out in fulness his charges against me. It is far better that he should discharge his thoughts upon me in my lifetime, than after I am dead. Under the circumstances I am happy in having the opportunity of reading the worst that can be said of me by a writer who has taken pains with his work and is well satisfied with it. I account it a gain to be surveyed from without by one who hates the principles which are nearest to my heart, has no personal knowledge of me to set right his misconceptions of my doctrine, and who has some motive or other to be as severe with me as he can possibly be. . . .

But I really feel sad for what I am obliged now to say. I am in warfare with him, but I wish him no ill; —it is very difficult to get up resentment towards persons whom one has never seen. It is easy enough to be irritated with friends or foes *vis-à-vis ;* but, though I am writing with all my heart against what he has said of me, I am not conscious of personal unkindness towards himself. I think it necessary to write as I am writing, for my own sake, and for the sake of the Catholic Priesthood; but I wish to impute nothing worse to him than that he has been furiously carried away by his feelings. Yet what shall I say of the up-shot of all his talk of my economies and equivocations and the like? What is the precise *work* which it is directed to effect? I am at war with him; but there is such a thing as legitimate warfare: war has its laws: there are things which may fairly be done, and things which may not be done. I say it with shame and with stern sorrow;—he has attempted a great transgression; he has attempted (as I may call it) *to poison the wells.* I will quote him and explain what I mean. . . . He says,—

" I am henceforth in doubt and fear, as much as any honest man can be, *concerning every word* Dr. Newman may write. *How can I tell that I shall not be the dupe of some cunning equivocation,* of one of the three kinds laid down as permissible by the blessed Alfonso da Liguori and his pupils, even when confirmed by an

oath because ' then we do not deceive our neighbour,
but allow him to deceive himself?' . . . . It is admis-
sible, therefore, to use words and sentences which have
a double signification, and leave the hapless hearer to
take which of them he may choose. *What proof have
I, then, that by ' mean it? I never said it!' Dr. Newman does not signify*, I did not say it, but I did mean
it ?"—Pp. 44, 45.

Now these insinuations and questions shall be
answered in their proper places ; here I will but say
that I scorn and detest lying, and quibbling, and
double-tongued practice, and slyness, and cunning,
and smoothness, and cant, and pretence, quite as
much as any Protestants hate them ; and I pray to be
kept from the snare of them. But all this is just now
by the bye ; my present subject is my Accuser ; what I
insist upon here is this unmanly attempt of his, in his
concluding pages, to cut the ground from under my
feet ;—to poison by anticipation the public mind
against me, John Henry Newman, and to infuse into
the imaginations of my readers, suspicion and mistrust
of everything that I may say in reply to him. This I
call *poisoning the wells.*

" I am henceforth in *doubt and fear*," he says, "as
much as any *honest* man can be, *concerning every word*
Dr. Newman may write. *How can I tell that I shall
not be the dupe of some cunning equivocation?*" . . . .

Well, I can only say, that, if his taunt is to take effect, I am but wasting my time in saying a word in
answer to his calumnies ; and this is precisely what he
knows and intends to be its fruit. I can hardly get
myself to protest against a method of controversy so

base and cruel, lest in doing so, I should be violating my self-respect and self-possession ; but most base and most cruel it is. We all know how our imagination runs away with us, how suddenly and at what a pace ; —the saying, " Cæsar's wife should not be suspected," is an instance of what I mean. The habitual prejudice, the humour of the moment, is the turning-point which leads us to read a defence in a good sense or a bad. We interpret it by our antecedent impressions. The very same sentiments, according as our jealousy is or is not awake, or our aversion stimulated, are tokens of truth or of dissimulation and pretence. There is a story of a sane person being by mistake shut up in the wards of a Lunatic Asylum, and that, when he pleaded his cause to some strangers visiting the establishment, the only remark he elicited in answer was, " How naturally he talks ! you would think he was in his senses." Controversies should be decided by the reason ; is it legitimate warfare to appeal to the misgivings of the public mind and to its dislikings ? Anyhow, if my accuser is able thus to practise upon my readers, the more I succeed, the less will be my success. If I am natural, he will tell them " Ars est celare artem ; " if I am convincing, he will suggest that I am an able logician ; if I show warmth, I am acting the indignant innocent ; if I am calm, I am thereby detected as a smooth hypocrite ; if I clear up difficulties, I am too plausible and perfect to be true. The more triumphant are my statements, the more certain will be my defeat.

So will it be if my Accuser succeeds in his manœuvre ; but I do not for an instant believe that he

will. Whatever judgment my readers may eventually
form of me from these pages, I am confident that they
will believe me in what I shall say in the course of
them. I have no misgiving at all, that they will be
ungenerous or harsh towards a man who has been so
long before the eyes of the world ; who has so many to
speak of him from personal knowledge ; whose natural
impulse it has ever been to speak out ; who has ever
spoken too much rather than too little ; who would
have saved himself many a scrape, if he had been wise
enough to hold his tongue ; who has ever been fair to
the doctrines and arguments of his opponents ; who
has never slurred over facts and reasonings which told
against himself ; who has never given his name or
authority to proofs which he thought unsound, or to
testimony which he did not think at least plausible ;
who has never shrunk from confessing a fault when he
felt that he had committed one ; who has ever consulted for others more than for himself ; who has given
up much that he loved and prized and could have re-
tained, but that he loved honesty better than name,
and Truth better than dear friends. . . .

What then shall be the special imputations, against
which I shall throw myself in these pages, out of the
thousand and one which my Accuser directs upon me ?
I mean to confine myself to one, for there is only one
about which I much care,—the charge of Untruthfulness. He may cast upon me as many other imputations as he pleases, and they may stick on me, as
long as they can, in the course of nature. They will
fall to the ground in their season.

And indeed I think the same of the charge of Untruthfulness, and select it from the rest, not because it is more formidable but because it is more serious. Like the rest, it may disfigure me for a time, but it will not stain: Archbishop Whately used to say, " Throw dirt enough, and some will stick ; " well, will stick, but not, will stain. I think he used to mean " stain," and I do not agree with him. Some dirt sticks longer than other dirt ; but no dirt is immortal. According to the old saying, Prævalebit Veritas. There are virtues indeed, which the world is not fitted to judge of or to uphold, such as faith, hope, and charity : but it can judge about Truthfulness ; it can judge about the natural virtues, and Truthfulness is one of them. Natural virtues may also become supernatural ; Truthfulness is such ; but that does not withdraw it from the jurisdiction of mankind at large. It may be more difficult in this or that particular case for men to take cognizance of it, as it may be difficult for the Court of Queen's Bench at Westminster to try a case fairly which took place in Hindostan : but that is a question of capacity, not of right. Mankind has the right to judge of Truthfulness in a Catholic, as in the case of a Protestant, of an Italian, or of a Chinese. I have never doubted, that in my hour, in God's hour, my avenger will appear, and the world will acquit me of untruthfulness, even though it be not while I live.

Still more confident am I of such eventual acquittal, seeing that my judges are my own countrymen. I consider, indeed, Englishmen the most suspicious and touchy of mankind ; I think them unreasonable, and unjust in their seasons of excitement ; but I had rather be an Englishman (as in fact I am,) than belong to any other race under heaven. They are as generous, as they are hasty and burly ; and their repentance for their injustice is greater than their sin.

For twenty years and more I have borne an imputation, of which I am at least as sensitive, who am the object of it, as they can be, who are only the judges. I have not set myself to remove it, first, because I never have had an opening to speak, and, next, because I never saw in them the disposition to hear. I have wished to appeal from Philip drunk to Philip sober. When shall I pronounce him to be himself again ? If I may judge from the tone of the public press, which represents the public voice, I have great reason to take heart at this time. I have been treated by contemporary critics in this controversy with great fairness and gentleness, and I am grateful to them for it. However, the decision on the time and mode of my defence has been taken out of my hands; and I am thankful that it has been so. I am bound now as a duty to myself, to the Catholic cause, to the Catholic Priesthood, to give account of myself without any delay, when I am so rudely and circumstantially charged with Untruthfulness. I accept the challenge; I shall do my best to meet it, and I shall be content when I have done so.

It is not my present accuser alone who entertains, and has entertained, so dishonourable an opinion of me and of my writings. It is the impression of large classes of men ; the impression twenty years ago and the impression now. There has been a general feeling

that I was for years where I had no right to be ; that
I was a " Romanist " in Protestant livery and service ;
that I was doing the work of a hostile Church in the
bosom of the English Establishment, and knew it, or
ought to have known it.   There was no need of argu-
ing about particular passages in my writings, when the
fact was so patent, as men thought it to be.

First it was certain, and I could not myself deny it,
that I scouted the name " Protestant."   It was certain
again, that many of the doctrines which I professed
were popularly and generally known as badges of the
Roman Church, as distinguished from the faith of the
Reformation.   Next, how could I have come by them ?
Evidently, I had certain friends and advisers who did
not appear ; there was some underground communication between Stonyhurst or Oscott and my rooms at
Oriel.   Beyond a doubt, I was advocating certain
doctrines, not by accident, but on an understanding
with ecclesiastics of the old religion.   Then men went
further, and said that I had actually been received
into that religion, and withal had leave given me to
profess myself a Protestant still.   Others went even
further, and gave it out to the world, as a matter of
fact, of which they themselves had the proof in their
hands, that I was actually a Jesuit.   And when the
opinions which I advocated spread, and younger men
went further than I, the feeling against me waxed
stronger and took a wider range.

And now indignation arose at the knavery of a conspiracy such as this :—and it became of course all the
greater in consequence of its being the received belief
of the public at large, that craft and intrigue, such as

they fancied they beheld with their eyes, were the very instruments to which the Catholic Church has in these last centuries been indebted for her maintenance and extension.

There was another circumstance still, which increased the irritation and aversion felt by the large classes, of whom I have been speaking, against the preachers of doctrines, so new to them and so unpalatable; and that was, that they developed them in so measured a way. If they were inspired by Roman theologians, (and this was taken for granted), why did they not speak out at once? Why did they keep the world in such suspense and anxiety as to what was coming next, and what was to be the upshot of the whole? Why this reticence, and half-speaking, and apparent indecision? It was plain that the plan of operations had been carefully mapped out from the first, and that these men were cautiously advancing towards its accomplishment, as far as was safe at the moment; that their aim and their hope was to carry off a large body with them of the young and the ignorant; that they meant gradually to leaven the minds of the rising generation, and to open the gates of that city, of which they were the sworn defenders, to the enemy who lay in ambush outside of it. And when in spite of the many protestations of the party to the contrary, there was at length an actual movement among their disciples, and one went over to Rome, and then another, the worst anticipations and the worst judgments which had been formed of them received their justification. And, lastly, when men first had said of me, " You will see, *he* will go, he is only biding his

time, he is waiting the word of command from Rome,"
and, when after all, after my arguments and denunciations of former years, at length I did leave the Anglican
Church for the Roman, then they said to each other,
" It is just as we said : we knew it would be so."

This was the state of mind of masses of men twenty
years ago, who took no more than an external and
common sense view of what was going on.   And partly
the tradition, partly the effect of that feeling, remains
to the present time   Certainly I consider that, in my
own case, it is the great obstacle in the way of my
being favourably heard, as at present, when I have to
make my defence.   Not only am I now a member of a
most un-English communion, whose great aim is considered to be the extinction of Protestantism and the
Protestant Church, and whose means of attack are
popularly supposed to be unscrupulous cunning and
deceit, but how came I originally to have any relations
with the Church of Rome at all? did I, or my opinions, drop from the sky? how came I, in Oxford, *in
gremio Universitatis*, to present myself to the eyes of
men in that full-blown investiture of Popery?   How
could I dare, how could I have the conscience, with
warnings, with prophecies, with accusations against
me, to persevere in a path which steadily advanced towards, which ended in, the religion of Rome?   And
how am I now to be trusted, when long ago I was
trusted, and was found wanting ?

It is this which is the strength of the case of my
Accuser against me ;—not the articles of impeachment
which he has framed from my writings, and which I
shall easily crumble into dust, but the bias of the

court. It is the state of the atmosphere; it is the vibration all around, which will echo his bold assertion of my dishonesty; it is that prepossession against me, which takes it for granted that, when my reasoning is convincing it is only ingenious, and that when my statements are unanswerable, there is always something put out of sight or hidden in my sleeve; it is that plausible, but cruel conclusion to which men are apt to jump, that when much is imputed, much must be true, and that it is more likely that one should be to blame, than that many should be mistaken in blaming him;—these are the real foes which I have to fight, and the auxiliaries to whom my Accuser makes his advances.

Well, I must break through this barrier of prejudice against me if I can; and I think I shall be able to do so. When first I read the Pamphlet of Accusation, I almost despaired of meeting effectively such a heap of misrepresentations and such a vehemence of animosity. What was the good of answering first one point, and then another, and going through the whole circle of its abuse; when my answer to the first point would be forgotten, as soon as I got to the second? What was the use of bringing out half a hundred separate principles or views for the refutation of the separate counts in the Indictment, when rejoinders of this sort would but confuse and torment the reader by their number and their diversity? What hope was there of condensing into a pamphlet of a readable length, matter which ought freely to expand itself into half a dozen volumes? What means was there, except the expenditure of interminable pages, to set right even one of that series of "single passing hints," to use my

Assailant's own language, which, "as with his finger tip he had delivered" against me ?

All those separate charges had their force in being illustrations of one and the same great imputation. He had already a positive idea to illuminate his whole matter, and to stamp it with a force, and to quicken it with an interpretation. He called me a *liar*,—a simple, a broad, an intelligible, to the English public a plausible arraignment ; but for me, to answer in detail charge one by reason one, and charge two by reason two, and charge three by reason three, and so on through the whole string both of accusations and replies, each of which was to be independent of the rest, this would be certainly labour lost as regards any effective result. What I needed was a corresponding antagonist unity in my defence, and where was that to be found? We see, in the case of commentators on the prophecies of Scripture, an exemplification of the principle on which I am insisting ; viz., how much more powerful even a false interpretation of the sacred text is than none at all ;—how a certain key to the visions of the Apocalypse, for instance, may cling to the mind (I have found it so in the case of my own), because the view, which it opens on us, is positive and objective, in spite of the fullest demonstration that it really has no claim upon our reception. The reader says, " What else can the prophecy mean ? " just as my Accuser asks, " What, then, does Dr. Newman mean ? " . . . . . I reflected, and I saw a way out of my perplexity.

Yes, I said to myself, his very question is about my *meaning;* " What does Dr. Newman mean ? " It pointed in the very same direction as that into which my musings had turned me already. He asks what I *mean*; not about my words, not about my arguments, not about my actions, as his ultimate point, but about that living intelligence, by which I write, and argue, and act. He asks about my Mind and its Beliefs and its sentiments; and he shall be answered;—not for his own sake, but for mine, for the sake of the Religion which I profess, and of the Priesthood in which I am unworthily included, and of my friends and of my foes, and of that general public which consists of neither one nor the other, but of well-wishers, lovers of fair play, sceptical cross-questioners, interested inquirers, curious lookers-on, and simple strangers unconcerned yet not careless about the issue,—for the sake of all these he shall be answered.

My perplexity had not lasted half an hour. I recognized what I had to do, though I shrank from both the task and the exposure which it would entail. I must, I said, give the true key to my whole life; I must show what I am, that it may be seen what I am not, and that the phantom may be extinguished which gibbers instead of me. I wish to be known as a living man, and not as a scarecrow which is dressed up in my clothes. False ideas may be refuted indeed by arguments, but by true ideas alone are they expelled. I will vanquish, not my Accuser, but my judges. I will indeed answer his charges and criticisms on me one by one,* lest any one should say that they are unanswerable, but such a work shall not be the scope

* This was done in the Appendix, of which the more important parts are preserved in the Notes.

6

nor the substance of my reply. I will draw out, as far as may be, the history of my mind; I will state the point at which I began, in what external suggestion or accident each opinion had its rise, how far and how they developed from within, how they grew, were modified, were combined, were in collision with each other, and were changed; again how I conducted myself towards them, and how, and how far, and for how long a time, I thought I could hold them consistently with the ecclesiastical engagements which I had made and with the position which I held. I must show,— what is the very truth,—that the doctrines which I held, and have held for so many years, have been taught me (speaking humanly) partly by the suggestion of Protestant friends, partly by the teaching of books, and partly by the action of my own mind : and thus I shall account for that phenomenon which to so many seems so wonderful, that I should have left "my kindred and my father's house" for a Church from which once I turned away with dread; so wonderful to them ! as if forsooth a Religion which has flourished through so many ages, among so many nations, amid such varieties of social life, in such contrary classes and conditions of men, and after so many revolutions, political and civil, could not subdue the reason and overcome the heart, without the aid of fraud in the process and the sophistries of the schools.—*Apologia*, ed. 1890, pp. xii–xxiii (1864).

THESE instances give us warning:—Is the enemy of Christ, and His Church, to arise out of a certain special falling away from GOD? And is there no reason to fear that some such Apostasy is gradually preparing, gathering, hastening on in this very day? For is there not at this very time a special effort made almost all over the world, that is, every here and there, more or less in sight or out of sight, in this or that place, but most visibly or formidably in its most civilized and powerful parts, an effort to do without Religion? Is there not an opinion avowed and growing, that a nation has nothing to do with Religion; that it is merely a matter for each man's own conscience?—which is all one with saying that we may let the Truth fail from the earth without trying to continue it in and on after our time. Is there not a vigorous and united movement in all countries to cast down the Church of Christ from power and place? Is there not a feverish and ever-busy endeavour to get rid of the necessity of Religion in public transactions? for example, an attempt to get rid of oaths, under a pretence that they are too sacred for affairs of common life, instead of providing that they be taken more reverently and more suitably? an attempt to educate without Religion?— that is, by putting all forms of Religion together,

83

which comes to the same thing;—an attempt to en-
force temperance, and the virtues which flow from it,
without Religion, by means of Societies which are
built on mere principles of utility? an attempt to make
expedience, and not *truth*, the end and the rule of measures of State and the enactments of Law? an attempt
to make numbers, and not the Truth, the ground of
maintaining, or not maintaining, this or that creed, as
if we had any reason whatever in Scripture for thinking that the many will be in the right, and the few in
the wrong? An attempt to deprive the Bible of its one
meaning to the exclusion of all other, to make people
think that it may have an hundred meanings all
equally good, or, in other words, that it has no meaning at all, is a dead letter, and may be put aside? an
attempt to supersede Religion altogether, as far as it
is external or objective, as far as it is displayed in ordinances, or can be expressed by written words,—to
confine it to our inward feelings, and thus, considering
how variable, how evanescent our feelings are, an attempt, in fact, to destroy Religion?

Surely, there is at this day a confederacy of evil,
marshalling its hosts from all parts of the world, organ-
izing itself, taking its measures, enclosing the Church
of Christ as in a net, and preparing the way for a
general Apostasy from it. Whether this very Apostasy
is to give birth to Antichrist, or whether he is still to be
delayed, as he has already been delayed so long, we
cannot know; but at any rate this Apostasy, and all
its tokens and instruments, are of the Evil One, and
savour of death. Far be it from any of us to be of
those simple ones who are taken in that snare which is

circling around us! Far be it from us to be seduced with the fair promises in which Satan is sure to hide his poison! Do you think he is so unskilful in his craft, as to ask you openly and plainly to join him in his warfare against the Truth? No; he offers you baits to tempt you. He promises you civil liberty; he promises you equality; he promises you trade and wealth; he promises you a remission of taxes; he promises you reform. This is the way in which he conceals from you the kind of work to which he is putting you; he tempts you to rail against your rulers and superiors; he does so himself, and induces you to imitate him; or he promises you illumination, —he offers you knowledge, science, philosophy, en-largement of mind. He scoffs at times gone by; he scoffs at every institution which reveres them. He prompts you what to say, and then listens to you, and praises you, and encourages you. He bids you mount aloft. He shows you how to become as gods. Then he laughs and jokes with you, and gets intimate with you; he takes your hand, and gets his fingers between yours, and grasps them, and then you are his.—*Discussions and Arguments*, ed. 1888, pp. 59–61 (1838).

Knowledge and Character.

A DISTINGUISHED Conservative statesman tells us from the town-hall of Tamworth that "in becoming wiser a man will become better;" meaning by wiser more conversant with the facts and theories of physical science; and that such a man will "rise at *once* in the scale of intellectual and *moral* existence." "That," he adds, "is my belief." He avows, also, that the fortunate individual whom he is describing, by being "accustomed to such contemplations, will feel the *moral dignity of his nature exalted.*" He speaks also of physical knowledge as "being the means of useful occupation and rational recreation;" of "the pleasures of knowledge" superseding "the indulgence of sensual appetite," and of its "contributing to the intellectual and *moral improvement* of the community." Accordingly, he very consistently wishes it to be set before "the female as well as the male portion of the population;" otherwise, as he truly observes, "great injustice would be done to the well-educated and virtuous" women of the place. They are to "have equal power and equal influence with others." It will be difficult to exhaust the reflections which rise in the mind on reading avowals of this nature.

The first question which obviously suggests itself is *how* these wonderful moral effects are to be wrought under the instrumentality of the physical sciences.

86

Can the process be analyzed and drawn out, or does it act like a dose or a charm which comes into general use empirically? Does Sir Robert Peel mean to say, that whatever be the occult reasons for the result, so it is; you have but to drench the popular mind with physics, and moral and religious advancement follows on the whole, in spite of individual failures? Yet where has the experiment been tried on so large a scale as to justify such anticipations? Or rather, does he mean, that, from the nature of the case, he who is imbued with science and literature, unless adverse influences interfere, cannot but be a better man? It is natural and becoming to seek for some clear idea of the meaning of so dark an oracle. To know is one thing, to do is another; the two things are altogether distinct. A man knows he should get up in the morning,—he lies a-bed; he knows he should not lose his temper, yet he cannot keep it. A labouring man knows he should not go to the ale-house, and his wife knows she should not filch when she goes out charing, but, nevertheless, in these cases, the consciousness of a duty is not all one with the performance of it. There are then, large families of instances, to say the least, in which men may become wiser, without becoming better; what, then, is the meaning of this great maxim in the mouth of its promulgators?

Mr. Bentham would answer, that the knowledge which carries virtue along with it, is the knowledge how to take care of number one—a clear appreciation of what is pleasurable, what painful, and what promotes the one and prevents the other. An uneducated man is ever mistaking his own interest, and standing in the way of his own true enjoyments. Useful Knowledge is that which tends to make us more useful to ourselves ;—a most definite and intelligible account of the matter, and needing no explanation. But it would be a great injustice, both to Lord Brougham and to Sir Robert, to suppose, when they talk of Knowledge being Virtue, that they are Benthamizing. Bentham had not a spark of poetry in him ; on the contrary, there is much of high aspiration, generous sentiment, and impassioned feeling in the tone of Lord Brougham and Sir Robert. They speak of knowledge as something "pulchrum," fair and glorious, exalted above the range of ordinary humanity, and so little connected with the personal interest of its votaries, that, though Sir Robert does *obiter* talk of improved modes of draining, and the chemical properties of manure, yet he must not be supposed to come short of the lofty enthusiasm of Lord Brougham, who expressly panegyrizes certain ancient philosophers who gave up riches, retired into solitude, or embraced a life of travel, smit with a sacred curiosity about physical or mathematical truth.

Here Mr. Bentham, did it fall to him to offer a criticism, doubtless would take leave to inquire whether such language was anything better than a fine set of words "signifying nothing,"—flowers of rhetoric, which bloom, smell sweet, and die. But it is impossible to suspect so grave and practical a man as Sir Robert Peel of using words literally without any meaning at all; and though I think at best they have not a very profound meaning, yet, such as it is, we ought to attempt to draw it out.

Now, without using exact theological language, we may surely take it for granted, from the experience of facts, that the human mind is at best in a very unformed or disordered state ; passions and conscience, likings and reason, conflicting,—might rising against right, with the prospect of things getting worse. Under these circumstances, what is it that the School of philosophy in which Sir Robert has enrolled himself proposes to accomplish ? Not a victory of the mind over itself—not the supremacy of the law—not the reduction of the rebels—not the unity of our complex nature—not an harmonizing of the chaos—but the mere lulling of the passions to rest by turning the course of thought; not a change of character, but a mere removal of temptation. This should be carefully observed. When a husband is gloomy, or an old woman peevish and fretful, those who are about them do all they can to keep dangerous topics and causes of offence out of the way, and think themselves lucky, if, by such skilful management, they get through the day without an outbreak. When a child cries, the nurserymaid dances it about, or points to the pretty black horses out of window, or shows how ashamed poll-parrot or poor puss must be of its tantarums. Such is the sort of prescription which Sir Robert Peel offers to the good people of Tamworth. He makes no pretence of subduing the giant nature, in which we were born, of smiting the lions of the domestic enemies of our piece, of overthrowing passion and fortifying reason ; he does but offer to bribe the foe for the nonce with gifts which will avail for that purpose just so long as they *will* avail, and no longer.

This was mainly the philosophy of the great Tully, except when it pleased him to speak as a disciple of the Porch. Cicero handed the recipe to Brougham, and Brougham has passed it on to Peel. If we examine the old Roman's meaning in *"O philosophia, vitæ dux,"* it was neither more nor less than this ;—that, *while* we were thinking of philosophy, we were not thinking of anything else ; we did not feel grief, or anxiety, or passion, or ambition, or hatred all that time, and the only point was to keep thinking of it. How to keep thinking of it was *extra artem.* If a man was in grief, he was to be amused; if disappointed, to be excited ; if in a rage, to be soothed ; if in love, to be roused to the pursuit of glory. No inward change was contemplated, but a change of external objects; as if we were all White Ladies or Undines, our moral life being one of impulse and emotion, not subjected to laws, not consisting in habits, not capable of growth. When Cicero was outwitted by Cæsar, he solaced himself with Plato ; when he lost his daughter, he wrote a treatise on consolation. Such, too, was the philosophy of that Lydian city, mentioned by the historian, who in a famine played at dice to stay their stomachs.

And such is the rule of life advocated by Lord Brougham ; and though, of course, he protests that knowledge " must invigorate the mind as well as entertain it, and refine and elevate the character, while it gives listlessness and weariness their most agreeable excitement and relaxation," yet his notions of vigour and elevation, when analyzed, will be found to resolve themselves into a mere preternatural excitement under the influence of some stimulating object, or the peace which is attained by there being nothing to quarrel with.

*   *   *

In morals, as in physics, the stream cannot rise higher than its source. Christianity raises men from earth, for it comes from heaven; but human morality creeps, struts, or frets upon the earth's level, without wings to rise. The Knowledge School does not contemplate raising man above himself; it merely aims at disposing of his existing powers and tastes, as is most convenient, or is practicable under circumstances. It finds him, like the victims of the French Tyrant, doubled up in a cage in which he can neither lie, stand, sit, nor kneel, and its highest desire is to find an attitude in which his unrest may be least. Or it finds him like some musical instrument, of great power and compass, but imperfect; from its very structure some keys must ever be out of tune, and its object, when ambition is highest, is to throw the *fault* of its nature where least it will be observed. It leaves man where it found him—man, and not an Angel—a sinner, not a Saint; but it tries to make him look as much like what he is not as ever it can. The poor indulge in low pleasures; they use bad language, swear loudly and recklessly, laugh at coarse jests, and are rude and boorish. Sir Robert would open on them a wider range of thought and more intellectual objects, by teaching them science; but what warrant will he give us that, if his object could be achieved, what they would gain in decency they would not lose in natural humility and faith? If so, he has exchanged a gross fault for a more subtle one. " Temperance topics " stop drinking; let us suppose it; but will much be gained, if those who give up spirits take to opium? *Naturam expellas furcâ, tamen usque recurret,* is at least a heathen truth, and universities and libraries which recur to heathenism many reclaim it from the heathen for their motto.

Nay, everywhere, so far as human nature remains hardly or partially Christianized, the heathen law remains in force; as is felt in a measure even in the most religious places and societies. Even there, where Christianity has power, the venom of the old Adam is not subdued. Those who have to do with our Colleges give us their experience, that in the case of the young committed to their care, external discipline may change the fashionable excess, but cannot allay the principle of sinning. Stop cigars, they will take to drinking parties; stop drinking, they gamble; stop gambling, and a worse license follows. You do not get rid of vice by human expedients; you can but use them according to circumstances, and in their place, as making the best of a bad matter. You must go to a higher source for renovation of the heart and of the will. You do but play a sort of "hunt the slipper" with the fault of our nature, till you go to Christianity.

I say, you must use human methods *in their place*, and there they are useful; but they are worse than useless out of their place. I have no fanatical wish to deny to any whatever subject of thought or method of reason a place altogether, if it chooses to claim it, in the cultivation of the mind. Mr. Bentham may despise verse-making, or Mr. Dugald Stewart logic, but the great and true maxim is to sacrifice none—to combine, and therefore to adjust, all. All cannot be first, and therefore each has its place, and the problem is to find it. It is at least not a lighter mistake to make what is secondary first, than to leave it out altogether. Here then it is that the Knowledge Society, Gower Street College, Tamworth Reading-room, Lord Brougham and Sir Robert Peel, are all so deplorably mistaken. Christianity, and nothing short of it, must be made the element and principle of all education. Where it has been laid as the first stone, and acknowledged as the governing spirit, it will take up into itself, assimilate, and give a character to literature and science. Where Revealed Truth has given the aim and direction to Knowledge, Knowledge of all kinds will minister to Revealed Truth. The evidences of Religion, natural theology, metaphysics,—or, again, poetry, history, and the classics,—or physics and mathematics, may all be grafted into the mind of a Christian, and give and take by the grafting. But if in education we begin with nature before grace, with evidences before faith, with science before conscience, with poetry before practice, we shall be doing much the same as if we were to indulge the appetites and passions, and turn a deaf ear to the reason. In each case we misplace what in its place is a divine gift. If we attempt to effect a moral improvement by means of poetry, we shall but mature into a mawkish, frivolous, and fastidious sentimentalism ;—if by means of argument, into a dry, unamiable longheadedness ;—if by good society, into a polished outside, with hollowness within, in which vice has lost its grossness, and perhaps increased its malignity ;—if by experimental science, into an uppish, supercilious temper much inclined to scepticism. But reverse the order of things : put Faith first and Knowledge second ; let the University minister to the Church, and then classical poetry becomes the type of Gospel truth, and physical science a comment on Genesis or Job, and Aristotle changes into Butler, and Arcesilas into Berkeley.*— *Discussions and Arguments*, ed. 1888, pp. 261–275 (1841).

* [On the supremacy of each science in its own field, of thought and the encroachments upon it of other sciences, *vide* the author's " University Teaching," Disc. 3, and " University Subjects," No. 7 and 10.]

PEOPLE say to me, that it is but a dream to suppose that Christianity should regain the organic power in human society which once it possessed. I cannot help that; I never said it could. I am not a politician; I am proposing no measures, but exposing a fallacy, and resisting a pretence. Let Benthamism reign, if men have no aspirations; but do not tell them to be romantic, and then solace them with glory; do not attempt by philosophy what once was done by religion. The ascendancy of Faith may be impracticable, but the reign of Knowledge is incomprehensible. The problem for statesmen of this age is how to educate the masses, and literature and science cannot give the solution.

Not so deems Sir Robert Peel; his firm belief and hope is, "that an increased sagacity will administer to an exalted faith; that it will make men not merely believe in the cold doctrines of Natural Religion, but that it will so prepare and temper the spirit and understanding, that they will be better qualified to comprehend the great scheme of human redemption." He certainly thinks that scientific pursuits have some considerable power of impressing religion upon the mind of the multitude. I think not, and will now say why.

95

Science gives us the grounds or premises from which religious truths are to be inferred; but it does not set about inferring them, much less does it reach the inference;—that is not its province. It brings before us phenomena, and it leaves us, if we will, to call them works of design, wisdom, or benevolence; and further still, if we will, to proceed to confess an Intelligent Creator. We have to take its facts, and to give them a meaning, and to draw our own conclusions from them. First comes Knowledge, then a view, then reasoning, and then belief. This is why Science has so little of a religious tendency; deductions have no power of persuasion. The heart is commonly reached, not through the reason, but through the imagination, by means of direct impressions, by the testimony of facts and events, by history, by description. Persons influence us, voices melt us, looks subdue us, deeds inflame us. Many a man will live and die upon a dogma: no man will be a martyr for a conclusion. A conclusion is but an opinion; it is not a thing which *is*, but which *we are* " *certain about ;* " and it has often been observed, that we never say we are certain without implying that we doubt. To say that a thing *must* be, is to admit that it *may not* be. No one, I say, will die for his own calculations; he dies for realities. This is why a literary religion is so little to be depended upon; it looks well in fair weather, but its doctrines are opinions, and, when called to suffer for them, it slips them between its folios, or burns them at its hearth. And this again is the secret of the distrust and raillery with which moralists have been so commonly visited. They say and do not. Why? Because they are contemplating the fitness of things, and they live by the square, when they should be realizing their high maxims in the concrete. Now Sir Robert thinks better of natural history, chemistry, and astronomy, than of such ethics ; but they too, what are they more than divinity *in posse?* He protests against "controversial divinity : " is *inferential* much better ?

I have no confidence, then, in philosophers who cannot help being religious, and are Christians by implication. They sit at home, and reach forward to distances which astonish us; but they hit without grasping, and are sometimes as confident about shadows as about realities. They have worked out by a calculation the lie of a country which they never saw, and mapped it by means of a gazetteer ; and like blind men, though they can put a stranger on his way, they cannot walk straight themselves, and do not feel it quite their business to walk at all.

Logic makes but a sorry rhetoric with the multitude ; first shoot round corners, and you may not despair of converting by a syllogism. Tell men to gain notions of a Creator from His works, and, if they were to set about it (which nobody does), they would be jaded and wearied by the labyrinth they were tracing. Their minds would be gorged and surfeited by the logical operation. Logicians are more set upon concluding rightly, than on right conclusions. They cannot see the end for the process. Few men have that power of mind which may hold fast and firmly a variety of thoughts. We ridicule "men of one idea ; " but a great many of us are born to be such, and we should be happier if we knew it. To most men argument makes

7

the point in hand only more doubtful, and considerably less impressive. After all, man is not a reasoning animal; he is a seeing, feeling, contemplating, acting animal. He is influenced by what is direct and precise. It is very well to freshen our impressions and convictions from physics, but to create them we must go elsewhere. Sir Robert Peel "never can think it possible that a mind can be so constituted, that, after being familiarized with the wonderful discoveries which have been made in every part of experimental science, it can retire from such contemplations without more enlarged conceptions of God's providence, and a higher reverence for His name." If he speaks of religious minds, he perpetrates a truism; if of irreligious, he insinuates a paradox.

Life is not long enough for a religion of inferences; we shall never have done beginning, if we determine to begin with proof. We shall ever be laying our foundations; we shall turn theology into evidences, and divines into textuaries. We shall never get at our first principles. Resolve to believe nothing, and you must prove your proofs and analyze your elements, sinking further and further, and finding "in the lowest depth a lower deep," till you come to the broad bosom of scepticism. I would rather be bound to defend the reasonableness of assuming that Christianity is true, than to demonstrate a moral governance from the physical world. Life is for action. If we insist on proofs for everything, we shall never come to action: to act you must assume, and that assumption is faith.

Let no one suppose that in saying this I am maintaining that all proofs are equally difficult, and all propositions equally debatable. Some assumptions are greater than others, and some doctrines involve postulates larger than others, and more numerous. I only say that impressions lead to action, and that reasonings lead from it. Knowledge of premises, and inferences upon them,—this is not to *live.* It is very well as a matter of liberal curiosity and of philosophy to analyze our modes of thought; but let this come second, and when there is leisure for it, and then our examinations will in many ways even be subservient to action. But if we commence with scientific knowledge and argumentative proof, or lay any great stress upon it as the basis of personal Christianity, or attempt to make man moral and religious by Libraries and Museums, let us in consistency take chemists for our cooks, and mineralogists for our masons.

Now I wish to state all this as matter of fact, to be judged by the candid testimony of any persons whatever. Why we are so constituted that Faith, not Knowledge or Argument, is our principle of action, is a question with which I have nothing to do; but I think it is a fact, and if it be such, we must resign ourselves to it as best we may, unless we take refuge in the intolerable paradox, that the mass of men are created for nothing, and are meant to leave life as they entered it. So well has this practically been understood in all ages of the world, that no Religion has yet been a Religion of physics or of philosophy. It has ever been synonymous with Revelation. It never has been a deduction from what we know: it has ever been an assertion of what we are to believe. It has never lived in a conclusion; it has ever been a message, or a history, or a vision. No legislator or priest ever dreamed of educating our moral nature by science or by argument. There is no difference here between true Religions and pretended. Moses was instructed, not to reason from the creation, but to work miracles. Christianity is a history, supernatural, and almost scenic : it tells us what its Author is, by telling us what He has done. I have no wish at all to speak otherwise than respectfully of conscientious Dissenters, but I have heard it said by those who were not their enemies, and who had known much of their preaching, that they had often heard narrow-minded and bigoted clergymen, and often Dissenting ministers of a far more intellectual cast; but that Dissenting teaching came to nothing,—that it was dissipated in thoughts which had no point, and inquiries which converged to no centre, that it ended as it began, and sent away its hearers as it found them;—whereas the instruction in the Church, with all its defects and mistakes, comes to some end, for it started from some beginning. Such is the difference between the dogmatism of faith and the speculations of logic.

Lord Brougham himself, as we have already seen, has recognized the force of this principle. He has not left his philosophical religion to argument; he has committed it to the keeping of the imagination. Why should he depict a great republic of letters, and an intellectual Pantheon, but that he feels that instances and patterns, not logical reasonings, are the living conclusions which alone have a hold over the affections, or can form the character?—*Discussions and Arguments*, ed. 1888, pp. 292–297 (1841).

Science and Religion.

WHEN Sir Robert Peel assures us from the Town-hall at Tamworth that physical science must lead to religion, it is no bad compliment to him to say that he is unreal. He speaks of what he knows nothing about. To a religious man like him, Science has ever suggested religious thoughts; he colours the phenomena of physics with the hues of his own mind, and mistakes an interpretation for a deduction. " I am sanguine enough to believe," he says, " that that superior sagacity which is most conversant with the course and constitution of Nature will be first to turn a deaf ear to objections and presumptions against Revealed Religion, and to acknowledge the complete harmony of the Christian Dispensation with all that Reason, assisted by Revelation, tells us of the course and constitution of Nature." Now, considering that we are all of us educated as Christians from infancy, it is not easy to decide at this day whether Science creates Faith, or only confirms it ; but we have this remarkable fact in the history of heathen Greece against the former supposition, that her most eminent empirical philosophers were atheists, and that it was their atheism which was the cause of their eminence. " The natural philosophies of Democritus and others," says Lord Bacon, " *who allow no God or mind* in the frame of things, but attribute the structure of the universe to infinite essays and trials of nature, or what they call fate or fortune, and assigned the causes of particular things to the necessity of matter, *without any intermixture of final causes*, seem, as far as we can judge from the remains of their philosophy, *much more solid*, and to have *gone deeper into nature*, with regard to physical causes, than the philosophies of Aristotle or Plato : and this only because they *never meddled with final causes*, which the others were perpetually inculcating."

Lord Bacon gives us both the fact and the reason for it. Physical philosophers are ever inquiring *whence* things are, not *why ;* referring them to nature, not to mind ; and thus they tend to make a system a substitute for a God. Each pursuit or calling has its own dangers, and each numbers among its professors men who rise superior to them. As the soldier is tempted to dissipation, and the merchant to acquisitiveness, and the lawyer to the sophistical, and the statesman to the expedient, and the country clergyman to ease and comfort, yet there are good clergymen, statesmen, lawyers, merchants, and soldiers, notwithstanding ; so there are religious experimentalists, though physics, taken by themselves, tend to infidelity ; but to have recourse to physics to *make* men religious is like recommending a canonry as a cure for the gout, or giving a youngster a commission as a penance for irregularities.

The whole framework of Nature is confessedly a tissue of antecedents and consequents ; we may refer all things forwards to design, or backwards on a physical cause. La Place is said to have considered he had a formula which solved all the motions of the solar system; shall we say that those motions came from this formula or from a Divine Fiat? Shall we have recourse for our theory to physics or to theology? Shall we assume Matter and its necessary properties to be eternal, ôr Mind with its divine attributes? Does the sun shine to warm the earth, or is the earth warmed because the sun shines? The one hypothesis will solve the phenomena as well as the other. Say not it is but a puzzle in argument, and that no one ever felt it in fact. So far from it, I believe that the study of Nature, when religious feeling is away, leads the mind, rightly or wrongly, to acquiesce in the atheistic theory, as the simplest and easiest. It is but parallel to that tendency in anatomical studies, which no one will deny, to solve all the phenomena of the human frame into material elements and powers, and to dispense with the soul. To those who are conscious of matter, but not conscious of mind, it seems more rational to refer all things to one origin, such as they know, than to assume the existence of a second origin such as they know not. It is Religion, then which suggests to Science its true conclusions; the facts come from Knowledge, but the principles come of Faith.*

There are two ways, then, of reading Nature—as a

---

* [This is too absolute, if it is to be taken to mean that the legitimate, and what may be called the objective, conclusion from the fact of Nature viewed in the concrete is not in favour of the being and providence of God.—*Vide* "Essay on Assent," pp. 336, 345, 369, and "Univ. Serm." p. 194.]

machíne and as a work. If we come to it with the
assumption that it is a creation, we shall study it with
awe ; if assuming it to be a system, with mere curiosity.   Sir Robert does not make this distinction.
He subscribes to the belief that the man " accustomed
to such contemplations, *struck with awe* by the manifold proofs of infinite power and infinite wisdom, will
yield more ready and hearty assent—yes, the assent of
the heart, and not only of the understanding, to the
pious exclamation, ' O Lord, how glorious are Thy
works ! ' "   He considers that greater insight into
Nature will lead a man to say, " How great and wise
is the Creator, who has done this ! "   True : but it is
possible that his thoughts may take the form of " How
clever is the creature who has discovered it ! " and
self-conceit may stand proxy for adoration.   This is
no idle apprehension.   Sir Robert himself, religious
as he is, gives cause for it ; for the first reflection that
rises in his mind, as expressed in the above passage,
before his notice of Divine Power and Wisdom, is, that
" the man accustomed to such contemplations will feel
the *moral dignity of his nature exalted.*"   But Lord
Brougham speaks out.   " The delight," he says, " is
inexpressible of *being able to follow*, as it were, with our
eyes, the marvellous works of the Great Architect of
Nature."   And more clearly still :   " One of the most
gratifying treats which science affords us is *the knowledge of the extraordinary powers* with which the human
mind is endowed.   No man, until he has studied
philosophy, can have a just idea of the great things
for which Providence has fitted his understanding, the
extraordinary disproportion which there is between his

natural strength and the powers of his mind, and the force which he derives from these powers. When we survey the marvellous truths of astronomy, we are first of all lost in the feeling of immense space, and of the comparative insignificance of this globe and its inhabitants. But there soon arises a *sense of gratification and of new wonder* at perceiving how so insignificant a creature has been *able to reach such a knowledge* of the unbounded system of the universe." So, this is the religion we are to gain from the study of Nature ; how miserable ! The god we attain is our own mind ; our veneration is even professedly the worship of self.

The truth is that the system of Nature is just as much connected with Religion, where minds are not religious, as a watch or a steam-carriage. The material world, indeed, is infinitely more wonderful than any human contrivance ; but wonder is not religion, or we should be worshipping our railroads. What the physical creation presents to us in itself is a piece of machinery, and when men speak of a Divine Intelligence as its Author, this god of theirs is not the Living and True, unless the spring is the god of a watch, or steam the creator of the engine. Their idol, taken at advantage (though it is *not* an idol, for they do not worship it), is the animating principle of a vast and complicated system ; it is subjected to laws, and it is connatural and co-extensive with matter. Well does Lord Brougham call it "the great architect of nature ;" it is an instinct, or a soul of the world, or a vital power ; it is not the Almighty God.*—*Discussions and Arguments,* ed. 1888, pp. 298--302 (1841).

* [*Vide* " University Teaching," Disc. 2.]

Now what is Theology? First, I will tell you what it is not. And here, in the first place (though of course I speak on the subject as a Catholic), observe that, strictly speaking, I am not assuming that Catholicism is true, while I make myself the champion of Theology. Catholicism has not formally entered into my argument hitherto, nor shall I just now assume any principle peculiar to it, for reasons which will appear in the sequel, though of course I shall use Catholic language. Neither, secondly, will I fall into the fashion of the day, of identifying Natural Theology with Physical Theology; which said Physical Theology is a most jejune study, considered as a science, and really is no science at all, for it is ordinarily nothing more than a series of pious or polemical remarks upon the physical world viewed religiously, whereas the word "Natural" properly comprehends man and society, and all that is involved therein, as the great Protestant writer, Dr. Butler, shows us. Nor, in the third place, do I mean by Theology polemics of any kind; for instance, what are called "The Evidences of Religion," or "the Christian Evidences;" for, though these constitute a science supplemental to Theology and are necessary in their place, they are not Theology itself, unless an army is synonymous with the body politic. Nor, fourthly, do I mean by Theology that vague thing called "Chris-tianity," or "our common Christianity," or "Christianity the law of the land," if there is any man alive who can tell what it is. I discard it, for the very reason that it cannot throw itself into a proposition. Lastly, I do not understand by Theology, acquaintance with the Scriptures; for, though no person of religious feelings can read Scripture but he will find those feelings roused, and gain much knowledge of history into the bargain, yet historical reading and religious feeling are not science. I mean none of these things by Theology, I simply mean the Science of God, or the truths we know about God put into system; just as we have a science of the stars, and call it astronomy, or of the crust of the earth, and call it geology.

For instance, I mean, for this is the main point, that, as in the human frame there is a living principle, acting upon it and through it by means of volition, so, behind the veil of the visible universe, there is an invisible, intelligent Being, acting on and through it, as and when He will. Further, I mean that this invisible Agent is in no sense a soul of the world, after the analogy of human nature, but, on the contrary, is absolutely distinct from the world, as being its Creator, Upholder, Governor, and Sovereign Lord. Here we are at once brought into the circle of doctrines which the idea of God embodies. I mean then by the Supreme Being, one who is simply self-dependent, and the only Being who is such; moreover, that He is without beginning or Eternal, and the only Eternal; that in consequence He has lived a whole eternity by Himself; and hence that he is all-sufficient, sufficient for His own blessedness, and all-blessed, and ever-blessed. Further, I mean a Being, who having these prerogatives, has the Supreme Good, or rather is the Supreme Good, or has all the attributes of Good in infinite intenseness; all wisdom, all truth, all justice, all love, all holiness, all beautifulness; who is omnipotent, omniscient, omnipresent; ineffably one, absolutely perfect; and such, that what we do not know and cannot even imagine of Him, is far more wonderful than what we do and can. I mean One who is sovereign over His own will and actions, though always according to the eternal Rule of right and wrong, which is Himself. I mean, moreover, that He created all things out of nothing, and preserves them every moment, and could destroy them as easily as He made them; and that, in consequence, He is separated from them by an abyss, and is incommunicable in all His attributes. And further, He has stamped upon all things, in the hour of their creation, their respective natures, and has given them their work and mission and their length of days, greater or less, in their appointed place. I mean, too, that He is ever present with His works, one by one, and confronts everything He has made by His particular and most loving Providence, and manifests Himself to each according to its needs; and has on rational beings imprinted the moral law, and given them power to obey it, imposing on them the duty of worship and service, searching and scanning them through and through with His omniscient eye, and putting before them a present trial and a judgment to come.

Such is what Theology teaches about God, a doctrine, as the very idea of its subject-matter presupposes, so mysterious as in its fulness to lie beyond any system, and in particular aspects to be simply external to nature, and to seem in parts even to be irreconcilable with itself, the imagination being unable to embrace what the reason determines. It teaches of a Being infinite, yet personal; all-blessed, yet ever operative; absolutely separate from the creature, yet in every part of the creation at every moment ; above all things, yet under everything. It teaches of a Being who, though the highest, yet in the work of creation, conservation, government, retribution, makes Himself, as it were, the minister and servant of all ; who, though inhabiting eternity, allows Himself to take an interest, and to have a sympathy, in the matters of space and time. His are all beings, visible and invisible, the noblest and the vilest of them. His are the substance, and the operation, and the results of that system of physical nature into which we are born. His too are the powers and achievements of the intellectual essences, on which he has bestowed an independent action and the gift of origination. The laws of the universe, the principles of truth, the relation of one thing to another, their qualities and virtues, the order and harmony of the whole, all that exists, is from Him ; and, if evil is not from Him, as assuredly it is not, this is because evil has no substance of its own, but is only the defect, excess, perversion, or corruption of that which has substance. All we see, hear, and touch, the remote sidereal firmament, as well as our own sea and land, and the elements which compose them and the ordinances they obey, are His. The primary atoms of matter, their properties, their mutual action, their disposition and collocation, electricity, magnetism, gravitation, light, and whatever other subtle principles or operations the wit of man is detecting or shall detect, are the work of His hands. From Him has been every movement which has convulsed and refashioned the surface of the earth. The most insignificant or unsightly insect is from Him, and good in its kind ; the ever-teeming, inexhaustible swarms of animalculæ, the myriads of living motes invisible to the naked eye, the restless, ever-spreading vegetation which creeps like a garment over the whole earth, the lofty cedar, the umbrageous banana, are His. His are the tribes and families of birds and beasts, their graceful forms, their wild gestures, and their passionate cries.

And so in the intellectual, moral, social, and political world. Man, with his motives and works, his languages, his propagation, his diffusion, is from Him. Agriculture, medicine, and the arts of life, are His gifts. Society, laws, government, He is their sanction. The pageant of earthly royalty has the semblance and the benediction of the Eternal King. Peace and civilization, commerce and adventure, wars when just, conquest when humane and necessary, have His co-operation, and His blessing upon them. The course of events, the revolution of empires, the rise and fall of states, the periods and eras, the progresses and the retrogressions of the world's history, not indeed the incidental sin, over-abundant as it is, but the great outlines and the results of human affairs, are from His disposition. The elements and types and seminal principles and constructive powers of the moral world, in ruins though it be, are to be referred to Him. He "enlighteneth every man that cometh into this world." His are the dictates of the moral sense, and the retributive reproaches of conscience. To Him must be ascribed the rich endowments of the intellect, the irradiation of genius, the imagination of the poet, the sagacity of the politician, the wisdom (as Scripture calls it), which now rears and decorates the Temple, now manifests itself in proverb or in parable. The old saws of nations, the majestic precepts of philosophy, the luminous maxims of law, the oracles of individual wisdom, the traditionary rules of truth, justice, and religion, even though imbedded in the corruption, or alloyed with the pride, of the world, betoken His original agency, and His long-suffering presence. Even where there is habitual rebellion against Him, or profound far-spreading social depravity, still the undercurrent, or the heroic outburst, of natural virtue, as well as the yearnings of the heart after what it has not, and its presentiment of its true remedies, are to be ascribed to the Author of all good. Anticipations or reminiscences of His glory haunt the mind of the self-sufficient sage, and of the pagan devotee; His writing is upon the wall, whether of the Indian fane, or of the porticoes of Greece. He introduces Himself, He all but concurs, according to His good pleasure, and in His selected season, in the issues of unbelief, superstition, and false worship, and He changes the character of acts by His overruling operation. He condescends, though he gives no sanction, to the altars and shrines of imposture, and He makes His own fiat the substitute for its sorceries. He speaks amid the

incantations of Balaam, raises Samuel's spirit in the
witch's cavern, prophesies of the Messias by the
tongue of the Sibyl, forces Python to recognize His
ministers, and baptizes by the hand of the misbe-
liever.   He is with the heathen dramatist in his denunciations of injustice and tyranny, and his auguries of
divine vengeance upon crime.   Even on the unseemly
legends of a popular mythology He casts His shadow,
and is dimly discerned in the ode or the epic, as in
troubled water or in fantastic dreams.   All that is
good, all that is true, all that is beautiful, all that is be-
nificent, be it great or small, be it perfect or fragment-
ary, natural as well as supernatural, moral as well as
material, comes from Him.

If this be a sketch, accurate in substance and as far
as it goes, of the doctrines proper to Theology, and
especially of the doctrine of a particular Providence,
which is the portion of it most on a level with human
sciences, I cannot understand at all how, supposing it
to be true, it can fail, considered as knowledge, to
exert a powerful influence on philosophy, literature,
and every intellectual creation or discovery whatever.
I cannot understand how it is possible, as the phrase
goes, to blink the question of its truth or falsehood.
It meets us with a profession and a proffer of the
highest truths of which the human mind is capable; it
embraces a range of subjects the most diversified and
distant from each other.   What science will not find
one part or other of its province traversed by its path?
What results of philosophic speculation are unques-
tionable, if they have been gained without inquiry as

to what Theology had to say to them ? Does it cast no light upon history ? has it no influence upon the principles of ethics ? is it without any sort of bearing on physics, metaphysics, and political science ? Can we drop it out of the circle of knowledge, without allowing, either that that circle is thereby mutilated, or on the other hand, that Theology is really no science ?

And this dilemma is the more inevitable, because Theology is so precise and consistent in its intellectual structure. When I speak of Theism or Monotheism, I am not throwing together discordant doctrines ; I am not merging belief, opinion, persuasion, of whatever kind, into a shapeless aggregate, by the help of ambiguous words, and dignifying this medley by the name of Theology. I speak of one idea unfolded in its just proportions, carried out upon an intelligible method, and issuing in necessary and immutable results ; understood indeed at one time and place better than at another, held here and there with more or less of inconsistency, but still, after all, in all times and places, where it is found, the evolution, not of half-a-dozen ideas, but of one.—*Idea of a University*, ed. 1891, pp. 60–67 (1852).

8

AND now I have said enough to explain the inconvenience which I conceive necessarily to result from
a refusal to recognize theological truth in a course of
Universal Knowledge ;—it is not only the loss of Theology, it is the perversion of other sciences. What it
unjustly forfeits, others unjustly seize. They have
their own department, and, in going out of it, attempt to
do what they really cannot do ; and that the more mis-
chievously, because they do teach what in its place is
true, though when out of its place, perverted or carried
to excess, it is not true. And, as every man has not
the capacity of separating truth from falsehood, they
persuade the world of what is false by urging upon it
what is true. Nor is it open enemies alone who en-
counter us here, sometimes it is friends, sometimes
persons who, if not friends, at least have no wish to
oppose Religion, and are not conscious they are doing
so ; and it will carry out my meaning more fully if I
give some illustrations of it.

As to friends, I may take as an instance the cultivation of the Fine Arts, Painting, Sculpture, Architecture, to which I may add Music. These high ministers of the Beautiful and the Noble are, it is plain,
special attendants and handmaids of Religion ; but
it is equally plain that they are apt to forget their

114

place, and, unless restrained with a firm hand, instead
of being servants, will aim at becoming principals.
Here lies the advantage, in an ecclesiastical point of
view, of their more rudimental state, I mean of the ancient style of architecture, of Gothic sculpture and
painting, and of what is called Gregorian music, that
these inchoate sciences have so little innate vigour and
life in them, that they are in no danger of going out of
their place, and giving the law to Religion. But the
case is very different when genius has breathed upon
their natural elements, and has developed them into
what I may call intellectual powers. When Painting,
for example, grows into the fulness of its function as a
simply imitative art, it at once ceases to be a dependant
on the Church. It has an end of its own, and that of
earth : Nature is its pattern, and the object it pursues
is the beauty of Nature, even till it becomes an ideal
beauty, but a natural beauty still. It cannot imitate
that beauty of Angels and Saints which it has never
seen. At first, indeed, by outlines and emblems it
shadowed out the Invisible, and its want of skill became
the instrument of reverence and modesty; but as time
went on and it attained its full dimensions as an art, it
rather subjected Religion to its own ends than minis-
tered to the ends of Religion, and in its long galleries
and stately chambers, did but mingle adorable figures
and sacred histories with a multitude of earthly, not to
say unseemly forms, which the Art had created, bor-
rowing withal a colouring and a character from that bad
company. Not content with neutral ground for its development, it was attracted by the sublimity of divine
subjects to ambitious and hazardous essays. Without

my saying a word more, you will clearly understand, Gentlemen, that under these circumstances Religion was bound to exert itself, that the world might not gain an advantage over it. Put out of sight the severe teaching of Catholicism in the schools of Painting, as men now would put it aside in their philosophical studies, and in no long time you would have the hierarchy of the Church, the Anchorite and Virgin-martyr, the Confessor and the Doctor, the Angelic Hosts, the Mother of God, the Crucifix, the Eternal Trinity, supplanted by a sort of pagan mythology in the guise of sacred names, by a creation indeed of high genius, of intense, and dazzling, and soul-absorbing beauty, in which, however, there was nothing which subserved the cause of Religion, nothing on the other hand which did not directly or indirectly minister to corrupt nature and the powers of darkness.

The art of Painting, however, is peculiar: Music and Architecture are more ideal, and their respective archetypes, even if not supernatural, at least are abstract and unearthly; and yet what I have been observing about Painting, holds, I think, analogously, in the marvellous development which Musical Science has undergone in the last century. Doubtless here too the highest genius may be made subservient to Religion; here too, still more simply than in the case of Painting, the Science has a field of its own, perfectly innocent, into which Religion does not and need not enter; on the other hand here also, in the case of Music as of Painting, it is certain that Religion must be alive and on the defensive, for, if its servants sleep, a potent enchantment will steal over it. Music, I suppose, though this is not the place to enlarge upon it, has an object of its own; as mathematical science also, it is the expression of ideas greater and more profound than any in the visible world, ideas, which centre indeed in Him whom Catholicism manifests, who is the seat of all beauty, order, and perfection whatever, still ideas after all which are not those on which Revelation directly and principally fixes our gaze. If then a great master in this mysterious science (if I may speak of matters which seem to lie out of my own province) throws himself on his own gift, trusts its inspirations, and absorbs himself in those thoughts which, though they come to him in the way of nature, belong to things above nature, it is obvious he will neglect everything else. Rising in his strength, he will break through the trammels of words, he will scatter human voices, even the sweetest, to the winds; he will be borne upon nothing less than the fullest flood of sounds which art has enabled him to draw from mechanical contrivances; he will go forth as a giant, as far as ever his instruments can reach, starting from their secret depths fresh and fresh elements of beauty and grandeur as he goes, and pouring them together into still more marvellous and rapturous combinations;—and well indeed and lawfully, while he keeps to that line which is his own; but, should he happen to be attracted, as he well may, by the sublimity, so congenial to him, of the Catholic doctrine and ritual, should he engage in sacred themes, should he resolve by means of his art to do honour to the Mass, or the Divine Office,—(he cannot have a more pious, a better purpose, and Religion will gracefully accept what he gracefully offers; but)—is it not certain, from the circumstances of the case, that he will be carried on rather to use Religion than to minister to it, unless Religion is strong on its own ground, and reminds him that, if he would do honour to the highest of subjects, he must make himself its scholar, must humbly follow the thoughts given him, and must aim at the glory, not of his own gift, but of the Great Giver?—*Idea of a University*, ed. 1891, pp. 78-81 (1852).

THE Prejudiced Man, then—for thus I shall personify that narrow, ungenerous spirit which energizes and operates so widely and so unweariedly in the Protestant community—the Prejudiced Man takes it for granted, or feels an undoubting persuasion,—not only that he himself is in possession of divine truth, for this is a matter of opinion, and he has a right to his own,—but that we, who differ from him, are universally impostors, tyrants, hypocrites, cowards, and slaves. This is a first principle with him; it is like divine faith in the Catholic, nothing can shake it. If he meets with any story against Catholics, on any or no authority, which does but fall in with this notion of them, he eagerly catches at it. Authority goes for nothing; likelihood, as he considers it, does instead of testimony; what he is now told is just what he expected. Perhaps it is a random report, put into circulation merely because it has a chance of succeeding, or thrown like a straw to the wind : perhaps it is a mere publisher's speculation, who thinks that a narrative of horrors will pay well for the printing: it matters not, he is perfectly convinced of its truth; he knew all about it beforehand; it is just what he always has said; it is the old tale over again a hundred times. Accordingly he buys it by the thousand, and sends it about with all speed in every

119

direction, to his circle of friends and acquaintance, to the newspapers, to the great speakers at public meetings ; he fills the Sunday and week-day schools with it ; loads the pedlars' baskets, perhaps introduces it into the family spiritual reading on Sunday evenings, consoled and comforted with the reflection that he has got something fresh and strong and undeniable, in evidence of the utter odiousness of the Catholic Religion.

Next comes an absolute, explicit, total denial or refutation of the precious calumny, whatever it may be, on unimpeachable authority. The Prejudiced Man simply discredits this denial, and puts it aside, not receiving any impression from it at all, or paying it the slightest attention. This, if he can : if he cannot, if it is urged upon him by some friend, or brought up against him by some opponent, he draws himself up, looks sternly at the objector, and then says the very same thing as before, only with a louder voice and more confident manner. He becomes more intensely and enthusiastically positive, by way of making up for the interruption, of braving the confutation, and of showing the world that nothing whatever in the universe will ever make him think one hair-breadth more favourably of Popery than he does think, than he ever has thought, and than his family ever thought before him, since the time of the fine old English gentleman.

If a person ventures to ask the Prejudiced Man what he knows of Catholics personally—what he knows of individuals, of their ways, of their books, or of their worship, he blesses himself that he knows nothing of them at all, and he never will ; nay, if they fall in his way, he will take himself out of it ; and if unawares he shall ever be pleased with a Catholic without knowing who it is, he wishes by anticipation to retract such feeling of pleasure. About our state of mind, our views of things, our ends and objects, our doctrines, our defence of them, our judgment on his objections to them, our thoughts about him, he absolutely refuses to be enlightened : and he is as sore if expostulated with on so evident an infirmity of mind, as if it were some painful wound upon him, or local inflammation, which must not be handled ever so tenderly. He shrinks from the infliction.

However, one cannot always make the whole world take one's own way of thinking; so let us suppose the famous story, to which the Prejudiced Man has pledged his veracity, utterly discredited and scattered to the winds by the common consent of mankind :— this only makes him the more violent. For it *ought*, he thinks, to be true, and it is mere special pleading to lay much stress on its not having all the evidence which it might have? for if it be not true, yet half a hundred like stories are. It is only impertinent to ask for evidence, when the fact has so often been established. What is the good of laboriously vindicating St. Eligius, or exposing a leading article in a newspaper, or a speaker at a meeting, or a popular publication, when the thing is notorious ; and to deny it is nothing else than a vexatious demand upon his time, and an insult to his common sense. He feels the same sort of indignation which the Philistine champion, Goliath, might have felt when David went out to fight with him. " Am I a dog, that thou comest to me with a staff? and the Philistine cursed him by his gods." And, as the huge giant, had he first been hit, not in the brain, but in the foot or the shoulder, would have yelled, not with pain, but with fury at the insult, and would not have been frightened at all or put upon the defensive, so our Prejudiced Man is but enraged so much the more, and almost put beside himself, by the presumption of those who, with their doubts or their objections, interfere with the great Protestant Tradition about the Catholic Church. To bring proof against us is, he thinks, but a matter of time; and we know in affairs of every day, how annoyed and impatient we are likely to become, when obstacles are put in our way in any such case. We are angered at delays when they are but accidental, and the issue is certain; we are not angered, but we are sobered, we become careful and attentive to impediments, when there is a doubt about the issue. The very same difficulties put us on our mettle in the one case, and do but irritate us in the other. If, for instance, a person cannot open a door, or get a key into a lock, which he has done a hundred times before, you know how apt he is to shake, and to rattle, and to force it, as if some great insult was offered him by its resistance: you know how surprised a wasp, or other large insect is, that he cannot get through a window-pane; such is the feeling of the Prejudiced Man, when we urge our objections—not softened by them at all, but exasperated the more; for what is the use of even incontrovertible arguments against a conclusion which he already considers to be infallible?

This, you see, is the reason why the most overwhelming refutations of the calumnies brought against us do us no good at all with the Protestant community. We were tempted, perhaps, to say to ourselves, " What *will* they have to say in answer to this? now at last the falsehood is put down forever, it will never show its face again?" Vain hope! just the reverse: like Milton's day-star, after sinking into the ocean, it soon "repairs its drooping head,"

> "And tricks its beams, and with new-spangled ore
> Flames in the forehead of the morning sky."

Certainly; for it is rooted in the mind itself; it has no uncertain holding upon things external; it does not depend on the accident of time, or place, or testimony, or sense, or possibility, or fact; it depends on the will alone. Therefore, "unhurt amid the war of elements," it "smiles" at injury, and "defies" defeat; for it is safe and secure, while it has the man's own will on its side. Such is the virtue of prejudice—it is ever reproductive; in vain is Jeffreys exposed; he rises again in Teodore; Teodore is put down; in vain, for future story-tellers and wonder-mongers, as yet unknown to fame, are below the horizon, and will come to view, and will unfold their tale of horror, each in his day, in long succession; for these whispers, and voices, and echoes, and reverberations, are but the response, and, as it were, the expression of that profound inward persuasion, and that intense illusion, which wraps the soul and steeps the imagination of the Prejudiced Man.

However, we will suppose him in a specially good

humour, when you set about undeceiving him on some point on which he misstates the Catholic faith. He is determined to be candour and fairness itself, and to do full justice to your argument. So you begin your explanation; you assure him he misconceives your doctrines; he has got a wrong view of facts. You appeal to original authorities, and show him how shamefully they have been misquoted; you appeal to history and prove it has been garbled. Nothing is wanted to your representation; it is triumphant. He is silent for a moment, then he begins with a sentiment. "What clever fellows these Catholics are!" he says, "I defy you to catch them tripping; they have a way out of everything. I thought we had you, but I fairly own I am beaten. This is how the Jesuits got on; always educated, subtle, well up in their books; a Protestant has no chance with them." You see, my Brothers, you have not advanced a step in convincing him.

Such is the Prejudiced Man at best advantage; but commonly under the same circumstances he will be grave and suspicious. "I confess," he will say, "I do *not* like these very complete explanations; they are too like a made-up case. I can easily believe there was exaggeration in the charge; perhaps money was only sometimes taken for the permission to sin, or only before the Reformation, but our friend professes to prove it never was taken; this is proving too much. I always suspect something behind, when everything is so very easy and clear." Or again, "We see before our eyes a tremendous growth of Popery; *how* does it grow? You tell me you are poor, your priests few, your friends without influence;

then how does it *grow*? It could not grow without
means! it is bad enough if you can assign a cause;
it is worse if you cannot. Cause there must be
somewhere, for effects imply causes. How did it get
into Oxford? tell me that. How has it got among
the Protestant clergy? I like all things above board;
I hate concealment, I detest plots. There is evidently something to be accounted for; and the more
cogently you prove that it is not referable to anything
which we see, the graver suspicions do you awaken,
that it is traceable to something which is hidden."
Thus our Prejudiced Man simply ignores the possible
existence of that special cause to which Catholics of
course refer the growth of Catholicism, and which
surely, if admitted, is sufficient to account for it—viz.,
that it is true. He will not admit the power of truth
among the assignable conjectural causes. He would
rather, I am sure, assign it to the agency of evil
spirits, than suspect the possibility of a religion being
true which he wills should be a falsehood.—*Present
Position of Catholics*, ed. 1889, pp. 236–243 (1851).

———

The Prejudiced Man travels, and then everything he
sees in Catholic countries only serves to make him more
thankful that his notions are so true; and the more he
sees of Popery, the more abominable he feels it to be.
If there is any Sin, any evil in a foreign population,
though it be found among Protestants also, still Popery
is clearly the cause of it. If great cities are the schools
of vice, it is owing to Popery. If Sunday is profaned,

if there is a carnival, it is the fault of the Catholic Church. Then, there are no private homes, as in England, families live on staircases; see what it is to belong to a Popish country. Why do the Roman labourers wheel their barrows so slow on the Forum? why do the Lazzaroni of Naples lie so listlessly on the beach? why, but because they are under the *malaria* of a false religion. Rage, as is well-known, is in the Roman like a falling sickness, almost as if his will had no part in it and he had no responsibility; see what it is to be a Papist. Bloodletting is as frequent and as much a matter of course in the South as hair-cutting in England; it is a trick borrowed from the convents, when they wish to tame down refractory spirits.—*Present Position of Catholics*, ed. 1889, pp. 249–250 (1851).

AND here I might conclude my subject, which has proposed to itself nothing more than to suggest, to those whom it concerns, that they would have more reason to be confident in their view of the Catholic religion, if it ever had struck them that it needed some proof, if there ever had occurred to their minds at least the possibility of truth being maligned, and Christ being called Beelzebub; but I am tempted, before concluding, to go on to try whether something of a monster indictment, similarly frightful and similarly fantastical to that which is got up against Catholicism, might not be framed against some other institution or power, of parallel greatness and excellence, in its degree and place, to the communion of Rome. For this purpose I will take the British Constitution, which is so specially the possession, and so deservedly the glory, of our own people; and in taking it I need hardly say, I take it for the very reason that it is so rightfully the object of our wonder and veneration. I should be but a fool for my pains, if I laboured to prove it otherwise; it is one of the greatest of human works, as admirable in its own line, to take the productions of genius in very various departments, as the Pyramids, as the wall of China, as the paintings of Raffaelle, as the Apollo Belvidere, as the plays of

Shakespeare, as the Newtonian theory, and as the exploits of Napoleon. It soars, in its majesty, far above the opinions of men, and will be a marvel, almost a portent, to the end of time; but for that very reason it is more to my purpose, when I would show you how even it, the British Constitution, would fare, when submitted to the intellect of Exeter Hall, and handled by practitioners, whose highest effort at dissection is to chop and to mangle.

I will suppose, then, a speaker, and an audience too, who never saw England, never saw a member of parliament, a policeman, a queen, or a London mob; who never read the English history, nor studied any one of our philosophers, jurists, moralists, or poets; but who has dipped into Blackstone and several English writers, and has picked up facts at third or fourth hand, and has got together a crude *farrago* of ideas, words, and instances, a little truth, a deal of falsehood, a deal of misrepresentation, a deal of nonsense, and a deal of invention. And most fortunately for my purpose, here is an account transmitted express by the private correspondent of a morning paper, of a great meeting held about a fortnight since at Moscow, under sanction of the Czar, on occasion of an attempt made by one or two Russian noblemen to spread British ideas in his capital. It seems the emperor thought it best in the present state of men's minds, when secret societies are so rife, to put down the movement by argument rather than by a military force; and so he instructed the governor of Moscow to connive at the project of a great public meeting which should be opened to the small faction of Anglo-maniacs, or

John-Bullists, as they are popularly termed, as well as to the mass of the population. As many as ten thousand men, as far as the writer could calculate, were gathered together in one of the largest *places* of the city; a number of spirited and impressive speeches were made, in all of which, however, was illustrated the fable of the "Lion and the Man," the man being the Russ, and the lion our old friend the British; but the most successful of all is said to have been the final harangue, by a member of a junior branch of the Potemkin family, once one of the imperial aides-de-camp, who has spent the last thirty years in the wars of the Caucasus. This distinguished veteran, who has acquired the title of Blood-sucker, from his extraordinary gallantry in combat with the Circassian tribes, spoke at great length; and the express contains a portion of his highly inflammatory address, of which, and of certain consequences which followed it, the British minister is said already to have asked an explanation of the cabinet of St. Petersburg: I transcribe it as it may be supposed to stand in the morning print:

The Count began by observing that the events of every day, as it came, called on his countrymen more and more importunately to choose their side, and to make a firm stand against a perfidious power, which arrogantly proclaims that there is nothing like the British Constitution in the whole world, and that no country can prosper without it; which is yearly aggrandizing itself in East, West, and South, which is engaged in one enormous conspiracy against all

9

States, and which was even aiming at modifying the old institutions of the North, and at dressing up the army, navy, legislature, and executive of his own country in the livery of Queen Victoria. "Insular in situation," he exclaimed, "and at the back gate of the world, what has John Bull to do with continental matters, or with the political traditions of our holy Russia?" And yet there were men in that very city who were so far the dupes of insidious propagandists and insolent traitors to their emperor, as to maintain that England had been a civilized country longer than Russia. On the contrary, he maintained, and he would shed the last drop of his blood in maintaining, that, as for its boasted Constitution, it was a crazy, old-fashioned piece of furniture, and an eyesore in the nineteenth century, and would not last a dozen years. He had the best information for saying so. He could understand those who had never crossed out of their island, listening to the songs about "Rule Britannia," and "*Rosbif,*" and "Poor Jack," and the "Old English Gentleman"; he understood and he pitied them; but that Russians, that the conquerors of Napoleon, that the heirs of a paternal government, should bow the knee, and kiss the hand, and walk backwards, and perform other antics before the face of a limited monarch, this was the incomprehensible foolery which certain Russians had viewed with so much tenderness. He repeated, there were in that city educated men, who had openly professed a reverence for the atheistical tenets and fiendish maxims of John-Bullism.

Here the speaker was interrupted by one or two murmurs of dissent, and a foreigner, supposed to be a

partner in a Scotch firm, was observed in the extremity
of the square, making earnest attempts to obtain a
hearing. He was put down, however, amid enthusiastic cheering, and the Count proceeded with a warmth
of feeling which increased the effect of the terrible
invective which followed. He said he had used the
words "atheistical" and "fiendish" most advisedly,
and he would give his reasons for doing so. What
was to be said to any political power which claimed
the attribute of Divinity? Was any term too strong
for such a usurpation? Now, no one would deny
Antichrist would be such a power: an Antichrist
was contemplated, was predicted in Scripture, it was
to come in the last times, it was to grow slowly, it
was to manifest itself warily and craftily, and then to
have a mouth speaking great things against the
Divinity and against His attributes. This prediction
was most literally and exactly fulfilled in the British
Constitution. Antichrist was not only to usurp, but
to profess to usurp the arms of heaven—he was to
arrogate its titles. This was the special mark of the
beast, and where was it fulfilled but in John-Bullism?
"I hold in my hand," continued the speaker, "a book
which I have obtained under very remarkable circumstances. It is not known to the British people, it is
circulated only among the lawyers, merchants, and
aristocracy, and its restrictive use is secured only by
the most solemn oaths, the most fearful penalties, and
the utmost vigilance of the police. I procured it
after many years of anxious search by the activity of
an agent, and the co-operation of an English book-
seller, and it cost me an enormous sum to make it my

own.   It is called 'Blackstone's Commentaries on the Laws of England,' and I am happy to make known to the universe its odious and shocking mysteries, known to few Britons, and certainly not known to the deluded persons whose vagaries have been the occasion of this meeting.   I am sanguine in thinking that when they come to know the real tenets of John Bull, they will at once disown his doctrines with horror, and break off all connection with his adherents.

"Now, I should say, gentlemen, that this book, while it is confined to certain classes, is of those classes, on the other hand, of judges, and lawyers, and privy councillors, and justices of the peace, and police magistrates, and clergy, and country gentlemen, the guide, and I may say, the gospel.   I open the book, gentlemen, and what are the first words which meet my eyes?   '*The King can do no wrong.*'   I beg you to attend, gentlemen, to this most significant assertion; one was accustomed to think that no child of man had the gift of impeccability; one had imagined that, simply speaking, impeccability was a divine attribute; but this British Bible, as I may call it, distinctly ascribes an absolute sinlessness to the King of Great Britain and Ireland.   Observe, I am using no words of my own, I am still but quoting what meets my eyes in this remarkable document.   The words run thus: 'It is an axiom of the law of the land that the *King himself can do no wrong.*'   Was I wrong, then, in speaking of the atheistical maxims of John Bullism?   But this is far from all: the writer goes on actually to ascribe to the Sovereign (I tremble while I pronounce the words) *absolute perfection;* for he speaks thus : ' The law ascribes to the King in his political capacity ABSOLUTE PERFECTION ; the *King can do no wrong!*'—(groans). One had thought that no human power could thus be described ; but the British legislature, judicature, and jurisprudence, have had the unspeakable effrontery to impute to their crowned and sceptred idol, to their doll,"—here cries of " shame, shame," from the same individual who had distinguished himself in an earlier part of the speech —" to this doll, this puppet whom they have dressed up with a lion and a unicorn, the attribute of ABSOLUTE PERFECTION !" Here the individual who had several times interrupted the speaker sprung up, in spite of the efforts of persons about him to keep him down, and cried out, as far as his words could be collected, " You cowardly liar, our dear good little Queen," when he was immediately saluted with a cry of "Turn him out," and soon made his exit from the meeting.

Order being restored, the Count continued: " Gentlemen, I could wish you would have suffered this emissary of a foreign potentate (immense cheering), who is insidiously aiming at forming a political party among us, to have heard to the end that black catalogue of charges against his Sovereign, which as yet I have barely commenced. Gentlemen, I was saying that the Queen of England challenges the divine attribute of ABSOLUTE PERFECTION ! but, as if this were not enough this Blackstone continues, ' The King, moreover, is not only incapable of *doing* wrong, but even of *thinking* wrong !! *he can never do an improper thing ; in him is no* FOLLY *or* WEAKNESS ! ! !'" (Shudders and cheers from the vast assemblage, which

lasted alternately some minutes.)   At the same time a
respectably dressed gentleman below the platform
begged permission to look at the book; it was immediately handed to him ; after looking at the passages, he
was observed to inspect carefully the title-page and
binding ; he then returned it without a word.

The Count, in resuming his speech, observed that
he courted and challenged investigation, he should be
happy to answer any question, and he hoped soon to
publish, by subscription, a translation of the work, from
which he had been quoting.   Then, resuming the subject where he had left it, he made some most forcible
and impressive reflections on the miserable state of
those multitudes, who, in spite of their skill in the
mechanical arts, and their political energy, were in the
leading-strings of so foul a superstition.   The passage
he had quoted was the first and mildest of a series of
blasphemies so prodigious, that he really feared to
proceed, not only from disgust at the necessity of uttering them, but lest he should be taxing the faith of his
hearers beyond what appeared reasonable limits.
Next, then, he drew attention to the point that the
English Sovereign distinctly claimed, according to the
same infamous work, to be the "*fount* of justice ; "
and, that there might be no mistake in the matter, the
author declared, " that she *is never bound in justice to
do anything.*"   What, then, is her method of acting ?
Unwilling as he was to defile his lips with so profane
a statement, he must tell them that this abominable
writer coolly declared that the Queen, a woman, only
did acts of reparation and restitution as a matter of
grace !   He was not a theologian, he had spent his

life in the field, but he knew enough of his religion to be able to say that grace was a word especially proper to the appointment and decrees of Divine Sovereignty. All his hearers knew perfectly well that nature was one thing, grace another; and yet here was a poor child of clay claiming to be the fount, not only of justice, but of grace. She was making herself a first cause of not merely natural, but spiritual excellence, and doing nothing more or less than simply emancipating herself from her Maker. The Queen, it seemed, never obeyed the law on compulsion, according to Blackstone; that is, her Maker could not compel her. This was no mere deduction of his own, as directly would be seen. Let it be observed, the Apostle called the predicted Antichrist "the wicked one," or, as it might be more correctly translated, " the lawless," because he was to be the proud despiser of all law; now, wonderful to say, this was the very assumption of the British Parliament. "The Power of Parliament," said Sir Edward Coke, "is so transcendent and absolute, that it cannot be *confined* within any bounds!! It has sovereign and uncontrollable authority!!" Moreover, the Judges had declared that " it is so high and mighty in its nature, that it *may make law*, and THAT WHICH IS LAW IT MAY MAKE NO LAW!" Here verily was the mouth speaking great things; but there was more behind, which, but for the atrocious sentiments he had already admitted into his mouth, he really should not have the courage, the endurance to utter. It was sickening to the soul, and intellect, and feelings of a Russ, to form the words on his tongue, and the ideas in his imagination. He would say what must be said as quickly as he could, and without comment. The gallant speaker then delivered the following passage from Blackstone's volume, in a very distinct and articulate whisper: "Some have not scrupled to call its power—the OMNIPOTENCE of Parliament!" No one can conceive the thrilling effect of these words; they were heard all over the immense assemblage; every man turned pale; a dead silence followed; one might have heard a pin drop. A pause of some minutes followed.

The speaker continued, evidently labouring under intense emotion:—"Have you not heard enough, my dear compatriots, of this hideous system of John-Bullism? was I wrong in using the words fiendish and atheistical when I entered upon this subject? and need I proceed further with blasphemous details, which cannot really add to the monstrous bearing of the passages I have already read to you? If the Queen 'cannot do wrong,' if she 'cannot even think wrong,' if she is 'absolute perfection,' if she has 'no folly, no weakness,' if she is the 'fount of justice,' if she is 'the fount of grace,' if she is simply 'above law,' if she is 'omnipotent,' what wonder that the lawyers of John-Bullism should also call her 'sacred!' what wonder that they should speak of her as 'majesty!' what wonder that they should speak of her as a 'superior being!' Here again I am using the words of the book I hold in my hand. 'The people' (my blood runs cold while I repeat them) 'are led to consider their Sovereign *in the light of a* SUPERIOR BEING.' 'Every one is under him,' says Bracton, 'and he is under no one.' Accordingly, the law-books call him 'Vicarius Dei in

terrâ,' ·the Vicar of God on earth ; ' a most astonishing fulfilment, you observe, of the prophecy, for Antichrist is a Greek word, which means ' Vicar of Christ.'
What wonder, under these circumstances, that Queen
Elizabeth, assuming the attribute of the Creator, once
said to one of her Bishops: ' Proud Prelate, *I made
you, and I can unmake you!*' What wonder that James
the First had the brazen assurance to say, that ' As it
is atheism and blasphemy in a creature to dispute the
Deity, so it is presumption and sedition in a subject to
dispute a King in the height of his power ! ' Moreover,
his subjects called him the ' breath of their nostrils ; '
and my Lord Clarendon, the present Lord Lieutenant
of Ireland, in his celebrated History of the Rebellion,
declares that the same haughty monarch actually on
one occasion called himself ' a God ; ' and in his great
legal digest, commonly called the ' Constitutions of
Clarendon,' he gives us the whole account of the King's
banishing the Archbishop, St. Thomas of Canterbury,
for refusing to do him homage. Lord Bacon, too, went
nearly as far when he called him ' Deaster quidam,'
' some sort of little god.' Alexander Pope, too, calls
Queen Anne a goddess: and Addison, with a servility
only equalled by his profaneness, cries out, "Thee, goddess, thee Britannia's isle adores.' Nay, even at this
very time, when public attention has been drawn to the
subject, Queen Victoria causes herself to be represented on her coins as the goddess of the seas, with a
pagan trident in her hand.

"Gentlemen, can it surprise you to be told, after
such an exposition of the blasphemies of England, that,
astonishing to say, Queen Victoria is distinctly pointed

out in the Book of Revelation as having the number of
the beast! You may recollect that number is 666;
now, she came to the throne in the year thirty-seven,
at which date she was eighteen years old. Multiply
then 37 by 18, and you have the very number 666, which
is the mystical emblem of the lawless King !!!

" No wonder then, with such monstrous pretensions,
and such awful auguries, that John-Bullism is, in act
and deed, as savage and profligate, as in profession it
is saintly and innocent. Its annals are marked with
blood and corruption. The historian Hallam, though
one of the ultra-bullist party, in his Constitutional
History, admits that the English tribunals are 'dis-
graced by the brutal manners and iniquitous partiality
of the bench.' ' The general behaviour of the bench,'
he says elsewhere, 'has covered it with infamy.' Soon
after, he tells us that the dominant faction inflicted on
the High Church Clergy ' the disgrace and remorse of
perjury.' The English Kings have been the curse and
shame of human nature. Richard the First boasted
that the evil spirit was the father of his family; of
Henry the Second St. Bernard said, ' From the devil he
came, and to the devil he will go;' William the Second
was killed by the enemy of man, to whom he had sold
himself, while hunting in one of his forests; Henry the
First died of eating lampreys; John died of eating
peaches; Clarence, a king's brother, was drowned in a
butt of malmsey wine; Richard the Third put to death
his Sovereign, his Sovereign's son, his two brothers,
his wife, two nephews, and half-a-dozen friends. Henry
the Eighth successively married and murdered no less
than six hundred women. I quote the words of the

'Edinburgh Review,' that, according to Hollinshed, no less than 70,000 persons died under the hand of the executioner in his reign. Sir John Fortescue tells us that in his day there were more persons executed for robbery in England in one year, than in France in seven. Four hundred persons a year were executed in the reign of Queen Elizabeth. Even so late as the last century, in spite of the continued protests of foreign nations, in the course of seven years there were 428 capital convictions in London alone. Burning of children, too, is a favourite punishment with John Bull, as may be seen in this same Blackstone, who notices the burning of a girl of thirteen given by Sir Matthew Hale. The valets always assassinate their masters; lovers uniformly strangle their sweethearts; the farmers and the farmers' wives universally beat their apprentices to death; and their lawyers in the inns of court strip and starve their servants, as has appeared from remarkable investigations in the law courts during the last year. Husbands sell their wives by public auction with a rope round their necks. An intelligent Frenchman, M. Pellet, who visited London in 1815, deposes that he saw a number of skulls on each side of the river Thames, and he was told they were found especially thick at the landing-places among the watermen. But why multiply instances, when the names of those two-legged tigers, Rush, Thistlewood, Thurtell, the Mannings, Colonel Kirk, Claverhouse, Simon de Monteforte, Strafford, the Duke of Cumberland, Warren Hastings, and Judge Jeffreys, are household words all over the earth? John-Bullism, through a space of 800 years, is *semper idem*, unchangeable in evil. One hundred and sixty offences are punishable with death. It is death to live with gipsies for a month; and Lord Hale mentions thirteen persons as having, in his day, suffered death thereon at one assize. It is death to steal a sheep, death to rob a warren, death to steal a letter, death to steal a handkerchief, death to cut down a cherry-tree. And, after all, the excesses of John-Bullism at home are mere child's play to the oceans of blood it has shed abroad. It has been the origin of all the wars which have desolated Europe; it has fomented national jealousy, and the antipathy of castes in every part of the world; it has plunged flourishing states into the abyss of revolution. The Crusades, the Sicilian Vespers, the wars of the Reformation, the Thirty Years' War, the War of Succession, the Seven Years' War, the American War, the French Revolution, all are simply owing to John-Bull ideas; and to take one definite instance, in the course of the last war, the deaths of two millions of the human race lie at his door; for the Whigs themselves, from first to last, and down to this day, admit and proclaim, without any hesitation or limitation, that that war was simply and entirely the work of John-Bullism, and needed not, and would not have been, but for its influence, and its alone.

" Such is that 'absolute perfection, without folly and without weakness,' which, revelling in the blood of man, is still seeking out her victims, and scenting blood all over the earth. It is that woman Jezebel, who fulfils the prophetic vision, and incurs the prophetic denunciation. And, strange to say, a prophet of her own has not scrupled to apply to her that very appellation.

Dead to good and evil, the children of Jezebel glory in the name; and ten years have not passed since, by a sort of infatuation, one of the very highest Tories in the land, a minister, too, of the established religion, hailed the blood-stained Monarchy under the very title of the mystical sorceress. Jezebel surely is her name, and Jezebel is her nature; for drunk with the spiritual wine-cup of wrath, and given over to believe a lie, at length she has ascended to heights which savour rather of madness than of pride; she babbles absurdities, and she thirsts for impossibilities. Gentlemen, I am speaking the words of sober seriousness; I can prove what I say to the letter; the extravagance is not in me but in the object of my denunciation. Once more I appeal to the awful volume I hold in my hands. I appeal to it, I open it, I cast it from me. Listen, then, once again; it is a fact; Jezebel has declared her own *omnipresence.* 'A consequence of the royal prerogatives,' says the antichristian author, 'is the legal UBIQUITY of the King!' 'His Majesty is always *present* in all his courts: his judges are the *mirror* by which the King's image is reflected;' and further, 'From this *ubiquity*' (you see he is far from shrinking from the word), 'from this *ubiquity* it follows that the Sovereign can never be NONSUIT!!' Gentlemen, the sun would set before I told you one hundredth part of the enormity of this child of Moloch and Belial. Inebriated with the cup of insanity, and flung upon the stream of recklessness, she dashes down the cataract of nonsense, and whirls amid the pools of confusion. Like the Roman emperor, she actually has declared herself immortal! she has declared her eternity!

Again, I am obliged to say it, these are no words of mine; the tremendous sentiment confronts me in black and crimson characters in this diabolical book. 'In the law,' says Blackstone, 'the Sovereign is said *never to die!*' Again, with still more hideous expressiveness, 'The law ascribes to the Sovereign an ABSOLUTE IMMORTALITY. THE KING NEVER DIES.'

" And now, gentlemen, your destiny is in your own hands. If you are willing to succumb to a power which has never been contented with what she was, but has been for centuries extending her conquests in both hemispheres, then the humble individual who has addressed you will submit to the necessary consequence; will resume his military dress, and return to the Caucasus; but if, on the other hand, as I believe, you are resolved to resist unflinchingly this flood of satanical imposture and foul ambition, and force it back into the ocean; if, not from hatred to the English—far from it—from *love* to them (for a distinction must ever be drawn between the nation and its dominant John-Bullism); if, I say, from love to them as brothers, from a generous determination to fight their battles, from an intimate consciousness that they are in their secret hearts *Russians*, that they are champing the bit of their iron lot, and are longing for you as their deliverers; if, from these lofty notions as well as from a burning patriotism, you will form the high resolve to annihilate this dishonour of humanity; if you loathe its sophisms, ' De minimis non curat lex,' and ' Malitia supplet ætatem,' and ' Tres faciunt collegium,' and ' Impotentia excusat legem,' and ' Possession is nine parts of the law,' and ' The greater the truth, the

greater the libel'—principles which sap the very foundations of morals ; if you wage war to the knife with its
blighting superstitions of primogeniture, gavelkind,
mortmain, and contingent remainders ; if you detest,
abhor, and adjure the tortuous maxims and perfidious
provisions of its *habeas corpus, quare impedit,* and *qui
tam* (hear, hear); if you scorn the mummeries of its wigs
and bands, and coifs, and ermine (vehement cheering) ;
if you trample and spit upon its accursed fee simple
and fee tail, villanage, and free soccage, fiefs, heriots,
seizins, feuds (a burst of cheers, the whole meeting in
commotion) ; its shares, its premiums, its post-obits, its
precentages, its tariffs, its broad and narrow gauge"
—Here the cheers became frantic, and drowned the
speaker's voice, and a most extraordinary scene of
enthusiasm followed. One half of the meeting was seen
embracing the other half ; till, as if by the force of a
sudden resolution, they all poured out of the square,
and proceeded to break the windows of all the British
residents. They then formed into procession, and
directing their course to the great square before the
Kremlin, they dragged through the mud, and then
solemnly burnt, an effigy of John Bull which had been
provided beforehand by the managing committee, a lion
and unicorn, and a Queen Victoria. These being
fully consumed, they dispersed quietly ; and by ten
o'clock at night the streets were profoundly still, and
the silver moon looked down in untroubled lustre on
the city of the Czars.

Now, my Brothers of the Oratory, I protest to you
my full conviction that I have not caricatured this par-

allel at all.   Were I, indeed, skilled in legal matters, I could have made it far more natural, plausible, and complete ; but, as for its extravagance, I say deliberately, and have means of knowing what I say, having once been a Protestant, and being now a Catholic—knowing what is said and thought of Catholics, on the one hand, and, on the other, knowing what they really *are*—I deliberately assert that no absurdities contained in the above sketch can equal—nay, that no conceivable absurdities can surpass—the absurdities which are firmly believed of Catholics by sensible, kind-hearted, well-intentioned Protestants.   Such is the consequence of having looked at things all on one side, and shutting the eyes to the other.—*Present Position of Catholics in England,* ed. 1889, pp. 24–41 (1851).

The Establishment is the keeper in ordinary of those national types and blocks from which Popery is ever to be printed off,—of the traditional view of every Catholic doctrine, the traditional account of every ecclesiastical event, the traditional lives of popes and bishops, abbots and monks, saints and confessors,—the traditional fictions, sophisms, calumnies, mockeries, sarcasms and invectives with which Catholics are to be assailed.

This, I say, is the special charge laid upon the Establishment. Unitarians, Sabellians, Utilitarians, Wesleyans, Calvinists, Swedenborgians, Irvingites, Freethinkers, all these it can tolerate in its very bosom ; no form of opinion comes amiss ; but Rome it cannot abide. It agrees to differ with its own children on a thousand points, one is sacred—that her Majesty the Queen is " The Mother and Mistress of all Churches ; " on one dogma it is infallible, on one it may securely insist without fear of being unseasonable or excessive—that " the Bishop of Rome hath no jurisdiction in this realm." Here is sunshine amid the darkness, sense amid confusion, an intelligible strain amid a Babel of sounds ; whatever befalls, here is sure footing ; it is, " No peace with Rome," " Down with the Pope," and " The Church in danger." Never has the Establishment failed in the use of these important and effective watchwords ; many are its shortcomings, but it is without reproach in the execution of this its special charge. Heresy, and scepticism, and infidelity, and fanaticism, may challenge it in vain ; but fling upon the gale the faintest whisper of Catholicism, and it recognizes by instinct the presence of its connatural foe. Forthwith, as during the last year, the atmosphere is tremulous with agitation, and discharges its vibrations far and wide. A movement is in birth which has no natural crisis or resolution. Spontaneously the bells of the steeples begin to sound. Not by an act of volition, but by a sort of mechanical impulse, bishop and dean, archdeacon and canon, rector and curate, one after another, each on his high tower, off they set, swinging and booming, tolling and chiming, with nervous intenseness, and thickening emotion, and deepening volume, the old ding-dong which has scared town and country this weary time ; tolling and chiming away, jingling and clamouring and ringing the changes on their poor half-dozen notes, all about " the Popish aggression," "insolent and insidious," " insidious and insolent," " insolent and atrocious," " atrocious and insolent," atrocious, insolent, and ungrateful," " ungrateful, insolent, and atrocious," " foul and offensive," " pestilent and horrid," " subtle and unholy," " audacious and revolting," " contemptible and shameless," " malignant," " frightful," " mad," " meretricious,"—bobs (I think the ringers call them), bobs, and bobs-royal, and triple-bob-majors, and grandsires,—to the extent of their compass and the full ring of their metal, in honour of Queen Bess, and to the confusion of the Holy

Father and the Princes of the Church.[1]—*Present Position of Catholics in England*, ed. 1889, pp. 75–77 (1851).

[1] The foregoing lecture in 1851 was, by an accidental coincidence, written simultaneously with an able pamphlet by Serjeant Bellasis, *apropos* of the conduct of the Anglican clergy of the day.

Two of my instances are despatched, and now I
come to my third. There is something so tiresome in
passing abruptly from one subject to another, that I
need your indulgence, my Brothers, in making this third
beginning; yet it has been difficult to avoid it, when
my very object is to show what extensive subject-
matters and what different classes of the community
are acted on by the Protestant Tradition. Now, I am
proceeding to the Legislature of the Nation, and will
give an instance of its operation in a respectable
political party.

In this case, its fountain springs up, as it were,
under our very feet, and we shall have no difficulty at
all in judging of its quality. Its history is as follows :—Coaches, omnibuses, carriages, and cars, day
after day drive up and down the Hagley Road; pas-
sengers lounge to and fro on the footpath; and close
alongside of it are discovered one day the nascent
foundations and rudiments of a considerable building.
On inquiring, it is found to be intended for a Catholic,
nay, even for a monastic establishment. This leads to
a good deal of talk, especially when the bricks begin
to show above the surface. Meantime the unsuspecting architect is taking his measurements, and ascer-
tains that the ground is far from lying level; and then,

148

since there is a prejudice among Catholics in favor of horizontal floors, he comes to the conclusion that the bricks of the basement must rise above the surface higher at one end of the building than at the other; in fact, that whether he will or no, there must be some construction of the nature of a vault or cellar at the extremity in question, a circumstance not at all inconvenient, considering it also happens to be the kitchen end of the building. Accordingly, he turns his necessity into a gain, and by the excavation of a few feet of earth, he forms a number of chambers convenient for various purposes, partly beneath, partly above the line of the ground. While he is thus intent on his work, loungers, gossipers, alarmists are busy at theirs too. They go round the building, they peep into the underground brickwork, and are curious about the drains;* they moralize about Popery and its

---

* It is undeniable, though the gentleman who has brought the matter before the public has accidentally omitted to mention it, that the Protestant feeling has also been excited by the breadth of the drain, which is considered excessive, and moreover *crosses the road.* There exists some nervousness on the subject in the neighbourhood, as I have been seriously given to understand. There is a remarkable passage, too, in the scientific report, which our accuser brings forward, and which has never been answered or perhaps construed : "One of the compartments was larger than the rest, and *was evidently to be covered in without the building over it.*" This is not the first time a dwelling of mine has been the object of a mysterious interest. When our cottages at Littlemore were in course of preparation, they were visited on horseback and on foot by many of the most distinguished residents of the University of Oxford. Heads of houses and canons did not scruple to investigate the building within and without, and some of them went so far as to inspect and theorize upon the

spread; at length they trespass upon the enclosure, they dive into the half-finished shell, and they take their fill of seeing what is to be seen, and imagining what is not. Every house is built on an idea; you do not build a mansion like a public office, or a palace like a prison, or a factory like a shooting-box, or a church like a barn. Religious houses, in like manner, have their own idea; they have certain indispensable peculiarities of form and internal arrangement. Doubtless, there was much in the very idea of an Oratory perplexing to the Protestant intellect, and inconsistent with Protestant notions of comfort and utility. Why should so large a room be here? why so small a room there? why a passage so long and wide? and why so long a wall without a window? the very size of the house needs explanation. Judgments which had employed themselves on the high subject of a Catholic hierarchy and its need, found no difficulty in dogmatizing on bedrooms and closets. There was much to suggest matter of suspicion, and to predispose the trespasser to doubt whether he had yet got to the bottom of the subject. At length one question flashed upon his mind: what can such a house have to do with cellars? cellars and monks, what can be their mutual relations? monks—to what possible use can they put pits, and holes, and corners, and outhouses, and sheds? A sensation was created; it brought other visitors; it spread; it became an impression, a belief; the truth lay bare; a tradition was born; a fact was

most retired portions of the premises. Perhaps some thirty years hence, in some " History of my own Times," speculations may be found on the subject, in aid of the Protestant Tradition.

elicited which henceforth had many witnesses. *Those cellars were cells.* How obvious when once stated! and every one who entered the building, every one who passed by, became, I say, in some sort, ocular vouchers for what had often been read of in books, but for many generations had happily been unknown to England, for the incarcerations, the torturings, the starvings, the immurings, the murderings proper to a monastic establishment.

Now I am tempted to stop for a while in order to *improve* (as the evangelical pulpits call it) this most memorable discovery. I will therefore briefly consider it under the heads of—1. THE ACCUSATION; 2. ITS GROUNDS; 3. THE ACCUSERS; and, 4. THE ACCUSED.

First.—THE ACCUSATION.—It is this,—that the Catholics, building the house in question, were in the practice of committing *murder.* This was so strictly the charge, that, had the platform selected for making it been other than we know it to have been, I suppose the speaker might have been indicted for libel. His words were these :—It was not usual for a coroner to hold an *inquest,* unless where a rumour had got abroad that there was a *necessity* for one; and how was a rumor to come *from the underground cells of the convents ?* Yes, he repeated, underground cells : and he would tell them something about such places. At this moment, in the parish of Edgbaston, within the borough of Birmingham, there was a large convent, of some kind or other, being erected, and the whole of the underground was fitted up with cells; *and what were those cells for ?* "

Secondly.—THE GROUNDS OF THE ACCUSATION.—

They are simple ; behold them : 1. That the house is
built level ; 2. and that the plot of earth on which it
is built is higher at one end than at the other.

Thirdly.—THE ACCUSERS.—This, too, throws light
upon the character of Protestant traditions. Not
weak and ignorant people only, not people at a distance—but educated men, gentlemen well connected,
high in position, men of business, men of character,
members of the legislature, men familiar with the lo-
cality, men who know the accused by name,—such are
the men who deliberately, reiteratedly, in spite of
being set right, charge certain persons with pitiless,
savage practices; with beating and imprisoning, with
starving, with murdering their dependents.

Fourthly.—THE ACCUSED.—I feel ashamed, my,
Brothers, of bringing my own matters before you
when far better persons have suffered worse imputations ; but bear with me. *I* then am the accused. A
gentleman of blameless character, a county member,
with whose near relatives I have been on terms of
almost fraternal intimacy for a quarter of a century,
who knows me by repute far more familiarly (I suppose) than any one in this room knows me, putting
aside my personal friends ; he it is who charges me,
and others like me, with delighting in blood, with enjoying the shrieks and groans of agony and despair,
with presiding at a banquet of dislocated limbs,
quivering muscles, and wild countenances. Oh, what
a world is this ! Could he look into our eyes and say
it ? Would he have the heart to say it, if he recollected of whom he said it ? For who are we ? Have
we lived in a corner? have we come to light suddenly

out of the earth? We have been nourished, for the greater part of our lives, in the bosom of the great schools and universities of Protestant England: we have been the foster sons of the Edwards and Henries, the Wykehams and Wolseys, of whom Englishmen are wont to make much ; we have grown up amid hundreds of contemporaries, scattered at present all over the country, in those special ranks of society which are the very walk of a member of the legislature. Our names are better known to the educated classes of the country than those of any others who are not public men. Moreover, if there be men in the whole world who may be said to live *in publico*, it is the members of a College at one of our Universities ; living, not in private houses, not in families, but in one or two apartments which are open to all the world, at all hours, with nothing, I may say, their own; with college servants, a common table,—nay, their chairs and their bedding, and their cups and saucers, down to their coal-scuttle and their carpet brooms,—a sort of common property, and the right of their neighbours. Such is that manner of life,—in which nothing, I may say, can be hid ; where no trait of character or peculiarity of conduct but comes to broad day—such is the life I myself led for above a quarter of a century, under the eyes of numbers who are familiarly known to my accusers ; such is almost the life which we all have led ever since we have been in Birmingham, with our house open to all comers, and ourselves accessible, I may almost say at any hour; and this being so, considering the *charge*, and the *evidence*, and the *accuser*, and the *accused*, could we Catholics desire a more apposite illustration of the formation and the value of a Protestant Tradition ? "

I set it down for the benefit of time to come; "though for no other cause," as a great author says, "yet for this: that posterity may know we have not loosely, through silence, permitted things to pass away as in a dream, there shall be for men's information extant thus much." One commonly forgets such things, from the trouble and inconvenience of having to remember them; let one specimen last, of many which have been suffered to perish, of the birth of an anti-Catholic tradition. The nascent fable has indeed failed, as the tale about the Belgian sin-table has failed, but it might have thriven: it has been lost by bad nursing; it ought to have been cherished awhile in those underground receptacles where first it drew breath, till it could comfortably bear the light; till its limbs were grown, and its voice was strong, and we on whom it bore had run our course, and gone to our account; and then it might have raised its head without fear and without reproach, and might have magisterially asserted what there was none to deny. But men are all the creatures of circumstances; they are hurried on to a ruin which they may see, but cannot evade: so has it been with the Edgbaston Tradition. It was spoken on the house-tops when it should have been whispered in closets, and it expired in the effort. Yet it might have been allotted, let us never forget, a happier destiny. It might have smouldered and spread through a portion of our Birmingham population; it might have rested obscurely on their memories, and now and then risen upon their tongues; there might have been flitting notions, misgivings, rumours, voices, that the horrors of the Inquisition were from time to time renewed in our subterranean chambers; and fifty years hence, if some sudden frenzy of the hour roused the anti-Catholic jealousy still lingering in the town, a mob might have swarmed about our innocent dwelling, to rescue certain legs of mutton and pats of butter from imprisonment, and to hold an inquest over a dozen packing-cases, some old hampers, a knife-board, and a range of empty blacking bottles.

Thus I close my third instance of the sort of evidence commonly adducible for the great Protestant Tradition; not the least significant circumstance about them all being this, that though in the case of all three that evidence is utterly disproved, yet in not one of the three is the charge founded on it withdrawn. In spite of Dr. Waddington, Dr. Maitland, and Mr. Rose, the editors of Mosheim still print and publish his slander on St. Eligius; in defiance of the Brussels protest, and the chair tariff of St. Gudule, the Kent clergyman and the *Times* still bravely maintain our traffic in sins; in violence to the common sense of mankind, the rack and the pulley are still affirmed to be busy in the dungeons of Edgbaston;—for Protestantism must be maintained as the Religion of Englishmen, and part and parcel of the Law of the land.— *Present Position of Catholics*, ed. 1889, pp. 118–125 (1851).

Catholic First Principles.

Now I have come to the point at which the maintenance of private opinion runs into bigotry. As Prejudice
is the rejection of reason altogether, so Bigotry is the im-
position of private reason,—that is of our own views and
theories of our own First Principles, as if they were the
absolute truth, and the standard of all argument, investigation, and judgment. If there are any men in the
world who ought to abstain from bigotry, it is Protestants.   They, whose very badge is the right of private
judgment should give as well as take, should allow others
what they claim themselves; but I am sorry to say, as I
have had occasion to say again and again, there is very
little of the spirit of reciprocity among them; they mono-
polize a liberty which, when they set out, they professed
was to be for the benefit of all parties. Not even the intellectual, not even the candid-minded among them, are free
from inconsistency here. They begin by setting up
principles of thought and action for themselves; then,
not content with applying them to their own thoughts
and actions, they make them the rule for criticising and
condemning our thoughts and actions too; this, I repeat,
is Bigotry. Bigotry is the infliction of our own unproved
First Principles on others, and the treating others with
scorn or hatred for not accepting them.   There are
principles, indeed, as I have already said, such as the

First Principles of morals, not peculiar or proper to the individual, but the rule of the world, because they come from the Author of our being, and from no private factory of man.   It is not bigotry to despise intemperance ; it is not bigotry to hate injustice or cruelty ; but whatever is local, or national, or sectional, or personal, or novel, and nothing more, to make that the standard of judging all existing opinions, without an attempt at proving it to be of authority, is mere ridiculous bigotry. "*In necessariis unitas, in dubiis libertas*," is ever the rule of a true philosopher.   And though I know in many cases it is very difficult to draw the line, and to decide what principles are, and what are not, independent of individuals, times and places, eternal and divine, yet so far we may safely assert,—that when the very persons who hold certain views, confess, nay, boast, nay, are jealously careful, that those views come of their own private judgment, they at least should be as jealous and as careful to keep them to their own place, and not to use them as if they came distinctly from heaven, or from the nature of things, or from the nature of man. Those persons, surely, are precluded, if they would be consistent, from using their principles as authoritative, who proclaim that they made them for themselves. Protestants, then, if any men alive, are, on their own showing, bigots, if they set up their First Principles as oracles and as standards of all truth.

This being considered, have we not, my Brothers, a curious sight before us ? This is what we call an enlightened age: we are to have large views of things ; everything is to be put on a philosophical basis ; reason is to rule : the world is to begin again ; a new and

transporting set of views is about to be exhibited to
the great human family. Well and good ; have them,
preach them, enjoy them, but deign to recollect the
while, that there have been views in the world before
you ; that the world has not been going on up to this day
without any principles whatever ; that the Old Religion
was based on principles, and that it is not enough to
flourish about your " new lamps," if you would make
us give up our " old " ones. Catholicism, I say, had
its First Principles before you were born : you say they
are false ; very well, prove them to be so : they are false,
indeed, if yours are true ; but not false merely because
yours are yours. While yours are yours it is self-evi-
dent, indeed, to you, that ours are false ; but it is not
the common way of carrying on business in the world,
to value English goods by French measures, or to pay
a debt in paper which was contracted in gold. Catholicism has its First Principles, overthrow them, if you
can ; endure them, if you cannot. It is not enough to
call them effete because they are old, or antiquated because they are ancient. It is not enough to look into
our churches, and cry, " It is all a form, *because* divine
favour cannot depend on external observances ; " or, " It
is all a bondage, *because* there is no such thing as sin ; "
or, " a blasphemy, *because* the Supreme Being cannot be
present in ceremonies ; " or, " a mummery, *because* prayer cannot move Him ; " or, " a tyranny, *because* vows
are unnatural ; " or, " hypocrisy, *because* no rational
man can credit it at all." I say here is endless assumption, unmitigated hypothesis, reckless assertion ; prove
your " because," " because," " because ; " prove your
First Principles, and if you cannot, learn philosophic

moderation. Why may not my First Principles contest the prize with yours? they have been longer in the world; they have lasted longer, they have done harder work, they have seen rougher service. You sit in your easy-chairs, you dogmatize in your lecture-rooms, you wield your pens: it all looks well on paper: you write exceedingly well: there never was an age in which there was better writing; logical, nervous, eloquent, and pure,—go and carry it all out in the world. Take your First Principles, of which you are so proud, into the crowded streets of our cities, into the formidable classes which make up the bulk of our population; try to work society by them. You think you can; I say you cannot—at least you have not as yet; it is yet to be seen if you can. "Let not him that putteth on his armour boast as he who taketh it off." Do not take it for granted that that is certain which is waiting the test of reason and experiment. Be modest until you are victorious. My principles, which I believe to be eternal, have at least lasted eighteen hundred years; let yours live as many months. That man can sin, that he has duties, that the Divine Being hears prayer, that He gives His favours through visible ordinances, that He is really present in the midst of them, these principles have been the life of nations; they have shown they could be carried out; let any single nation carry out yours, and you will have better claim to speak contemptuously of Catholic rites, of Catholic devotions, of Catholic belief.—*Present Position of Catholics*, ed. 1889, pp. 291–5(1851).

STARTING then with the being of a God,(which, as I have said, is as certain to me as the certainty of my own existence, though when I try to put the grounds of that certainty into logical shape I find a difficulty in doing so in mood and figure to my satisfaction), I look out of myself into the world of men, and there I see a sight which fills me with unspeakable distress. The world seems simply to give the lie to that great truth, of which my whole being is so full; and the effect upon me is, in consequence, as a matter of necessity, as confusing as if it denied that I am in existence myself. If I looked into a mirror, and did not see my face, I should have the sort of feeling which actually comes upon me, when I look into this living busy world, and see no reflection of its Creator. This is, to me, one of those great difficulties of this absolute primary truth, to which I referred just now. Were it not for this voice, speaking so clearly in my conscience and my heart, I should be an atheist, or a pantheist, or a polytheist when I looked into the world. I am speaking for myself only; and I am far from denying the real force of the arguments in proof of a God, drawn from the general facts of human society and the course of history, but these do not warm me or en-

lighten me ; they do not take away the winter of my
desolation, or make the buds unfold and the leaves
grow within me, and my moral being rejoice. The
sight of the world is nothing else than the prophet's
scroll, full of " lamentations, and mourning, and
woe."

To consider the world in its length and breadth, its
various history, the many races of man, their starts,
their fortunes, their mutual alienation, their conflicts;
and then their ways, habits, governments, forms of
worship ; their enterprises, their aimless courses, their
random achievements and acquirements, the impotent
conclusion of long-standing facts, the tokens so faint
and broken of a superintending design, the blind
evolution of what turn out to be great powers or truths,
the progress of things, as if from unreasoning elements,
not towards final causes, the greatness and littleness
of man, his far-reaching aims, his short duration, the
curtain hung over his futurity, the disappointments of
life, the defeat of good, the success of evil, physical
pain, mental anguish, the prevalence and intensity of
sin, the pervading idolatries, the corruptions, the dreary
hopeless irreligion, that condition of the whole race, so
fearfully yet exactly described in the Apostle's words,
" having no hope and without God in the world,"—all
this is a vision to dizzy and appal ; and inflicts upon
the mind the sense of a profound mystery, which is
absolutely beyond human solution.

What shall be said to this heart-piercing, reason-
bewildering fact ? I can only answer, that either there
is no Creator, or this living society of men is in a true
sense discarded from His presence. Did I see a boy

11

of good make and mind, with the tokens on him of a refined nature, cast upon the world without provision, unable to say whence he came, his birth-place or his family connections, I should conclude that there was some mystery connected with his history, and that he was one, of whom, from one cause or other, his parents were ashamed. Thus only should I be able to account for the contrast between the promise and the condition of his being. And so I argue about the world ;—*if* there be a God, *since* there is a God, the human race is implicated in some terrible aboriginal calamity. It is out of joint with the purposes of its Creator. This is a fact, a fact as true as the fact of its existence ; and thus the doctrine of what is theologically called original sin becomes to me almost as certain as that the world exists, and as the existence of God.

And now, supposing it were the blessed and loving will of the Creator to interfere in this anarchical condition of things, what are we to suppose would be the methods which might be necessarily or naturally involved in His purpose of mercy? Since the world is in so abnormal a state, surely it would be no surprise to me, if the interposition were of necessity equally extraordinary—or what is called miraculous. But that subject does not directly come into the scope of my present remarks. Miracles as evidence, involve a process of reason, or an argument; and of course I am thinking of some mode of interference which does not immediately run into argument. I am rather asking what must be the face-to-face antagonist, by which to withstand and baffle the fierce energy of passion and the all-corroding, all-dissolving scepticism of the intellect in religious inquiries? I have no intention at all of denying, that truth is the real object of our reason, and that, if it does not attain to truth, either the premiss or the process is in fault; but I am not speaking here of right reason, but of reason as it acts in fact and concretely in fallen man. I know that even the unaided reason, when correctly exercised, leads to a belief in God, in the immortality of the soul, and in a future retribution; but I am considering the faculty of reason actually and historically; and in this point of view, I do not think I am wrong in saying that its tendency is towards a simple unbelief in matters of religion. No truth, however sacred, can stand against it, in the long run; and hence it is that in the pagan world, when our Lord came, the last traces of the religious knowledge of former times were all but disappearing from those portions of the world in which the intellect had been active and had had a career.

And in these latter days, in like manner, outside the Catholic Church things are tending,—with far greater rapidity than in that old time from the circumstance of the age,—to atheism in one shape or other. What a scene, what a prospect, does the whole of Europe present at this day! and not only Europe, but every government and every civilization through the world, which is under the influence of the European mind! Especially, for it most concerns us, how sorrowful, in the view of religion, even taken in its most elementary, most attenuated form, is the spectacle presented to us by the educated intellect of England, France, and Germany! Lovers of their country and of their race, religious men, external to the Catholic Church, have attempted various expedients to arrest fierce wilful human nature in its onward course, and to bring it into subjection. The necessity of some form of religion for the interests of humanity, has been generally acknowledged : but where was the concrete representative of things invisible, which would have the force and the toughness necessary to be a breakwater against the deluge? Three centuries ago the establishment of religion, material, legal, and social, was generally adopted as the best expedient for the purpose, in those countries which separated from the Catholic Church ; and for a long time it was successful; but now the crevices of those establishments are admitting the enemy. Thirty years ago, education was relied upon : ten years ago there was a hope that wars would cease forever, under the influence of commercial enterprise and the reign of the useful and fine arts ; but will any one venture to say that there is anything anywhere on this earth, which will afford a fulcrum for us, whereby to keep the earth from moving onwards ?

The judgment, which experience passes whether on establishments or on education, as a means of maintaining religious truth in this anarchical world, must be extended even to Scripture, though Scripture be divine. Experience proves surely that the Bible does not answer a purpose for which it was never intended. It may be accidentally the means of the conversion of individuals ; but a book, after all, cannot make a stand against the wild living intellect of man, and in this day it begins to testify, as regards its own structure and contents, to the power of that universal solvent, which is so successfully acting upon religious establishments.

Supposing then it to be the Will of the Creator to interfere in human affairs, and to make provisions for retaining in the world a knowledge of Himself, so definite and distinct as to be proof against the energy of human scepticism, in such a case,—I am far from saying that there was no other way,—but there is nothing to surprise the mind, if He should think fit to introduce a power into the world, invested with the prerogative of infallibility in religious matters. Such a provision would be a direct, immediate, active, and prompt means of withstanding the difficulty; it would be an instrument suited to the need ; and, when I find that this is the very claim of the Catholic Church not only do I feel no difficulty in admitting the idea, but there is a fitness in it, which recommends it to my mind. And thus I am brought to speak of the Church's infallibility, as a provision, adapted by the mercy of the Creator, to preserve religion in the world, and to restrain that freedom of thought, which of course in itself is one of the greatest of our natural gifts, and to rescue it from its own suicidal excesses. And let it be observed that, neither here nor in what follows, shall I have occasion to speak directly of Revelation in its subject-matter, but in reference to the sanction which it gives to truths which may be known independently of it,—as it bears upon the defence of natural religion. I say, that a power, possessed of infallibility in religious teaching, is happily adapted to be a working instrument, in the course of human affairs, for smiting hard and throwing back the im-

mense energy of the aggressive, capricious, untrust-
worthy intellect :—and in saying this, as in the other
things that I have to say, it must still be recollected
that I am all along bearing in mind my main purpose,
which is a defence of myself.—*Apologia*, ed. 1890,
pp. 241–246 (1864).

THE Protestant, I say, laughs at the very idea of miracles or supernatural acts as occurring at this day; his First Principle is rooted in him; he repels from him the idea of miracles; he laughs at the notion of evidence for them; one is just as likely as another; they are all false. Why? Because of his First Principle: there are no miracles since the Apostles. Here, indeed, is a short and easy way of getting rid of the whole subject, not by reason, but by a First Principle which he calls reason. Yes, it *is* reason, granting his First Principle is true; it is *not* reason, supposing his First Principle is false. It is reason, if the private judgment of an individual, or of a sect, or of a philosophy, or of a nation, be synonymous with reason; it is not reason, if reason is something not local, nor temporal, but universal. Before he advances a step in his argument, he ought to prove his First Principle true; he does not attempt to do so, he takes it for granted; and he proceeds to apply it, gratuitous, personal, peculiar as it is, to all our accounts of miracles taken together, and thereupon and thereby triumphantly rejects them all. This, forsooth, is his spontaneous judgment, his instinctive feeling, his common sense,—a mere private opinion of his own, a Protestant opinion; a lecture-room opinion; not a world-wide opinion, not an in-

stinct ranging through time and space, but an assumption and presumption, which, by education and habit,
he has got to think as certain, as much of an axiom, as
that two and two make four; and he looks down upon
us, and bids us consider ourselves beaten, all because
the savour of our statements and narratives and reports
and legends is inconsistent with his delicate Protestant
sense,—all because our conclusions are different, not
from our principles and premisses, but from his.

And now for the structure he proceeds to raise on
this foundation of sand. If, he argues, in matter of
fact, there be a host of stories about relics and miracles circulated in the Catholic Church, which, as a
matter of First Principle, cannot be true; to what must
we attribute them? indubitably to enormous stupidity
on the one hand, and enormous roguery on the other.
This, observe, is an immediate and close inference :—
clever men must see through the superstition ; those
who do not see through it must be dolts. Further,
since religion is the subject-matter of the alleged
fictions, they must be what are called pious frauds, for
the sake of gain and power. Observe, my Brothers,
there is in the Church a vast tradition and testimony
about miracles : how is it to be accounted for ? If
miracles *can* take place, then the *truth* of the miracle
will be a natural explanation of the *report*, just as the
fact of a man dying satisfactorily accounts for the
news that he is dead ; but the Protestant cannot so explain it, because he thinks miracles cannot take place ;
so he is necessarily driven, by way of accounting for
the report of them, to impute that report to fraud. He
cannot help himself. I repeat it ; the whole mass of

accusations which Protestants bring against us under this head, Catholic credulity, imposture, pious frauds, hypocrisy, priestcraft, this vast and varied superstructure of imputation, you see, all rests on an assumption, on an opinion of theirs, for which they offer no kind of proof. What then, in fact, do they say more than this, *If* Protestantism be true, you Catholics are a most awful set of knaves?—Here, at least, is a most intelligible and undeniable position.

Now, on the other hand, let me take our own side of the question, and consider how we ourselves stand relatively to the charge made against us. Catholics, then, hold the mystery of the Incarnation; and the Incarnation is the most stupendous event which ever can take place on earth; and after it and henceforth, I do not see how we can scruple at any miracle on the mere ground of its being unlikely to happen. No miracle can be so great as that which took place in the Holy House of Nazareth; it is indefinitely more difficult to believe than all the miracles of the Breviary, of the Martyrology, of Saints' lives, of legends, of local traditions, put together; and there is the grossest inconsistency on the very face of the matter, for any one so to strain out the gnat and to swallow the camel, as to profess what is inconceivable, yet to protest against what is surely within the limits of intelligible hypothesis. If, through divine grace, we once are able to accept the solemn truth that the Supreme Being was born of a mortal woman, what is there to be imagined which can offend us on the ground of its marvellousness? Thus, you see, it happens that, though First Principles are commonly assumed, not proved, ours in this case admits, if not of proof, yet of recommendation, by means of that fundamental truth which Protestants profess as well as we. When we start with assuming that miracles are not unlikely, we are putting forth a position which lies imbedded, as it were, and involved, in the great revealed fact of the Incarnation.

So much is plain on starting; but more is plain too. Miracles are not only not unlikely, they are positively likely; and for this simple reason, because, for the most part, when God begins He goes on. We conceive that when He first did a miracle, He began a series; what He commenced, He continued: what has been, will be. Surely this is good and clear reasoning. To my own mind, certainly, it is incomparably more difficult to believe that the Divine Being should do one miracle and no more, than that He should do a thousand; that He should do one great miracle only, than that He should do a multitude of less besides. This beautiful world of nature, His own work, He broke its harmony; He broke through His own laws which He had imposed on it; He worked out His purposes, not simply through it, but in violation of it. If He did this only in the lifetime of the Apostles, if He did it but once, eighteen hundred years ago and more, that isolated infringement looks as the mere infringement of a rule: if Divine Wisdom would not leave an infringement, an anomaly, a solecism on His work, He might be expected to introduce a series of miracles, and turn the apparent exception into an additional law of His providence. If the Divine Being does a thing once, He is, judging by human reason, likely to do it again. This surely is common sense. If a beggar gets food at a gentleman's house once, does he not send others thither after him? If you are attacked by thieves once, do you forthwith leave your windows open at night? If an acquaintance were convicted of a fraud, would you let that be the signal for reposing confidence in him, as a man who could not possibly deceive you? Nay, suppose you yourselves were once to see a miracle, would you not feel that experience to be like passing a line? should you, in consequence of it, declare, "I never will believe another if I hear of one?" would it not, on the contrary, predispose you to listen to a new report? would you scoff at it and call it priestcraft for the reason that you had actually seen one with your own eyes? I think you would not; then I ask what is the difference of the argument, whether you have seen one or believe one? You believe the Apostolic miracles, therefore be inclined beforehand to believe later ones. Thus you see, our First Principle, that miracles are not unlikely now, is not at all a strange one in the mouths of those who believe that the Supreme Being came miraculously into this world, miraculously united Himself to man's nature, passed a life of miracles and then gave His Apostles a greater gift of miracles, than He exercised Himself. So far on the principle itself; and now, in the next place, see what comes of it.

This comes of it,—that there are two systems going on in the world, one of nature, and one above nature; and two histories, one of common events, and one of miracles; and each system and each history has its own order. When I hear of the miracle of a Saint, my first feeling would be of the same kind as if it were a report of any natural exploit or event. Supposing, for instance, I heard a report of the death of some public man; it would not startle me, even if I did not at once credit it, for all men must die. Did I read of any great feat of valor, I should believe it, if imputed to Alexander or Cœur de Lion. Did I hear of any act of baseness, I should disbelieve it, if imputed to a friend whom I knew and loved. And so, in like manner, were a miracle reported to me as wrought by a member of Parliament, or a Bishop of the Establishment, or a Wesleyan preacher, I should repudiate the notion : were it referred to a saint, or the relic of a saint, or the intercession of a saint, I should not be startled at it, though I might not at once believe it. And I certainly should be right in this conduct, supposing my First Principle be true. Miracles to the Catholic are facts of history and biography, and nothing else; and they are to be regarded and dealt with as other facts; and as natural facts, under circumstances, do not startle Protestants, so supernatural, under circumstances, do not startle the Catholic.[1] They may or may not have taken place in particular cases; he may be unable to determine

---

[1] Douglas, succeeding Middleton, lays down the sceptical and Protestant First Principle thus : " The history of miracles (to make use of the words of an author, whose authority you will think of some weight) is of a kind totally *different* from that of common events ; the one to be *suspected always of course*, without the *strongest* evidence to *confirm* it ; the other to be *admitted of course*, without *as strong* reason to *suspect* it," etc.—*Criterion*, p. 26.

which; he may have no distinct evidence; he may suspend his judgment, but he will say, "It is very possible;" he never will say, "I cannot believe it."

Take the history of Alfred: you know his wise, mild, beneficent, yet daring character, and his romantic vicissitudes of fortune. This great king has a number of stories, or, as you may call them, legends, told of him. Do you believe them all? no. Do you, on the other hand, think them incredible? no. Do you call a man a dupe or a blockhead for believing them? no. Do you call an author a knave and a cheat who records them? no. You go into neither extreme, whether of implicit faith or of violent reprobation. You are not so extravagant; you see that they suit his character, they *may* have been; yet this is so romantic, that has so little evidence, a third is so confused in dates or in geography, that you are in matter of fact indisposed towards them. Others are probably true, others certainly. Nor do you force every one to take your own view of particular stories; you and your neighbours think differently about this or that in detail and agree to differ. There is in the Museum at Oxford, a jewel or trinket said to be Alfred's; it is shown to all comers: I never heard the keeper of the Museum accused of hypocrisy or fraud for showing, with Alfred's name appended, what he might or might not himself believe to have belonged to that great king: nor did I ever see any party of strangers, who were looking at it with awe, regarded by any self-complacent bystander with scornful compassion. Yet the relic is not to a certainty Alfred's. The world pays civil honour to it on the probability; we pay religious honour to relics, if so be, on the probability. Is the Tower of London shut against sightseers, because the coats of mail or pikes there may have half legendary tales connected with them? why then may not the country people come up in joyous companies, singing and piping, to see the Holy Coat at Trèves? There is our Queen again, who is so truly and justly popular; she roves about in the midst of tradition and romance; she scatters myths and legends from her as she goes along; she is a being of poetry, and you might fairly be sceptical whether she had any personal existence. She is always at some beautiful, noble, bounteous work or other, if you trust the papers. She is doing alms-deeds in the Highlands; she meets beggars in her rides at Windsor; she writes verses in albums, or draws sketches, or is mistaken for the housekeeper by some blind old woman, or she runs up a hill, as if she were a child. Who finds fault with these things? he would be a cynic, he would be white-livered, and would have gall for blood, who was not struck with this grace-ful, touching evidence of the love which her subjects bear her. Who could have the head, even if he had the heart, who could be so cross and peevish, who could be so solemn and perverse, as to say that some of the stories *may* be simple lies, and all of them might have stronger evidence than they carry with them? Do you think she is displeased at them? Why, then, should He, the Great Father, who once walked the earth, look sternly on the unavoidable mistakes of His own subjects and children in their devotion to Him and His? Even granting they mistake some cases in particular, from the infirmity of human nature, and the

contingencies of evidence, and fancy there is or has
been a miracle here or there when there is not;—
though a tradition, attached to a picture, or to a shrine,
or to a well, be very doubtful;—though one relic be
sometimes mistaken for another, and St. Theodore
stands for St. Eugenius, or St. Agathocles;—still, once
take into account our First Principle, that He is likely
to continue miracles among us, which is as good as the
Protestant's, and I do not see why He should feel
much displeasure with us on account of this error, or
should cease to work wonders in our behalf. In the
Protestant's view, indeed, who assumes that miracles
never are, our thaumatology is one great falsehood;
but that is *his* First Principle, as I have said so often,
which he does not prove but assume. If *he*, indeed,
upheld *our* system, or *we* held *his* principle, in either
case he or we should be impostors; but though we
should be partners to a fraud, if we thought like Protestants, we surely are not, because we think like
Catholics.

Such, then, is the answer which I make to those
who would urge against us the multitude of miracles
recorded in our Saints' Lives and devotional works,
for many of which there is little evidence, and for some
next to none. We think them true in the sense in
which Protestants think the details of English history
true. When they say that, they do not mean to say
there are no mistakes in it, but no mistakes of consequence, none which alter the general course of history.
Nor do they mean they are equally sure of every part;
for evidence is fuller and better for some things than

for others.   They do not stake their credit on the truth
of Froissart or Sully, they do not pledge themselves for
the accuracy of Doddington or Walpole, they do not
embrace as an Evangelist, Hume, Sharon Turner, or
Macaulay.   And yet they do not think it necessary, on
the other hand, to commence a religious war against
all our historical catechisms, and abstracts, and dic-
tionaries, and tales and biographies, through the
country; they have no call on them to amend and
expurgate books of archæology, antiquities, heraldry,
architecture, geography, and statistics, to rewrite our
inscriptions, and to establish a censorship on all new
publications for the time to come.   And so as regards
the miracles of the Catholic Church; if, indeed,
miracles never can occur, then, indeed, impute the narratives to fraud; but till you prove they are not likely,
we shall consider the histories which have come down
to us true on the whole, though in particular cases they
may be exaggerated or unfounded.   Where, indeed,
they can certainly be proved to be false, there we shall
be bound to do our best to get rid of them; but till
that is clear, we shall be liberal enough to allow others
to use their private judgment in their favour, as we use
ours in their disparagement.   For myself, lest I appear
in any way to be shrinking from a determinate judgment on the claims of some of those miracles and relics,
which Protestants are so startled at, and to be hiding
particular questions in what is vague and general, I
will avow distinctly, that, putting out of the question
the hypothesis of unknown laws of nature (that is, of
the professed miracle being not miraculous), I think it
impossible to withstand the evidence which is brought

for the liquefaction of the blood of St. Januarius at Naples, and for the motion of the eyes of the pictures of the Madonna in the Roman States. I see no reason to doubt the material of the Lombard crown at Monza ; and I do not see why the Holy Coat at Trèves may not have been what it professes to be. I firmly believe that portions of the True Cross are at Rome and elsewhere, that the Crib of Bethlehem is at Rome, and the bodies of St. Peter and St. Paul also. I believe that at Rome too lies St. Stephen, that St. Matthew lies at Salerno, and St. Andrew at Amalfi. I firmly believe that the relics of the saints are doing innumerable miracles and graces daily, and that it needs only for a Catholic to show devotion to any saint in order to receive special benefits from his intercession. I firmly believe that saints in their life-time have before now raised the dead to life, crossed the sea without vessels, multiplied grain and bread, cured incurable diseases, and superseded the operation of the laws of the universe in a multitude of ways. Many men, when they hear an educated man so speak, will at once impute the avowal to insanity, or to an idiosyncrasy, or to imbecility of mind, or to decrepitude of powers, or to fanaticism, or to hypocrisy. They have a right to say so, if they will ; and we have a right to ask them why they do not say it of those who bow down before the Mystery of mysteries, the Divine Incarnation. If they do not believe this, they are not yet Protestants ; if they do, let them grant that He who has done the greater may do the less.—*Present Position of Catholics*, ed. 1889, pp. 303-313 (1851).

12

In the bosom of the woods which stretched for many miles from the immediate environs of Sicca, and placed on a gravel slope reaching down to a brook, which ran in a bottom close by, was a small, rude hut, of a kind peculiar to Africa, and commonly ascribed to the wandering tribes, who neither cared, nor had leisure, for a more stable habitation. Some might have called it a tent, from the goat's-hair cloth with which it was covered ; but it looked, as to shape, like nothing else than an inverted boat, or the roof of a house set upon the ground. Inside it was seen to be constructed of the branches of trees, twisted together or wattled, the interstices, or rather the whole surface, being covered with clay. Being thus stoutly built, lined, and covered, it was proof against the tremendous rains, to which the climate, for which it was made, was subject. Along the centre ridge or backbone, which varied in height from six to ten feet from the ground, it was supported by three posts or pillars ; at one end it rose conically to an open aperture, which served for chimney, for sky-light, and for ventilator. Hooks were suspended from the roof for baskets, articles of clothing, weapons, and implements of various kinds ; and a second cone, excavated in the ground with the vertex downward, served as a storehouse for grain.

The door was so low, that an ordinary person must bend double to pass through it.

However, it was in the winter months only, when the rains were profuse, that the owner of this respectable mansion condescended to creep into it. In summer she had a drawing-room, as it may be called, of nature's own creation, in which she lived, and in one quarter of which she had her lair. Close above the hut was a high plot of level turf, surrounded by old oaks, and fringed beneath with thick underwood. In the centre of this green rose a yew tree of primeval character. Indeed, the whole forest spoke of the very beginnings of the world, as if it had been the immediate creation of that Voice which bade the earth clothe itself with green life. But the place no longer spoke exclusively of its Maker. Upon the trees hung the emblems and objects of idolatry, and the turf was traced with magical characters. Littered about were human bones, horns of wild animals, wax figures, spermaceti taken from vaults, large nails, to which portions of flesh adhered, as if they had had to do with malefactors, metal plates engraved with strange characters, bottled blood, hair of young persons, and old rags. The reader must not suppose any incantation is about to follow, or that the place we are describing will have a prominent place in what remains of our tale; but even if it be the scene of only one conversation, and one event, there is no harm in describing it, as it appeared on that occasion.

The old crone, who was seated in this bower of delight, had an expression of countenance in keeping, not with the place, but with the furniture with which it was adorned : that furniture told her trade. Whether the root of superstition might be traced deeper still, and the woman and her traps were really and directly connected with the powers beneath the earth, it is impossible to determine : it is certain she had the will, it is certain that that will was from their inspiration ; nay, it is certain that she thought she really possessed the communications which she desired ; it is certain, too, she so far deceived herself as to fancy that what she learned by mere natural means came to her from a diabolical source. She kept up an active correspondence with Sicca. She was consulted by numbers : she was up with the public news, the social gossip, and the private and secret transactions of the hour ; and had, before now, even interfered in matters of state, and had been courted by rival political parties. But in the high cares and occupations of this interesting person, we are not here concerned ; but with a conversation which took place between her and Juba, about the same hour of the evening as that of Cæcilius's escape, but on the day after it, while the sun was gleaming almost horizontally through the tall trunks of the trees of the forest.

" Well, my precious boy, " said the old woman, " the choicest gifts of great Cham be your portion ! You had excellent sport yesterday, I'll warrant. The rats squeaked, eh ? and you beat the life out of them. That scoundrel sacristan, I suppose, has taken up his quarters below. "

" You may say it, " answered Juba. " The reptile ! he turned right about, and would have made himself an honest fellow, when it couldn't be helped. "

"Good, good!" returned Gurta, as if she had got something very pleasant in her mouth; "ah! that is good! but he did not escape on that score, I do trust."

"They pulled him to pieces all the more cheerfully," said Juba.

"Pulled him to pieces, limb by limb, joint by joint, eh?" answered Gurta. "Did they skin him?—did they do anything to his eyes, or his tongue?—Anyhow, it was too quickly, Juba. Slowly, leisurely, gradually. Yes, it's like a glutton to be quick about it. Taste him, handle him, play with him,—that's luxury! but to bolt him,—faugh!"

"Cæso's slave made a good end," said Juba: "he stood up for his views, and died like a man."

"The gods smite him! but he has gone up,—up:" and she laughed. "Up to what they call bliss and glory;—such glory! but he's out of our domain, you know. But he did not die easy?"

"The boys worried him a good deal," answered Juba: "but it's not quite in my line, mother, all this. I think you drink a pint of blood morning and evening, and thrive on it, old woman. It makes you merry; but it's too much for my stomach."

"Ha, ha, my boy!" cried Gurta: "you'll improve in time, though you make wry faces, now that you're young. Well, and have you brought me any news from the capitol? Is any one getting a rise in the world, or a downfall? How blows the wind? Are there changes in the camp? This Decius, I suspect, will not last long."

"They all seem desperately frightened," said Juba,

15

" lest they should not smite your friends hard enough, Gurta. Root and branch is the word. They'll have to make a few Christians for the occasion, in order to kill them : and I almost think they're about it," he added, thoughtfully. " They have to show that they are not surpassed by the rabble. 'Tis a pity Christians are so few, isn't it, mother?"

"Yes, yes," she said; "but we must crush them, grind them, many or few : and we shall, we shall! Callista's to come."

" I don't see they are worse than other people," said Juba; "not at all, except that they are commonly sneaks. If Callista turns, why should not I turn too, mother, to keep her company, and keep your hand in?"

" No, no, my boy," returned the witch, " you must serve *my* master. You are having your fling just now, but you will buckle to in good time. You must one day take some work with my merry men. Come here, child," said the fond mother, " and let me kiss you."

" Keep your kisses for your monkeys, and goats, and cats," answered Juba : " they're not to my taste, old dame. Master! my master! I won't have a master! I'll be nobody's servant. I'll never stand to be hired, nor cringe to a bully, nor quake before a rod. Please yourself, Gurta; I'm a free man. You're my mother by courtesy only."

Gurta looked at him savagely. " Why you're not going to be pious and virtuous, Juba? A choice saint you'll make! You shall be drawn for a picture."

" Why shouldn't I, if I choose?" said Juba. " If I must take service, willy, nilly, I'd any. day prefer the other's to that of your friend. I've not left the master to take the man."

" Blaspheme not the great gods," she answered, " or they'll do you a mischief yet."

"I say again," insisted Juba, "if I must lick the earth, it shall not be where your friend has trod. It shall be in my brother's fashion, rather than in yours, Gurta."

"Agellius!" she shrieked out with such disgust, that it is wonderful she uttered the name at all. "Ah! you have not told me about him, boy. Well, is he safe in the pit, or in the stomach of an hyena ?"

"He's alive," said Juba ; "but he has not got it in him to be a Christian. Yes, he's safe with his uncle."

"Ah! Jucundus must ruin him, debauch him, and then we must make away with him. We must not be in a hurry," said Gurta, "it must be body and soul."

" No one shall touch him, craven as he is," answered Juba. " I despise him, but let him alone."

" Don't come across me," said Gurta, sullenly ; " I'll have my way. Why, you know I could smite you to the dust, as well as him, if I chose."

" But you have not asked me about Callista," answered Juba. " It is really a capital joke, but she has got into prison for certain, for being a Christian. Fancy it! they caught her in the streets, and put her in the guard-house, and have had her up for examination. You see they want a Christian for the nonce : it would not do to have none such in prison; so they will flourish with her till Decius bolts from the scene.

" The furies have her !" cried Gurta : " she *is* a Christian, my boy : I told you so, long ago."

"Callista a Christian!" answered Juba, "ha ! ha!
She and Agellius are going to make a match of it, of
some sort or other. They're thinking of other things
than paradise."

" She and the old priest, more likely, more likely,"
said Gurta. " He's in prison with her,—in the pit, as
I trust."

" Your master has cheated you for once, old woman,"
said Juba.

Gurta looked at him fiercely, and seemed waiting
for his explanation. He began singing :—

" She wheedled and coaxed, but he was no fool ;
   He'd be his own master, he'd not be her tool;
   Not the little black moor should send him to school.

" She foamed and she cursed,—'twas the same thing to him ;
   She laid well her trap ; but he carried his whim :—
   The priest scuffled off, safe in life and in limb."

Gurta was almost suffocated with passion. "Cyprianus has not escaped, boy ?" she asked at length.

" I got him off," said Juba, undauntedly.

A shade, as of Erebus, passed over the witch's
face ; but she remained quite silent.

" Mother, I am my own master," he continued. " I
must break your assumption of superiority. I'm not
a boy, though you call me so. I'll have my own way.
Yes, I saved Cyprianus. You're a bloodthirsty old
hag! Yes, *I've* seen your secret doings. Did not I
catch you the other day, practising on that little child ?
You had nailed him up by hands and feet against the
tree, and were cutting him to pieces at your leisure,

as he quivered and shrieked the while. You were examining or using his liver for some of your black purposes. It's not in my line; but you gloated over it; and when he wailed, you wailed in mimicry. You were panting with pleasure."

Gurta was still silent, and had an expression on her face, awful from the intensity of its malignity. She had uttered a low piercing whistle.

"Yes!" continued Juba, "you revelled in it. You chattered to the poor babe, when it screamed, as a nurse to an infant. You called it pretty names, and squeaked out your satisfaction each time you stuck it. You old hag! I'm not of your breed, though they say I am of your blood. *I* don't fear you," he said, observing the expression of her countenance, " I don't fear the immortal devil! " And he continued his song :—

> " She beckoned the moon, and the moon came down ;
> The green earth shrivelled beneath her frown ;
> But a man's strong will can keep his own."

While he was talking and singing, her call had been answered from the hut. An animal of some wonderful species had crept out of it, and proceeded to creep and crawl, moeing and twisting as it went, along the trees and shrubs which rounded the grass plot. When it came up to the old woman, it crouched at her feet, and then rose up upon its hind legs and begged. She took hold of the uncouth beast and began to fondle it in her arms, muttering something in its ear. At length, when Juba stopped for a moment in his song, she suddenly flung it right at him, with great force, saying, "Take that!" She then gave utterance to a low inward laugh, and leaned herself back against the trunk of the tree under which she was sitting, with her knees drawn up almost to her chin.

The blow seemed to act on Juba as a shock on his nervous system, both from its violence and its strange.ness. He stood still for a moment, and then, without saying a word, he turned away, and walked slowly down the hill, as if in a maze. Then he sat down. . . .

In an instant up he started again with a great cry, and began running at the top of his speed. He thought he heard a voice speaking in him; and, however fast he ran, the voice, or whatever it was, kept up with him. He rushed through the underwood, trampling and crushing it under his feet, and scaring the birds and small game which lodged there. At last, exhausted, he stood still for breath, when he heard it say loudly and deeply, as if speaking with his own organs, "You cannot escape from yourself!" Then a terror seized him; he fell down and fainted away.

When his senses returned, his first impression was of something in him not himself. He felt it in his breathing; he tasted it in his mouth. The brook which ran by Gurta's encampment had by this time become a streamlet, though still shallow. He plunged into it; a feeling came upon him as if he ought to drown himself, had it been deeper. He rolled about in it, in spite of its flinty and rocky bed. When he came out of it, his tunic sticking to him, he tore it off his shoulders, and let it hang round his girdle in shreds, as it might. The shock of the water, however,

acted as a sedative upon him, and the coolness of the
night refreshed him. He walked on for a while in
silence.

Suddenly the power within him began uttering, by
means of his organs of speech, the most fearful blasphemies, words embodying conceptions which, had they
come into his mind, he might indeed have borne with
patience before this, or uttered in bravado, but which
now filled him with inexpressible loathing, and a
terror to which he had hitherto been quite a stranger.
He had always in his heart believed in a God, but he
now believed with a reality and intensity utterly new
to him. He felt it as if he saw Him ; he felt there
was a world of good and evil beings. He did not love
the good, or hate the evil ; but he shrank from the
one, and he was terrified at the other; and he felt
himself carried away, against his will, as the prey of
some dreadful, mysterious power, which tyrannized
over him.

The day had closed—the moon had risen. He
plunged into the thickest wood, and the trees seemed
to him to make way for him. Still they seemed to
moan and to creak as they moved out of their place.
Soon he began to see that they were looking at him,
and exulting over his misery. They, of an inferior
nature, had had no gift which they could abuse and
lose ; and they remained in that honour and perfection
in which they were created. Birds of the night flew
out of them, reptiles slunk away ; yet soon he began
to be surrounded, wherever he went, by a circle of
owls, bats, ravens, crows, snakes, wild cats, and apes
which were always looking at him, but somehow made

way, retreating before him, and yet forming again, and in order, as he marched along.

He had passed through the wing of the forest which he entered, and penetrated into the more mountainous country. He ascended the heights; he was a taller, stronger man than he had been; he went forward with a preternatural vigour, and flourished his arms with the excitement of some vinous or gaseous intoxication. He heard the roar of the wild beasts echoed along the woody ravines which were cut into the solid mountain rock, with a reckless feeling, as if he could cope with them. As he passed the dens of the lion, leopard, hyena, jackal, wild boar, and wolf, there he saw them sitting at the entrance, or stopping suddenly as they prowled along, and eyeing him, but not daring to approach. He strode along from rock to rock, and over precipices, with the certainty and ease of some giant in Eastern fable. Suddenly a beast of prey came across him; in a moment he had torn up by the roots the stump of a wild vine plant, which was near him, had thrown himself upon his foe before it could act on the aggressive, had flung it upon its back, forced the weapon into its mouth, and was stamping on its chest. He knocked the life out of the furious animal; and crying "Take that," tore its flesh, and, applying his mouth to the wound, sucked a draught of its blood.

He has passed over the mountain, and has descended its side. Bristling shrubs, swamps, precipitous banks, rushing torrents, are no obstacle to his course. He has reached the brow of a hill, with a deep placid river at the foot of it, just as the dawn begins to break. It is a lovely prospect, which every step he takes is

becoming more definite and more various in the day-
light. Masses of oleander, of great beauty, with their
red blossoms, fringed the river, and tracked out its
course into the distance. The bank of the hill below
him, and on the right and left, was a maze of fruit
trees, about which nature, if it were not the hand of
man, had had no thought except that they should be
all together there. The wild olive, the pomegranate,
the citron, the date, the mulberry, the peach, the apple,
and the walnut, formed a sort of spontaneous orchard.
Across the water groves of palm trees waved their long
and graceful branches in the morning breeze. The
stately and solemn ilex, marshalled into long avenues,
showed the way to substantial granges or luxurious
villas. The green turf or grass was spread out beneath, and here and there flocks and herds were
emerging out of the twilight and growing distinct
upon the eye. Elsewhere the ground rose up into
sudden eminences crowned with chestnut woods, or
with plantations of cedar and acacia, or wildernesses
of the cork tree, the turpentine, the carooba, the
white poplar, and the Phenician juniper, while overhead
ascended the clinging tendrils of the hop, and an underwood of myrtle clothed their stems and roots. A profusion of wild flowers carpeted the ground far and near.

Juba stood and gazed till the sun rose opposite to
him, envying, repining, hating, like Satan looking in
upon Paradise. The wild mountains, or the locust-
smitten tract would have better suited the tumult of
his mind. It would have been a relief to him to have
retreated from so fair a scene, and to have retraced
his steps, but he was not his own master, and was

hurried on. Sorely against his determined strong
resolve and will, crying out and protesting and
shuddering, the youth was forced along into the fulness of beauty and blessing with which he was so
little in tune. With rage and terror he recognized
that he had no part in his own movements, but was a
mere slave. In spite of himself he must go forward
and behold a peace and sweetness which witnessed
against him. He dashed down through the thick
grass, plunged into the water, and without rest or res-
pite began a second course of aimless toil and travail
through the day.

The savage dogs of the villages howled and fled from
him as he passed by; beasts of burden, on their way to
market, which he overtook or met, stood still, foamed
and trembled; the bright birds, the blue jay and
golden oriole, hid themselves under the leaves and
grass; the storks, a religious and domestic bird,
stopped their sharp clattering note from the high tree
or farmhouse turret, where they had placed their nests;
the very reptiles skulked away from his shadow, as if it
were poisonous. The boors who were at their labour
in the fields suspended it to look at one whom the
Furies were lashing and whirling on. Hour passed
after hour, the sun attained its zenith, and then de-
clined, but this dreadful compulsory race continued.
O what would he have given for one five minutes of
oblivion, of slumber, of relief from the burning thirst
which now consumed him! but the master within him
ruled his muscles and his joints, and the intense pain
of weariness had no concomitant of prostration of
strength. Suddenly he began to laugh hideously; and

he went forward dancing and singing loud, and playing antics. He entered a hovel, made faces at the children, till one of them fell into convulsions, and he ran away with another; and, when some country people pursued him, he flung the child in their faces saying, "Take that," and said he was Pentheus, King of Thebes, of whom he had never heard, about to solemnize the orgies of Bacchus, and he began to spout a chorus of Greek, a language he had never learnt or heard spoken.

Now it is evening again, and he has come up to a village grove, where the rustics were holding a feast in honour of Pan. The hideous brutal god, with yawning mouth, horned head, and goat's feet, was placed in a rude shed, and a slaughtered lamb, decked with flowers, lay at his feet. The peasants were frisking before him, boys and women, when they were startled by the sight of a gaunt, wild, mysterious figure, which began to dance too. He flung and capered about with such vigour that they ceased their sport to look on, half with awe and half as a diversion. Suddenly he began to groan and to shriek, as if contending with himself, and willing and not willing some new act; and the struggle ended in his falling on his hands and knees, and crawling like a quadruped towards the idol. When he got near, his attitude was still more servile; still groaning and shuddering, he laid himself flat on the ground, and wriggled to the idol as a worm, and lapped up with his tongue the mingled blood and dust which lay about the sacrifice. And then again, as if nature had successfully asserted her own dignity, he jumped up high in the air, and, falling on the god, broke him to pieces, and scampered away out of pursuit, before the lookers-on recovered from the surprise.

Another restless, fearful night amid the open country; . . . but it seemed as if the worst had passed, and, though still under the heavy chastisement of his pride, there was more in Juba of human action and of effectual will. The day broke and he found himself on the road to Sicca. The beautiful outline of the city was right before him. He passed his brother's cottage and garden; it was a wreck. The trees torn up, the fences broken down, and the room pillaged of the little that could be found there. He went on to the city, crying out Agellius; the gate was open, and he entered. He went on to the Forum; he crossed to the house of Jucundus; few people as yet were stirring in the place. He looked up at the wall. Suddenly, by the help of projections and other irregularities of the brick-work, he mounted up upon the flat roof, and dropped down, along the tiles, through the *impluvium* into the middle of the house. He went softly into Agellius's closet, where he was asleep, he roused him with the name of Callista, threw his tunic upon him, which was by his side, put his boots into his hands, and silently beckoned him to follow him. When he hesitated, he still whispered to him Callista, and at length seized him and led him on. He unbarred the street door, and with a movement of his arm, more like a blow than a farewell, thrust him into the street. Then he barred again the door upon him, and lay down himself upon the bed which Agellius had left. His good angel, we may suppose, had gained a point in his favour, for he lay quiet and fell into a heavy sleep.—*Callista*, ed. 1856, chap. 23 (1855).

O WISDOM of the world ! and strength of the world !
what are you when matched beside the foolishness
and the weakness of the Christian ?   You are great in
resources, manifold in methods, hopeful in prospects ;
but one thing you have not,—and that is peace.   You
are always tumultuous, restless, apprehensive.   You
have nothing you can rely upon.   You have no rock
under your feet.   But the humblest, feeblest Christian
has that which is impossible to you.   Callista had
once felt the misery of maladies akin to yours.   She
had passed through doubt, anxiety, perplexity, despon-
dency, passion ; but now she was in peace.   Now she
feared the torture or the flame as little as the breeze
which arose at nightfall, or the busy chatter of the
grasshoppers at the noonday.   Nay, rather, she did
not think of torture and death at all, but was possessed by a peace which bore her up, as if bodily, on
its mighty wings.   For hours she remained on her
knees, after Cæcilius left her : then she lay down on
her rushes and slept her last mortal sleep.

She slept sound ; she dreamed.   She thought she
was no longer in Africa, but in her own Greece, more
sunny and bright than before ; but the inhabitants
were gone.   Its majestic mountains, its rich plains, its
expanse of waters, all silent : no one to converse with,

no one to sympathize with. And, as she wandered on and wondered, suddenly its face changed, and its colours were illuminated tenfold by a heavenly glory, and each hue upon the scene was of a beauty she had never known, and seemed strangely to affect all her senses at once, being fragrance and music, as well as light. And there came out of the grottos, and glens, and woods, and out of the seas, myriads of bright images, whose forms she could not discern; and these came all around her, and became a sort of scene or landscape, which she could not have described in words, as if it were a world of spirits, not of matter. And as she gazed, she thought she saw before her a well-known face, only glorified. She, who had been a slave, now was arrayed more brilliantly than an oriental queen; and she looked at Callista with a smile so sweet, that Callista felt she could but dance to it.

And as she looked more earnestly, doubting whether she should begin or not, the face changed, and now was more marvellous still. It had an innocence in its look, and also a tenderness, which bespoke both Maid and Mother, and so transported Callista, that she must needs advance towards her, out of love and reverence. And the Lady seemed to make signs of encouragement: so she began a solemn measure, unlike all dances of earth, with hands and feet, serenely moving on towards what she heard some of them call a great action and a glorious consummation, though she did not know what they meant. At length she was fain to sing as well as dance; and her words were, " In the Name of the Father, and of the Son, and of the Holy

Ghost;" on which another said, "A good beginning
of the sacrifice." And when she had come close to
this gracious figure, there was a fresh change. The
face, the features were the same; but the light of Divinity now seemed to beam through them, and the
hair parted, and hung down long on each side of the
forehead; and there was a crown of another fashion
from the Lady's round about it, made of what looked
like thorns. And the palms of the hands were spread
out as if towards her, and there were marks of wounds
in them. And the vestment had fallen, and there was
a deep opening in the side. And as she stood en-
tranced before Him, and motionless, she felt a consciousness that her own palms were pierced like His,
and her feet also. And she looked round, and saw
the likeness of His face and of His wounds upon all
that company. And now they were suddenly moving
on, and bearing something, or some one, heaven-
wards; and they too began to sing, and their words
seemed to be, "Rejoice with Me, for I have found My
sheep," ever repeated. They went up through an
avenue or long grotto, with torches of diamonds, and
amethysts, and sapphires, which lit up its spars and
made them sparkle. And she tried to look, but could
not discover what they were carrying, till she heard
a very piercing cry, which awoke her.—*Callista*, ed.
1856, chap. xxxi. (1855).

NOTES.

1.—*Site of a University*. This selection is taken from the third chapter of the *Rise and Progress of Universities*, a series of papers originally published in Dublin in 1854, under the title *Office and Work of Universities*, to supplement Newman's more formal and elaborate *Discourses on University Teaching* (1852). Throughout these papers, Newman's manner and method are characteristic. He makes no parade of logical divisions or of abstract definitions; he is unpretentious, almost colloquial in style; he has, as he says of himself in the *Apologia*, "a lounging, free-and-easy way of carrying things on." Yet despite this ease, unpretentiousness, lack of formality, and apparent aimlessness, he guides the reader unerringly to a perfect intellectual possession of the subject under discussion. He takes up in a pleasantly familiar tone one after another of the great Universities and describes the characteristically good points in each; and in this seemingly unsystematic fashion he gives the reader, without wearying him, a thorough comprehension of the aims and the ideal conditions of University life. Later chapters are *Free Trade in Knowledge—the Sophists: Discipline,—Macedonian and Roman Schools: Supply and Demand —the Schoolmen: Professors and Tutors.*

4 : 8.—*A confined triangle*. The passage that follows is a remarkable bit of descriptive writing. The reader should note the skilful definition of the outlines of the scene, the constant use of sensations other than those of sight, the sensitive registration of motions of various kinds, the continuous emphasis on details that a painter would be powerless to reproduce, and finally the breadth of handling by means of which details are made constantly subordinate to total effect. All these points in Newman's method contribute to the life, vivacity, symmetry, and imaginative glow of the

description.   The easy air of mastery is also characteristic of Newman ; the tone never grows artificial and the note is never forced.
The tone is almost colloquial throughout, and at the very climax
of the description Newman does not hesitate to make his "agent
of a London Company" "bless his stars."

11 : 1.— *To-day I have confined myself.*   This is an extract from
the seventh of the nine *Discourses on University Teaching* that
Newman delivered in 1852 to the Catholics of Dublin.   Newman's
task was two-fold : first, to win over prelates and gentry to thorough sympathy with the plan for the higher education of Catholics ; secondly, to organize the new institution and to determine
its aims and policy.   He remained Rector of the University down
to 1858, when he returned to England, taking up his residence at
Birmingham, where the rest of his life was spent.   It should be
borne in mind, in reading these extracts, that one important part of
Newman's task was to prove to rather narrowly religious ecclesiastics the need of general culture and of a knowledge of the world.
Accordingly, while a large part of the *Discourses* is devoted to
demonstrating the incompleteness of any curriculum that refuses
to recognize theology as a science and to include theological truth
as a legitimate subject of study, yet Newman never forgets that
he is also championing liberal knowledge both against the prejudice of bigots and against the utilitarian objections of the practical man.   These discourses illustrate strikingly the range of
Newman's sympathies.   He appreciates the good in all modes of
life and types of character, while never for a moment falling into
the dilettante's fallacy that all lives or all characters are equally
good.

14 : 1.— *Pride under such training.*— Newman's insight into
the springs of human action, his skill in tracing out the interplay
of motives, his intuitive knowledge of the structure and working
of individual minds and hearts were important sources of his power
over men.   His works are full of evidences of this subtle comprehension of character.   Sometimes he analyzes a mood, explaining
minutely its origin and its reaction in conduct and life.   See, for example, his account of *detachment* in chap. xi. of the *Rise and Progress of Universities.*   Sometimes, as in the text, he follows out a
single quality in all its ramifications.   Sometimes he develops a

type of character in all its details of feeling and thought and action. See, for example, in the present extract the description of the gentleman and in the preceding extract the description of the cultivated man of the world. In all these cases Newman's complete mastery of the details of moral life is conspicuous, and illustrates both the <u>intensity of his imaginative sympathy with souls and the keenness of his analysis.</u>

19.—*Knowledge. . . . Learning.* In the first four of his Discourses on *University Teaching* Newman argues for the inclusion of theology in a university curriculum. Science, he maintains, is an organic whole made up of many complementary parts, of which parts theology is the most important. A university, then, that excludes theology from its list of studies offers its students not simply incomplete knowledge, but mutilated knowledge; the truth that is left after theology is taken away is weakened and vitiated throughout, and cannot perfectly fulfil its functions, because it lacks the aid of the missing parts. In his plea for theology Newman is contending against the ideal of education in accordance with which London University had been founded in 1825-8. Cf. *Notes* 88 : 5. A suggestive argument for this unecclesiastical ideal may be found in the *Edinburgh Review* of Feb., 1826. Regarded still more comprehensively, Newman's plea for theology is meant to counteract <u>anti-dogmatic theories of religion which teach that religion is merely a matter of feeling, that nothing certain can be known about God or the future life</u>, and that one set of ideas about the unseen world is as good as another, provided each be held sincerely and conduce on the whole to morality. Finally, Newman's plea for theology was sure to win for him the sympathy and confidence of even the most conservative of the Catholic ecclesiastics whom he was addressing, and to conciliate their favor for the new university. To plead for theology, then, was the first part of Newman's task. The second part was to convince his hearers, many of whom were almost fanatical in their adherence to the Roman Catholic Church and in their intense distrust of the tendencies of modern science, that a liberal education is essential to fit men for the best kind of life. To this end he devotes *Discourses V.-VIII.* The fifth *Discourse* demonstrates that knowledge is its own end, and is to be pursued, not because of its practical value in the mechanical arts, or because of its ameliorating effect on character, but simply and solely because of the infinite desirableness for every individual of being able to comprehend "the relative disposition of things," and "to map out the universe." This disinterested knowledge of things in their causes is shown to be the end of Liberal Education. Such Liberal Knowledge is then discriminated from Useful Knowledge, which aims to minimize bodily discomforts and to supply temporal wants. At this point the passage on Bacon occurs, which is quoted, p. 41. Then follows *Discourse VI.*, most of which is given in the present *Selection*. The extracts, pp. 11, 14, and 44, are from these same *Discourses*, and are parts of a continuous plea for the value of a liberal education in forming a man for his proper place in the world.

28 : 19.—*The world is all before it.* An adaptation of the fourth line from the end of the *Paradise Lost* :

> The world was all before them, where to choose
> Their place of rest, and Providence their guide."

28 : 30.—*The judgment-stricken king.* See the *Bacchæ* of Euripides, 918-9. Pentheus, King of Thebes, who has defied Dionysus, and has been smitten with madness, speaks :

> Καὶ μὴν ὁρᾶν μοι δύο μὲν ἡλίους δοκῶ,
> δισσὰς δὲ Θήβας καὶ πόλισμ' ἑπτάστομον.

'Lo, I seem to see two suns and a double Thebes as well, the city of seven gates.'

34 : 28.—Τετράγωνος. See Aristotle, *Eth. N.*, I., x., 11 : ἀεὶ γὰρ ἢ μάλιστα πάντων πράξει καὶ θεωρήσει τὰ κατ' ἀρετήν, καὶ τὰς τύχας οἴσει κάλλιστα καὶ πάντη πάντως ἐμμελῶς ὅ γ' ὡς ἀληθῶς ἀγαθὸς καὶ τετράγωνος ἄνευ ψόγου. 'For most persistently and strenuously of all men will he pursue in deed and thought the things of virtue, and endure the chances of life most nobly and most fittingly,— that man, I mean, who is truly good and four-square without flaw.'

Aristotle and his followers are called the Peripatetics, because the master is supposed to have lectured to his pupils while walking about in the courts of the Lyceum.

34 : 28.—*Nil admirari.* See Zeller's account of the ethics of the Stoics, in Zeller's *Stoics, Epicureans*, etc., Reichel's translation, pp. 235-7 : " The right relation, therefore, towards emotions—indeed, the only one morally tenable—is an attitude of absolute hostility. The wise man must be emotionless." Cf. Horace, *Epistles* I. 6 :

> " Nil admirari prope res est una, Numici,
>   Solaque, quæ possit facere et servare beatum."

'To shun emotion is the sole way, Numicius, to win to happiness and to retain it.'

For the name Stoic see *Notes* 90 : 3.

34 : 30.—*Felix qui potuit.* From Virgil's *Georgics*, II., 490-2.

' Happy is he who has come to know the sequences of things, and is thus above all fear, master of the dread march of fate, and careless of the wild noise of greedy Acheron.'

41: 11.—*True to his friend.* The allusion is to Bacon's faithlessness to his early patron, the Earl of Essex. At the Queen's request Bacon drew up the charges against Essex when he was put on trial for treason, and conducted the case against him with such vigor as to secure his conviction and execution. The precise degree of blame attaching to Bacon's conduct is still debated.

41 : 11.—*Faithful in his trust.* Bacon was tried and condemned for bribery and forced to resign his post as Lord Chancellor in 1621.

41 : 18.—*Idols of the den.* See Bacon's *Novum Organum : Works*, Ed. Spedding, Boston, 1868, VIII., 76-8. " There are four classes of Idols which beset men's minds. To these for distinction's sake I have assigned names,—calling the first class, *Idols of the Tribe ;* the second, *Idols of the Cave ;* the third, *Idols of the Market Place ;* the fourth, *Idols of the Theatre.*" . . .

" The Idols of the Tribe have their foundation in human nature itself, and in the tribe or race of men. . . . The human understanding is like a false mirror, which, receiving rays irregularly, distorts and discolours the nature of things by mingling its own nature with it." . . .

"The Idols of the Cave are the idols of the individual man. For every one . . . . has a cave or den of his own, which refracts and discolours the light of nature.". . .

" There are also Idols formed by the intercourse and association of men with each other, which I call Idols of the Market-place, on account of the commerce and consort of men there."

"Lastly, there are Idols which have immigrated into men's minds from the various dogmas of philosophies, and also from wrong laws of demonstration. These I call Idols of the Theatre; because in my judgment all the received systems are but so many stage-plays, representing worlds of their own creation after an unreal and scenic fashion."

41 : 23.—*I agree with Lord Macaulay.* See Macaulay's essay on *Lord Bacon,* originally published in the *Edinburgh Review* for July, 1837. "The philosophy which [Bacon] taught was essentially new. It differed from that of the celebrated ancient teachers, not merely in method, but also in object. Its object was the good of mankind, in the sense in which the mass of mankind always have understood and always will understand the word good." . . . .
" What then was the end which Bacon proposed to himself? It was, to use his own emphatic expression, 'fruit.' It was the multiplying of human enjoyments and the mitigating of human sufferings. . . . Two words form the key of the Baconian doctrine, Utility and Progress." Macaulay's panegyric on the Philosophy of Utility is often urged in proof of his Philistinism. See Morison's *Life of Macaulay,* chap. iii., and Leslie Stephen's *Hours in a Library,* 3d series. With Macaulay's sneers at the "cant," the "sterile exuberance," the "unprofitableness" of Platonism and Aristotelianism, Newman could not have sympathized; nor would Macaulay have agreed with what Newman says of the "low aim" and the "intellectual narrowness" of the Baconian school of thought.

44 : 1.—*Here, then . . . . you are involved.* This extract, and the following one on St. Philip Neri, come at the very end of the last, or ninth, of the *Discourses on University Teaching.* In *Discourses V.–VIII.* Newman has vindicated the rights of Liberal Education, and has shown that knowledge is worth pursuing for its own sake, apart from its effects upon character or from its

practical results. Now, in closing, he devotes a Discourse to de-
fining the duties of the Church toward knowledge. He divides
all secular knowledge into Science or the Book of Nature, and
Literature or the Book of Man, and considers the duties of the
Church toward each. In relation to Science the Church must be
on the watch to hold in check "the wild living intellect of man."
The Church must defend theology against men of Science, who are
ever ready to judge of things divine by human standards and to
exalt observation and experiment into the sole tests of truth. The
Church must make good for Theology a place among the Sciences;
it must secure to Theology its own methods of study and criteria of
truth, and, above all, must prevent the insidious encroachments of
private judgment and rationalism upon the domain of revelation.
The duty of the Church toward the second division of knowledge,
Literature, is defined in the text.

45 : 17.—*Quicquid agunt.* See Juvenal, *Satires,* I., 85-6 :

> " Quidquid agunt homines, votum, timor, ira, voluptas,
> Gaudia, discursus, nostri est farrago libelli."

> " What ever since that Golden Age was done,
> What human kind desires, and what they shun,
> Rage, passions, pleasures, impotence of will,
> Shall this satirical collection fill."
>
> *Dryden.*

46 : 5.—*Jabel and Tubalcain.* See Gen. iv. 20-2. Jabal,—
Vulgate, Jabel,—"was the father of such as dwell in tents, and of
such as have cattle." Tubal-cain was "an instructor of every
artificer in brass and iron."

46 : 9.—*Beseleel.* See Exodus xxxi., 2. Bezaleel,—Vulgate,
Beseleel,—was one of the makers of the tabernacle.

51 : 1.—*Such at least is the lesson.* The reference is to the last
paragraph of the preceding Selection.

51 : 5.—*St. Philip Neri* (1515-1595). He spent most of his
life at Rome. He was the founder of the Brotherhood of the Oratory. Despite his far-reaching influence over men he took no
part in public affairs. Almost his sole interference in such matters is said to have been on the occasion of Pope Clement's refusal to be reconciled with Henry IV. of France on the latter's

abjuration of Calvinism. It was owing to Neri's influence on the Pope through the Pope's confessor that Clement VIII. was led to receive Henry once more into the Church. See Bacci's *Life of St. Philip Neri*, translated by F. W. Faber, London, 1847, and Faber's *Spirit and Genius of St. Philip Neri*, London, 1850. St. Philip was Newman's ideal. Soon after joining the Catholic Church Newman was received into the Brotherhood of the Oratory, and the last thirty-two years of his life (1858–90) were spent in the Edgbaston Oratory, Birmingham.

55 : 1.—*The author of the Christian Year.* John Keble (1792–1866) took double first-class honors at Oxford in 1811, was at once elected fellow of Oriel College, and remained at Oxford, filling various positions, till 1823. In this year, on the death of his mother, he left Oxford to make his home with his father, at Fairford, Gloucestershire, where he remained, refusing offers of promotion in the Church, until his father's death in 1835. In this same year he was married, and in 1836 he was made vicar of Hursley in Hampshire, where he spent the rest of his life fulfilling the duties of the priest of a country parish. His *Christian Year* was published anonymously in 1827. By 1867 it had passed through 109 editions, each numbering 3,000 or 5,000 copies. In 1846 was published his second important book of verse, *Lyra Innocentium ;* it is from Newman's review of this volume that the extract in the text is taken. Keble wrote seven of the *Tracts for the Times*, edited Hooker's *Works*, and published a volume of lectures on poetry, which he had delivered during his tenure of the Professorship of Poetry at Oxford, 1831–41.

55 : 3.—*Ken and Herbert.* Ken (1637–1711) was Bishop of Bath and Wells from 1685 to 1691. He was fearless towards princes,—witness his treatment of William II. of Holland, Charles II. and James II. of England,—and utterly self-forgetful in his devotion to the needs of his people. " His Morning and Evening Hymns," Macaulay has said, " are still repeated daily in thousands of dwellings." The Tractarians held him in high reverence. Tract lxxv. contained a special service in his memory drawn up by Newman, and two of Isaac Williams's poems were devoted to his honor. George Herbert (1593–1633) was rector of Bemerton, near Salisbury, from 1629 to 1633, and author of the *Temple* (1633).

His best-known poem begins "Sweet day, so cool, so calm, so bright." Other familiar poems are "I made a posie while the day ran by," and " Who is the honest man ?" The latter may have suggested Wordsworth's " Who is the happy warrior ? "

56 : 27.—*Socinianism.* Lælius Socinus and Faustus Socinus, uncle and nephew, were Italians, who during the latter part of the sixteenth century did much to spread anti-Trinitarian doctrines. Socinianism stands in the text for a rationalizing religion, a religion devoid of mystery and appealing solely to the intellect.

57 : 20—*Miraturque novas frondes et non sua poma.* 'The tree marvels at strange foliage and fruit not its own.' The quotation is from Virgil's *Georgics*, II., 81, where the poet is describing the process of grafting.

61 : 14.—*He hated . . . . heresy.* " He delighted to see his little nephew under his teaching snapping at all the Roundheads, and kissing all the Cavaliers." (Tulloch's *Movements of Religious Thought*, Lecture iii.) " A member of a family with which he had been intimate had adopted Liberal opinions in theology. . . . . He came to call one day when the erring brother happened to be at home and learning that he was in the house, he refused to enter, and remained sitting in the porch." Froude's *Short Studies*, IV., 176.

62 : 8.—*The first Whig.* " The first Whig was the Devil." *Boswell's Johnson*, ed. G. B. Hill, III., 326.

62 : 18.—*Doctrines of 1776.* Neither Keble nor Newman had the faith in human nature that underlies modern democratic theories. See the famous passage in the *Apologia*, describing fallen humanity : " I look out of myself into the world of men, and there I see a sight which fills me with unspeakable distress. . . . . The sight of the world is nothing else than the prophet's scroll, full of 'lamentations, and mourning, and woe.' " *Selections*, p. 160.

64 : 20.—*The new fashion.* This " new fashion " is, of course, the Tractarian mode of thought. The Selection suggests the view that worldly-wise Dons took of the Tractarian agitation. *Loss and Gain : The Story of a Convert*, was published anonymously in 1848. Newman's name was placed on the title-page in 1874. The book gives a remarkably sympathetic and suggestive picture of Oxford life during the years when the ideas of the Tractarians were finding lodgment and fructifying in the best minds.

67 : 6.—*In the Edinburgh.* The criticisms of the *Edinburgh Review* upon Oxford were for a time very searching and severe. They were probably in part provoked by a clever skit, called *Advice to a Young Reviewer, with a Specimen of the Art,* which had been published at Oxford in 1807 by Copleston, University Professor of Poetry. In the *Edinburgh* for Jan., 1808, Lord Brougham in a review of La Place made the charge that Oxford undergraduates had no opportunity of going " beyond the mere elements of geometry " in their study of mathematics. In the number for July, 1809, Payne Knight assailed the recent Oxford edition of Strabo, ridiculed its Latinity and made it the pretext of a severe attack on the laziness and amateurishness of Oxford scholarship and on the limitations of its curriculum. In the October number for 1809, Sydney Smith, in the course of a favorable notice of Edgeworth's *Professional Education,* blamed the Oxford training for its disregard of the needs of practical life, and its blindly reverential insistence on a dry-as-dust classical scholarship. In 1810, these articles provoked from the pen of Dr. Copleston an elaborate defence of Oxford methods, published under the title, *Replies to the Calumnies of the Edinburgh Review against Oxford.* In April, 1810, Playfair, Sydney Smith, and Payne Knight united in a satirical review of Dr. Copleston's *Replies.* The reviewers admitted that they had hardly taken into account the Oxford Reforms of 1802, but contended that nevertheless their charges of neglect of the sciences and of amateurishness in scholarship were just.

Like most of the *Edinburgh's* attacks on " things as they were," the Oxford articles made at the time a great stir ; and although after 1821 the *Edinburgh* took a much friendlier tone toward the University, the memory of the earlier articles still rankled in the breasts of the dons. It should be noted that Dr. Copleston was for many years (1814–1826) the Provost of Newman's old college, Oriel. Cf. Newman's eloquent tribute to him in the *Idea of a University,* ed. 1891, pp. 154–8. It was a favourite charge that attacks on Oxford came from the pens of disappointed aspirants for honors. In his *Introduction*, for example, Copleston asserts that most of the abuse of Oxford proceeds from "that hireling tribe of turncoats, who, disappointed of honours or rewards here adequate to their own fancied merits, have carried over to the enemy, as the most acceptable passport, some local information, and have courted the favor of their new employers, by mean detraction aud extravagant abuse of their former friends." Similarly, in his Autobiographical Memoir for 1821, Newman speaks of certain strictures on Oxford in the July number of the *Edinburgh*, and notes the fact that the writer of the article was a few months before the unsuccessful candidate for an Oriel fellowship. *Letters and Correspondence*, I., 65. For Newman's account of the earlier attacks of the *Edinburgh* on Oxford and of Copleston's reply, see his *Idea of a University*, ed. 1891, pp. 153-8.

68 : 1.—*Mr. Kingsley begins.* This extract is taken from the concluding part of *Mr. Kingsley and Dr. Newman : a Correspondence*, with which the original editions of the *Apologia* opened. In subsequent editions the correspondence was omitted.

The words of Kingsley that led to the controversy were as follows :—" Truth for its own sake had never been a virtue with the Roman clergy. Father Newman informs us that it need not be, and on the whole ought not to be ; that cunning is the weapon which Heaven has given to the saints wherewith to withstand the brute male force of the wicked world which marries and is given in marriage. Whether his notion be doctrinally correct or not, it is at least historically so." This passage occurred in an unsigned review of Froude's *History of England* in *Macmillan's Magazine* for January, 1864. Newman at once wrote to the editor, protesting against the passage. Kingsley acknowledged the authorship of the article and referred in justification of his charge to a sermon on *Wisdom and Innocence*, which Newman had preached at Oxford, in 1843. After an exchange of several letters, Kingsley finally consented to insert in *Macmillan's Magazine* for February, 1864, the following note :—

" To the Editor of *Macmillan's Magazine*.

Sir : In your last number I made certain allegations against the teaching of Dr. John Henry Newman, which I thought were justified by a sermon of his, entitled ' Wisdom and Innocence.'

(Sermon 20 of 'Sermons bearing on Subjects of the Day.') Dr. Newman has by letter expressed, in the strongest terms, his denial of the meaning which I have put upon his words. It only remains, therefore, for me to express my hearty regret at having so seriously mistaken him."

Newman, who was by no means content with this explanation, forthwith published the entire correspondence between Kingsley and himself, adding, as his sole comment, an ironical summary. By way of rejoinder, Kingsley published an excessively bitter pamphlet, *What then does Dr. Newman mean?* in which while nominally professing to believe in Newman's truthfulness, he substantially charges him with systematic duplicity, with misrepresentation and falsehood. It was in answer to this pamphlet that the *Apologia* was written; the line of thought that led to its composition, is traced in the extract, pp. 79–82. Newman's ironical summary of his correspondence with Kingsley is given in the *Selections*, p. 68.

70 : 31.—*Alfonso da Liguori* (1696–1787). He was a famous Roman Catholic casuist, author of many works for the guidance both of laity and of clergy in delicate questions of conscience. A full account of his teachings may be found in the *Encyclopædia Britannica*, art. Liguori.

75 : 5.—*For twenty years and more.* In a letter of 1864, Newman speaks of having been subject to lying attacks ever since 1833, the year when the Tractarian movement began. In the present passage the date that he has in mind is probably that of the publication of Tract xc., *i.e.*, 1841. His interpretation of the thirty-nine articles was vehemently assailed as conscious prevarication, and wilful misconstruction.

76 : 16.—*Stonyhurst or Oscott.* Stonyhurst, in Lancashire, is a boy's college, "the Catholic Eton;" it celebrated its centenary in July, 1894. Near Oscott, a village four miles from Birmingham, is St. Mary's Roman Catholic College.

83 : 4. *Some such Apostasy.* Cf. Newman's declarations in the first chapter of the *Apologia :* "The vital question was, how were we to keep the Church from being liberalized?" . . . . "It was the success of the Liberal cause that fretted me inwardly." In his notes at the end of the *Apologia*, Newman enumerates

eighteen propositions characteristic of Liberal theology, to all of
which he objects. Among them are the following:

" No religious tenet is important unless reason shows it to be
so."

" No one can believe what he does not understand."

" No theological doctrine is anything more than an opinion
which happens to be held by bodies of men."

" There is a right of Private Judgment."

" It is lawful to rise in arms against legitimate princes."

" The people are the legitimate source of power."

" Virtue is the child of knowledge and Vice of ignorance."

84 : 11.—*To deprive the Bible of its one meaning.* It is the
Protestant doctrine of the right of private judgment in the interpretation of Scripture that Newman here attacks.

84 : 18.—*Expressed by written words.* Newman contends here
against the anti-dogmatic principle. Cf. his definition of his position in 1833. " First was the principle of dogma; my battle was
with liberalism; by liberalism I mean the anti-dogmatic principle
and its developments. . . . . From the age of fifteen, dogma has
been the fundamental principle of my religion: I know no other
religion; I cannot enter into the idea of any other sort of religion;
religion, as a mere sentiment, is to me a dream and a mockery."
Apologia, ed. 1890, p. 49.

84 : 27.—*Antichrist.* See *Notes,* **131 : 12.**

85 : 2.—*Satan.* Newman's belief in the world of evil spirits
was intense and absolute. See a letter of Elizabeth Mozley's
quoted in Newman's *Letters and Correspondence*, I., 335: " One
sees that Dr. Newman's great power . . . . is a certain vivid
realization of the unseen. . . . . 'How can people say what
is, or is not, natural to evil spirits? What is a grotesque manifestation to us may not be so to them. What do we know
about an evil spirit?' The words were nothing, but there was an
intensity of realization in his face as he said them, of a reality
and of his ignorance about it, that was a key to me as to the
source of his influence over others." Cf. *Notes,* **178.**

86 : 1.—*Conservative Statesman.* The letters on the *Tamworth
Reading-room* appeared in the *Times* in February, 1841, by way
of comment on a speech that Sir Robert Peel had delivered upon

14

the establishment of a Library and Reading-room in the town of Tamworth. In their treatment of knowledge and their ideas about education these letters contrast strikingly with Newman's *Discourses on University Teaching.* They illustrate his intense distrust of secular knowledge and of intellectual excellence, pursued as ends in themselves, and without regard to religious culture. They are also pervaded by an anti-democratic manner of thought and feeling that, despite Newman's universal courtesy and complete unpretentiousness both of demeanor and of temper, is nevertheless distinctive of his whole character. He only half veils his contempt for the smattering of knowledge that common people can derive from journals and reading-rooms and Libraries of Useful Knowledge. He is thoroughly academic in his sympathies and prejudices; he is a typical ecclesiastic in his feeling that the multitude must be treated with tender condescension and friendly solicitude, but never for a moment as equals or as essentially and individually deserving.

87 : 27.—*Mr. Bentham* (1748–1832). He was the founder of the Utilitarian school in morals, politics, and philosophy.

88 : 5.—*Lord Brougham* (1778–1868). He was one of the prime movers in the cause of popular education; in 1825 he formed the famous Society for the Diffusion of Useful Knowledge. In 1828, largely through his instrumentality, London University, now University College, was opened for instruction; the new institution was totally independent of the Church, was anti-theological, if not anti-religious, was meant to give freer and better opportunities for the study of the sciences than the old universities offered, and has always remained identified with Free Thought and Positivism. Brougham's *Discourse* on his inauguration as Lord Rector of Glasgow University (1825) will be found in his *Speeches*, Vol. III., ed. 1838, p. 69, together with various other important addresses on popular education. In the preceding letter Newman has commented very severely on this Inaugural.

88 : 8.—*Not a spark of poetry.* In his computation of pleasures and pains with a view to deciding the relative values of causes of action, Bentham laid it down as a rule that, in quality, "push-pin was worth as much as poetry."

88 : 26.—*Signifying nothing.*

" It is a tale
Told by an idiot, full of sound and fury,
Signifying nothing." —*Macbeth*, Act V., Sc. 5.

90 : 3.—*Porch.* The Stoic philosophers were called philosophers of the Porch, because Zeno, founder of the school, taught in a porch (Geek στοά). The Stoics taught that virtue consisted in recognizing the limitations that the law of nature imposes on the individual, and in regulating the appetites and desires in accordance with the dictates of reason.—Cf. *Notes*, **34** : 28.

90 : 5.—*O philosophia.* Newman misquotes. See Cicero, *Tuscul. Quæst.*, bk. v., 2: "O vitæ philosophia dux! O virtutis indagatrix, expultrixque vitiorum!" 'O philosophy, guide of life! Searcher out of virtue and scourge of vice!'

90 : 16.—*White Ladies or Undines.* In the mythology of the Scottish Highlands White Ladies were mysterious maidens who were held captive in lonely regions under some spell, and who appeared to solitary wayfarers or shepherds and offered them gifts of flowers or corn in return for assistance. In the system of Paracelsus, an Undine was a water-sprite. Newman's immediate allusion is probably to de la Motte Fouqué's well-known story, *Undine,* in which a water-sprite marries the Knight Sir Huldbrand and so receives a human soul. Newman's question, then, is whether rational men are to be dealt with, as are these semi-human creatures, purely by external expedients; whether reasonable beings can be transformed in character, simply by a change of surroundings.

90 : 19.—*When Cicero was outwitted.* Cicero had sided with Pompey against Cæsar, and on the defeat of Pompey at Pharsalia in 48 B. C. was forced out of public life. He took refuge in study and composition. In a letter to Varro in 46 B. C. he declares, " As soon as I was back in Rome, I had a reconciliation with my old friends, my books." *Ad. Fam.*, IX., i. In 45 B. C. he composed his *Academica*, dealing wholly with philosophical questions and discussing incidentally many of Plato's doctrines. Cf. Newman's *Hist. Sketches,* I., 285 : [Cicero] " then published the *De claris Oratoribus* and *Orator ;* and a year later, when he was sixty-three, his *Academicæ Quæstiones,* in the retirement from public business to which he was driven by the dictatorship of Cæsar."

90 : 21.—*A treatise on consolation.* Cicero's daughter Tullia died in 45 B. C., and his treatise *De Consolatione seu de Luctu Minuendo* was written soon afterwards.

90 : 22.—*That Lydian City.* " In the days of Atys the son of Manes, there was great scarcity through the whole land of Lydia. For some time the Lydians bore the affliction patiently, but finding that it did not pass away, they set to work to devise remedies for the evil. Various expedients were discovered by various persons; dice, and huckle-bones, and ball, and all such games were invented, except tables, the invention of which they do not claim as theirs. The plan adopted against the famine was to engage in games one day so entirely as not to feel any craving for food, and the next day to eat and abstain from games."—*Herodotus*, I., 94. (Rawlinson's translation.)

91 : 11.—*French Tyrant.* Newman has in mind Scott's account of Louis the Eleventh's iron cages for prisoners: " At this formidable castle [Loches] were also those dreadful places of confinement called *cages*, in which the wretched prisoner could neither stand upright, nor stretch himself at length, an invention, it is said, of the Cardinal Balue."—*Quentin Durward* I., chap. xv. In point of fact these cages were eight feet long and about seven feet high. Philippe de Comines was confined in one of them for eight months; Balue himself, their supposed inventor, was enclosed in a cage for fourteen years. See Comines, *Memoirs*, bk. vi., chap. xii.

92 : 3.—*Naturam expellas.* See *Horace, Epistles*, I., x , 24–5 :

> " Naturam expellas furcâ, tamen usque recurret,
> Et mala perrumpet furtim fastidia victrix."

' Though you drive nature out with a pitchfork yet will she always make her way back and stealthily destroy your mischievous squeamishness and subdue you to her will.'

92 : 30.—*Mr. Bentham . . . verse-making.* Cf. *Notes*, **88** : 8.

92 : 31.—*Mr. Dugald Stewart.* Stewart's attack on the pretensions of the Aristotelian logic is to be found in his *Elements of the Human Mind*, Part II., chap. iii. A sentence at the opening of section iii. sums up his position: "The general result of the foregoing reflections is, That neither the means employed by the school logic for the assistance of the *discursive faculty*,

nor the accomplishment of that end, were it really attained,
are of much consequence in promoting the enlargement of
the mind, or in guarding it against the influence of erroneous
opinions."

93 : 5.—*Knowledge Society.* In 1825 was formed the "Society
for Promoting the Diffusion of Useful Knowledge;" among the
foremost of the original members were Brougham, Lord John
Russell, and Dr. Lushington. The main object of the society
was the cheap publication of good literature. Elementary treatises on the sciences were written to order and widely dissemi-
nated. One of the most famous and successful ventures of the
Society was the *Penny Magazine*, of which 200,000 copies were
sold per week. See Martineau's *History of the Peace*, bk. iii.,
chap. xi. Cf. Peacock's *Crotchet Castle*, chap. xvii., where Dr.
Folliott sneers at "the march of mind" and at the "learned
friend," who writes penny tracts on chemistry; the "learned
friend" was Lord Brougham.

93 : 5.—*Gower Street College.* See *Notes,* **88 : 5.**

94 : 7.—*Arcesilas.* Arcesilaus or Arcesilas (315-241 B. C.) was
the head of the New Academy; it was under him that Platonism
first became radically sceptical. His doubts were "directed not
only to knowledge derived from the senses, but to rational knowledge as well." (Zeller's *Stoics, Epicureans, and Sceptics*, Reichel's
translation, p. 501.) With Berkeley, on the other hand, the same
analysis that leads to idealism leads to belief in God as an Infinite
Spirit, the supporter and regulator of ideas. In Arcesilaus, then,
idealism is the occasion of scepticism; in Berkeley it is made the
basis of religious faith. Cf. Newman's article on *Cicero*, in the
*Encyclopædia Metropolitana, Greek and Roman Philosophy and
Science*, (London, 1853), p. 218. "Mistaking the profession of
ignorance, which Socrates had used against the sophists on
physical questions, for an actual scepticism on points connected
with *morals*, [Arcesilas] fell into the opposite extreme, and
declared, first, that nothing could be known, and therefore,
secondly, that nothing should be advanced."

97 : 14.—*The lie of a country.* English usage favors *lie* rather
than *lay* in this sense. Cf. E. A. Freeman, *Venice*, p. 312, and

also " the lie and issue of the whole matter " in Newman's *Grammar of Assent*, ed. 1889, p. 76.

98 : 25.—*Scepticism.* This is one of the passages that seem to justify the charge of scepticism sometimes brought against Newman, the charge that he fled to the Church because he was afraid of his reason.   Later, in this same discussion he declares : " I believe that the study of nature, when religious feeling is away, leads the mind, rightly or wrongly, to acquiesce in the atheistic theory, as the simplest and easiest." *Selections*, p. 103.   Again, throughout the whole of Tract 85, there is observable a sceptical bias ; Newman is contending against rationalism and private judgment and in favor of submission to the authority of the Anglican Church, and his argument is that if a man begins choosing for himself among the doctrines of the Church, he will soon be choosing among the doctrines of the Bible ; that if he doubts about ecclesiastical miracles, he will soon be doubting about Balaam and Jonah.   In other words, if reason be allowed to question the authority of the Church, it will soon question and reject the authority of the Bible.   Hence, the only safe course is for the individual to submit unhesitatingly in matters of faith to the voice of the Church.   This argument seems, as Mr. Leslie Stephen has pointed out, essentially sceptical.   " A conclusion peremptorily asserted in this fashion is simply scepticism afraid of itself.   It orders us to believe because, if we don't believe, we shall doubt. That is virtually to admit that doubt is the legitimate and normal result of reasoning, which is, I take it, the essential characteristic of scepticism." *Nineteenth Century*, XXIX., 201.   In the same strain with that of this passage, Prof. Huxley has asserted that a " Primer of Infidelity " can be compiled from Cardinal Newman's works. *Nineteenth Century*, XXV., p. 948.   Elaborate defences of Newman against these charges of scepticism may be found in Wilfrid Ward's *Witnesses to the Unseen* (published originally in the *Nineteenth Century*, XXIX., reissued with other essays in 1893) and in R. H. Hutton's *Cardinal Newman*, chap. v.   Moreover, there are several crucial passages in Newman's works that the reader should have in mind, while trying to decide on the fundamental trend of Newman's thought.   Such passages are the following : " I know that even the unaided reason, when correctly exercised, leads to a belief in God, in the immortality of the soul, and in a future retribution." *Selections*, p. 163. " By Religion I mean the knowledge of God, of His Will, and of our duties towards Him; and there are three main channels which Nature furnishes for our acquiring this knowledge, viz., our own minds, the voice of mankind, and the course of the world, that is, of human life and human affairs. The informations which these three convey to us teach us the Being and Attributes of God, our responsibility to Him, our dependence on Him, our prospect of reward or punishment, to be somehow brought about, according as we obey or disobey Him. And the most authoritative of these three means of knowledge, as being specially our own, is our own mind." *Grammar of Assent*, ed. 1889, p. 389. " Truth certainly, as such, rests upon grounds intrinsically and objectively and abstractedly demonstrative, but it does not follow from this that the arguments producible in its favour are unanswerable and irresistible. . . . . The fact of revelation is in itself demonstrably true, but it is not therefore true irresistibly. . . . . I cannot convert men, when I ask for assumptions which they refuse to grant to me; and without assumptions no one can prove anything about anything." *Grammar of Assent*, p. 410.

98 : 28.—*Life is for action.* This is the sum and substance of Newman's plea against rationalism. Man is not mere intellect; life is not pure thought. Truth, though ultimately always demonstrable by logical processes, is constantly reached in practical life by short cuts, of which logic can give but a sorry account. The principle of life is faith or belief, the voluntary acceptance of ideas and propositions according as they commend themselves to the whole nature of the man who receives them. " Belief . . . being concerned with things concrete, not abstract, which variously excite the mind from their moral and imaginative properties, has for its objects, not only directly what is true, but inclusively what is beautiful, useful, admirable, heroic; objects which kindle devotion, rouse the passions, and attach the affections; and thus it leads the way to actions of every kind, to the establishment of principles, and the formation of character, and is thus again intimately connected with what is individual and personal." *Grammar of Assent*, ed. 1889, pp. 90-1. The real aim

or the *Grammar of Assent* is to define the faculty, viz., the Illative Sense, which makes these justly discriminating choices of
truth in concrete matters, to study its relation to other faculties
of the mind, to suggest the best discipline for it, to illustrate its
action in all departments of life, and to trace in detail the process
by which Newman's own Illative Sense leads him to accept the
truth of Christianity and Catholicism. The whole of this passage from the *Tamworth Reading-room* will be found quoted in
the *Grammar of Assent*, pp. 92–97.

101 : 24.—*Democritus and others.* The passage occurs in
Bacon's *De Augmentis*, bk. iii. chap. 4. See Lord Bacon's *Works*,
ed. Ellis and Spedding, 1858, IV., 363-4.

106 : 1.—*Now what is Theology?* This is part of Newman's
plea for giving Theology a place among the sciences. His
purpose in making this plea and its relation to the rest of the
argument in his *Discourses on University Teaching* have been explained, *Notes*, **19.** Cf. with this account of Theology that given
in the *Grammar of Assent*, pp. 147–8.

117 : 1.—*Music . . . has an object of its own.* Newman was a
thoroughly-trained musician and played admirably on the violin.
See his *Letters and Correspondence*, I., 71, and also *Newman as a
Musician*, in *Month*, LXXIII., 1.

119 : 1.—*The prejudiced man.* This extract is taken from Newman's *Lectures on the Present Position of Catholics in England*,
which were delivered in 1851, before the Brothers of the Oratory
in Birmingham, and published in the same year. The object of
the lectures, as defined by Newman, was not " to prove the
divine origin of Catholicism, but to remove some of the moral
and intellectual impediments which prevent Protestants from
acknowledging it. Protestants cannot be expected to do justice
to a religion whose professors they hate and scorn." During
1851, the feeling against Catholics was exceptionally intense. In
the autumn of the preceding year had occurred what was called
the "Papal aggression." The Pope had raised Dr. Wiseman to
the rank of a Cardinal, and made him the first Catholic Archbishop of Westminster and Primate of England; he had also re-
distributed England into Catholic dioceses, over which he appointed Catholic bishops, whose titles included the names of

English towns. This establishment of a Romish hierarchy in England excited in the breasts of many worthy Protestants the utmost consternation. On November 4, Lord John Russell published with reference to the whole affair, the famous Durham letter, the tone of which is fairly represented by the following extract: " There is an assumption of power in all the documents which have come from Rome, a pretension to supremacy over the realm of England, and a claim to sole and undecided sway, which is inconsistent with the Queen's supremacy, with the rights of our bishops and clergy, and with the spiritual independence of the nation as asserted even in Roman Catholic times." On November 5, the Pope and Cardinal Wiseman were burned in effigy and the anti-Catholic demonstrations were almost riotous. As soon as Parliament met, in February, 1851, a bill was read for the first time by a majority of 332, forbidding Roman Catholic ecclesiastics to assume the new titles the Pope had assigned them, and this bill, though fiercely opposed in its later stages, became law in April, 1851. It was in the midst of this atmosphere of intense feeling that Newman's lectures were delivered in the summer of 1851.

123 : 9.—*And tricks its beams.* The quotation is from near the close of *Lycidas ;* Newman substitutes "its " for "his " to suit the context.

123 : 15.—*Unhurt amid the war of elements.* See Addison's *Cato,* Act V., Scene i. :

> " The soul, secured in her existence, smiles
> At the drawn dagger, and defies its point.
> The stars shall fade away, the sun himself
> Grow dim with age, and nature sink in years ;
> But thou shalt flourish in immortal youth,
> Unhurt amidst the war of elements,
> The wrecks of matter, and the crash of worlds. "

123 : 19.—*Jeffreys . . . . Teodore.* " Only two years have I been [in Birmingham], and each of these two has been signalised by accusations against Catholics, similar, in the disreputableness of their authors, and in the enormity of their falsehood, and in the brilliancy of their success, to the calumnies of Maria Monk. Two years ago it was Jeffreys ; last year it was Teodore.

You recollect how Jeffreys acted his part, how he wept, and prayed, and harangued, and raised a whole population against an innocent company of monks; and how he was convicted of fraud and confessed his guilt, and was sent to prison. You also recollect how an impostor, called Teodore, declaimed such shocking things, and wrote such indecent pamphlets against us, that they cannot have been intended for any other purpose than to afford merriment to the haunts of profligacy and vice; yet he was followed for a time, was admitted into Protestant places of worship, and honoured as a truth-telling oracle, till at length he was plainly detected to be what every one from the first would have seen he really was, were it usual to do the same common justice to Catholics which every Protestant considers his due." Newman's *Present Position of Catholics in England*, Lecture IV.

127 : 20.—*I should be but a fool.* Newman feels himself bound as a Catholic to be almost ludicrously emphatic in his professions of loyalty and patriotism. Cf. the passage in the *Apologia*, ed. 1890, p. xvi.: " I had rather be an Englishman (as in fact I am), than belong to any other race under heaven."

128 : 7.—*Exeter Hall.* The great gathering place of dissenters in London.

128 : 10.—*I will suppose, then, a speaker.* The very effective parody that follows may have been suggested by Whately's *Historic Doubts relative to Napoleon Buonaparte* (1819). This pamphlet parodied Hume's attack on the credibility of miracles by an elaborate proof that Napoleon Buonaparte was a myth. Whately strongly influenced Newman for several years beginning with 1822; " he, emphatically, opened my mind," writes Newman, " and taught me to think and to use my reason." (*Apologia*, ed. 1890, p. 11.) Another similar parody by an Oriel man was Copleston's *Advice to a Young Reviewer, with a Specimen of the Art* (1807). This was a mock-review of " Mr. Milton's 'L'Allegro,'" and imitated very cleverly the tone and manner of the early *Edinburgh Review* articles. Newman doubtless, as an Oriel man, had been well trained in the Academic irony these pieces of writing illustrate.

129 7.—*The Lion and the Man.* Newman's allusion is to a fable with which he had begun his first Lecture. The Lion, who was

being entertained by the Man, was led through the Man's beautiful palace to inspect its works of art. In all the paintings and
sculpture and carvings he found men and lions portrayed, but the
men were always victorious and the lions vanquished; in the
pictures, the lions were always running away from the hunter,
and in the carvings they were wrought into the legs or the arms of
chairs or the brackets of mantels. When at length the Lion was
asked for his opinion of the decorations, he admitted their beauty
and skill, but added that Lions would have fared better, if Lions
had been the artists. So, according to Newman, Catholics would
have fared better in English art and literature during the last
three hundred years, had not Protestants always been the por-
trayers and Catholics the portrayed.

129 : 23.—*The Count began.* The reader will not need to be told
that, in the ironical passage that follows, John Bullism stands for
Roman Catholicism, the British Constitution for the ordinances
and institutions of the Catholic Church, the Kings and Queens
of England for the Popes, and Blackstone's Commentaries for
any esoteric work, on the mysteries of ecclesiasticism. Russians,
of course, correspond to Protestants, and Newman's contention
is that, to any good Catholic, current Protestant ideas about
Roman Catholicism seem precisely as grotesque as the Russian
Count's ravings about the British Constitution seem to an enlightened Englishman. The skill should be noted with which throughout this whole passage Newman plays upon British prejudice.

131 : 12.—*Antichrist.* See I. John iv. 18: "This is that spirit
of Antichrist, whereof ye have heard that it should come." Cf. I.
John ii. 18. The favorite Protestant interpretation of these passages identified Antichrist with the Papacy. Newman's own
imagination "was stained by the effects of this doctrine up to the
year 1843." (*Apologia*, ed. 1890, p. 7.) In the 83d *Tract for the
Times*, however, on the *Patristical Idea of Antichrist* (1838), he
seems to suggest that the sceptical spirit of modern science is the
spirit of Antichrist; see especially *Discussions and Arguments*,
ed. 1888, p, 98. Cf. also the *Protestant Idea of Antichrist* (1840),
Essays Critical and Historical, II., 112-185, where Newman
argues at length against the identification of the Mediæval Church
with Antichrist.

133 : 15.—*You cowardly liar.* Newman means to suggest that a good Catholic's devotion to the Pope is as praiseworthy as a loyal Englishman's love for the Queen ; and that a Catholic's in-dignation when he is forced to listen to stupid slanders against the Pope is as justifiable as the patriotic outburst of wrath in the text.

135 : 3.—*Divine Sovereignty.* The argument is plain. The Russian Count's malice and stupidity are the counterparts of Protestant prejudice. His misinterpretations of the British Con-stitution correspond to Protestants' misconstruction of Catholic doctrines and ceremonial. His grotesque horror over the blas-phemy of innocent legal fictions satirizes Protestant denunciations of the wickedness of the reverential phraseology and elaborate etiquette of the Papal Court. Cf. *Present Position of Catholics,* p. 79, where Newman represents the Prejudiced Man as exclaim-ing, " The Pope not the man of sin! why, it is a fact that the Romanists distinctly maintain that ' the Pope is God, and God is the Pope.' "

136 : 31.—*Bracton,* an English judge, who died in 1268. His *De Legibus et Consuetudinibus Angliæ* is one of the earliest dis-cussions of the law of England.

137 : 13.—*Lord Clarendon.* George Villiers, fourth Earl of Clarendon, was Lord Lieutenant of Ireland, from 1847 to 1852, in Lord John Russell's Government. The *History of the Rebellion* was, of course, the work of Edward Hyde, first Earl of Clarendon (1608–1674), and was published 1702-4. The Constitutions of Clarendon were famous enactments, whereby in 1164 Henry II. greatly limited the power of the Church.

138 : 1.—*The number of the beast.* See *Revelations* xiii. 18 : " Let him that hath understanding count the number of the beast: for it is the number of a man; and his number is six hun-dred three score and six." The beast is often identified with Antichrist.

138 : 19.—*The English Kings.* This rigmarole about the crimes of English monarchs corresponds, in Newman's opinion, to the collections of scandals about the Popes to which Protestants give credence, and on which they base their hostility to the Papacy.

140 : 1.—*One hundred and sixty offences.* The Count is merely a century behind in his knowledge of English law.

142 : 29.—*De minimis, etc.* There is no reason for expounding these legal terms and maxims; their grotesque misconstruction and misapplication is plain enough to produce the effect Newman desires.

145 : 11.—*Sabellians.* The Sabellian heresy originated in the third century. It taught that the Deity is one in substance but triple in manifestation, and that the so-called persons of the Trinity are merely the forms in which an indivisible Monad energizes in the universe. God is immanent in the Universe, and merely reveals himself, becomes vocal in its phenomena. Ultimately, the Infinite Monad shall withdraw again into itself and become silent; then, the visible universe shall be no more. See E. de Pressensé, *Heresy and Christian Doctrine* (translated by Annie Harwood), London, 1873, pp. 146-150.

145 : 12.—*Irvingites.* To the ordinary readers of to-day, Edward Irving (1792-1834) is best known through Carlyle's *Reminiscences;* but between 1827 and 1834 Irving was a very prominent figure in the religious world of London. The most fanatical of his followers became dreamers of dreams, seers of visions, and speakers in unknown tongues. Finally, the manifestations grew so grotesque, that the saner members of the congregation refused to sanction them and compelled Irving and the extremists to withdraw to a new place of worship. The sect of the Irvingites still exists; their chief place of worship is in Gordon Square, London.

146 : 8.—*As during the last year,* i. e., during 1850-51. The allusion is to the so-called " Papal Aggression," the attempt of the Pope to establish a Roman Catholic hierarchy in England. Cf. *Notes*, **119** : 1.

148 : 1.—*Two of my instances.* Newman has been illustrating Protestant ignorance of all things Catholic, and the prejudice of Protestants in commenting on the things of which they are ignorant. He has been bringing home to his readers the intense hostility with which English Protestants approach whatever pertains to the Catholic Church. His first illustration has been a series of misinterpretations which for over a hundred years and by half a dozen famous Protestant historians had been imposed on a few innocent phrases of a certain Catholic writer, St. Eloi or St. Eligius. Ever since the publication of Mosheim's *Ecclesiastical History* (1755), St. Eloi had been represented as teaching that "true Christianity consisted, not in the absence of fraud and injustice, or again, of immorality, hatred, or strife, but in merely coming to church, paying tithes, burning candles, and praying to the saints." But careful examination of St. Eloi's writings showed that the quotation urged against him had been torn from a context that corrected its deficiencies, and imposed on it a totally new meaning.

Newman's second instance was a scandalous charge that had recently been brought against the Catholic Cathedral of St. Gudule, Brussels. A certain enthusiastic Protestant clergyman had asserted at an anti-Catholic meeting, that on one of the doors of the Cathedral at Brussels there was posted a list of all the sins possible to human nature, with the prices for which each would be forgiven. According to Newman, however, this list of sins was merely a price-list of the various kinds of chairs in the Cathedral, on feast-days, and on ordinary days.

Newman's third instance follows in the text.

153 : 4.—*Edwards and Henries.* Cf. *Idea of a University,* ed. 1891, p. 155: "Edward the Second, flying from the field of Bannockburn, is said to have made a vow to the Blessed Virgin to found a religious house in her honour, if he got back in safety. Prompted and aided by his Almoner, he decided on placing this house in the city of Alfred," *i. e.*, in Oxford. This is Newman's account of the foundation in 1326 of Oriel College, Oxford. Newman was elected Fellow of Oriel in 1823. Henry VIII. usually shares with Cardinal Wolsey the honor of founding Christ Church, Oxford, 1525–1532. Henry VI. founded Eton in 1440. William of Wykeham, Bishop of Winchester, founded Winchester College, Winchester, and New College, Oxford, between 1373 and 1393. Wolsey's share in the establishment of Christ Church, Oxford, has already been noted.

Newman is simply emphasizing the fact that he and his Catholic friends have been trained in the great English Colleges and

Universities, and may claim a common share with Protestants in the best traditions of English culture.

154 : 13.—*The Belgian sin-table.* Cf. *Notes*, **148 : 1.**

155 :18.—*Mosheim.* It was in Mosheim's *Ecclesiastical History* that St. Eligius was first calumniated in the fashion of which Newman has complained in the earlier parts of this Lecture.

159 : 12.—*Try to work society.* That religious unbelief tends to the disintegration of society is a familiar argument in favor of established creeds. Roman Catholics are apt to point with a certain complacency to the social disturbances so characteristic of recent years, and to urge that they are the necessary expression of the modern spirit. If you teach that society is founded solely on expediency, and if you encourage every man to judge for himself on questions of politics and morals and religion, can you wonder, they ask, if there result savage attacks of all kinds on the established order?

160 : 1.—*Starting then with the being.* This passage comes from chapter iv. of the *Apologia*, where Newman is describing the position of his mind since 1845. "From the time that I became a Catholic, of course I have no further history of my religious opinions to narrate. . . . I have been in perfect peace and contentment; I never have had one doubt. I was not conscious to myself, on my conversion, of any change, intellectual or moral, wrought in my mind. I was not conscious of firmer faith in the fundamental truths of Revelation, or of more self-command; I had not more fervour; but it was like coming into port after a rough sea; and my happiness on that score remains to this day without interruption." (*Apologia*, ed. 1890, p. 238.) After this preliminary account of the results of his change of faith, Newman goes on to explain why he found little or no difficulty in accepting those additional articles of the Catholic faith which, as an Anglican, he had rejected. He admits that there are difficulties attendant on some of these articles ; but difficulties are connected with every point of religious belief, most of all with the belief in God,—the belief which is nevertheless " borne in upon our minds with most power." " Ten thousand difficulties," however, " do not make one doubt ; " . . . " difficulty and doubt are incommensurate." Newman next considers the doctrines of Transubstantiation and the Trinity, and points out that both have to do with things in themselves, not with phenomena, and hence are truths beyond the control or criticism of science, which deals wholly with phenomena. Finally, he undertakes to prove, in the passage given in the text, that the system of the Catholic Church " is in no sense dishonest, and that therefore the upholders and teachers of that system, as such, have a claim to be acquitted in their own persons of that odious imputation."

160 : 7.—*Unspeakable distress.* The nature of Newman's re-action upon the great spectacle of human folly, wickedness, and woe should be carefully noted. His distress is caused not so much by intense sympathy with a struggling humanity, as by the impingement of a vast mass of disorderly evil upon his con-sciousness, by the resulting shock to his spiritual sensitiveness, and by the threat to the integrity of his spiritual life.

160 : 18.—*This voice.* Newman postulates a God in obedience to the dictates of his moral consciousness. Cf. his *Grammar of Assent*, ed. 1889, p. 417 : "I assume the presence of God in our conscience, and the universal experience, as keen as our experience of bodily pain, of what we call a sense of sin or guilt. This sense of sin, as of something not only evil in itself, but an affront to the good God, is chiefly felt as regards one or other of three viola-tions of His law. He Himself is Sanctity, Truth, and Love ; and the three offences against His Majesty are impurity, inveracity, and cruelty." This consciousness of guilt, Newman urges, is really a consciousness of the violation of a law ; and law implies a Lawgiver. This interpretation of conscience is what Newman has in mind when he speaks of assuming " the presence of God in our conscience." Cf. *Grammar of Assent*, ed. 1889, p. 63, where Newman traces in detail the "induction from particular experi-ences of conscience," by means of which we have "a warrant for concluding the Ubiquitous Presence of One Supreme Master."

160: 22.—*Arguments in proof of a God.* Apart from this testi-mony of the moral consciousness, the so-called demonstrations of the existence of God seem to Newman, on the whole, of doubtful worth. Cf. *Discussions and Arguments*, ed. 1888, p. 299 : "The whole framework of Nature is confessedly a tissue of antecedents and consequents; we may refer all things forwards to design, or backwards on a physical cause. . . . The one hypothesis will solve the phenomena as well as the other. . . . I believe that the study of Nature, when religious feeling is away, leads the mind, rightly or wrongly, to acquiesce in the atheistic theory, as the simplest and easiest." This assertion, although limited by Newman in a foot-note (*Selections*, p. 103), seems nevertheless to express his prevailing opinion. Cf. *Discussions and Arguments*, p. 295: "I would rather be bound to defend the reasonableness of assuming that Christianity is true, than to demonstrate a moral governance from the physical world." In the fourth of his *University Sermons*, p. 70, Newman speaks of the ineffectiveness of the argument from design, and of a possible "unsoundness in the intellectual basis of the argument." Even in the passage in the *Grammar of Assent*, ed. 1889, p. 72, where he summarizes apparently with more respect, the argument based on the prevalence of order in the universe, he admits that the argument tends merely to prove the existence of "mind at least as wide and as enduring in its living action, as the immeasurable ages and spaces of the universe on which that agency has left its traces." Finally, in the *Grammar of Assent*, p. 66, he expressly notes that the argument for a great First Cause is unconvincing. From these passages, then, it is plain that Newman found in the moral consciousness the surest grounds for his belief in God; and that he did not pretend, even on these grounds, to demonstrate the existence of God, but merely postulated it in obedience to an instinct as imperative as that which leads us to postulate the existence of an outside world. Cf. *Grammar of Assent*, p. 63.

167.—*Miracles.* Newman's various pleas for miracles have exposed him to severe attacks on the score of insincerity, credulousness, and illogicalness. Newman published two Essays on Miracles, the first, in 1826, the second, in 1842, as a preface to a new translation of Fleury's *Ecclesiastical History*. For the relations between the two *Essays* see the *Apologia*, ed. 1890, pp. 20–23, and Note B, at the end of the *Apologia*, on Ecclesiastical Miracles. Newman's ideas of the comparative credibility of Scripture miracles and of ecclesiastical miracles will be found still fur-

ther expounded in the correspondence with the Bishop of Nor-
wich, appended to the *Present Position of Catholics*. For criticisms
of Newman's treatment of miracles see E. A. Abbott's *Philomythus*; Kingsley's *What, then, does Dr. Newman mean?*; Prof.
Huxley's article in the *Nineteenth Century*, XXV., p. 948; and
Leslie Stephen's *Newman's Theory of Belief* in *An Agnostic's
Apology*. A vigorous reply to Mr. Abbott may be found in Wilfrid Ward's *Philalethes* in *Witnesses to the Unseen and Other
Essays*. Cf. R. H. Hutton, *Cardinal Newman*, chap. v.

169 : 21.—*Breviary.* The daily service-book of Catholic priests;
to be distinguished from the Missal which contains the service
of the Mass. Beside homilies, prayers and psalms, appropriate
for every saint's day, the Breviary contains many legends of the
lives and the deaths of the saints.

174 : 6.—*Holy Coat.* The Empress Helena, Mother of Con-
stantine the Great, is said to have presented to the Cathedral of
Trèves, which she founded, the original seamless coat of Jesus.
The relic was exhibited in 1844 to vast crowds of pilgrims from
all parts of the world; the next exhibition, that of 1891, was also
successful. Argenteuil in France possesses a rival Holy Coat,
which was last exhibited in the spring of 1894.

176 : 2.—*Froissart.* Jean Froissart (1337–1410), whose *Chro-
nique* deals with the history of France during the last seventy-five
years of the fourteenth century.

176 : 2.—*Sully.* The famous minister of Henry the Fourth of
France. His *Memoires* recite the events of his administration
under that monarch.

176 : 3.—*Doddington.* The allusion is to George Bubb Doding-
ton, Lord Melcombe (1691–1762), whose great wealth, shameless
intrigues for office, ostentatious bad taste, and occasional wit
have combined to preserve his memory. Thomson dedicated to
him his *Summer*, and Hogarth in the *Analysis of Beauty* has
immortalized his wig. His *Diary* (1784) contains much amusing
gossip about Court life under George II.

176 : 4.—*Sharon Turner* (1768–1847). He is best remembered
by his *History of the Anglo-Saxons*, published 1799–1805. He also
wrote a somewhat portentous *Sacred History of the World as displayed in the Creation and subsequent Events*.

177 : 1.—*St. Januarius.* See Edward Kinesman, *Lives of the Saints*, p. 742: " The most stupendous miracle is that seen to this day in the Church of St. Gennaro, in Naples, viz., the blood of St. Januarius, kept in two glass vials. When either vial, held in the right hand, is presented to the head of the saint, the congealed blood first melts, and then goes on apparently to boil." The miracle is said to be wrought in the sight of large concourses of people, thrice yearly, on Sept. 19, Dec. 20, and about the first of May. See Alban Butler, *Lives of the Saints*, ed. 1814, IX., 251. Murat, when King of Naples, is said to have commanded the Bishop, who was hostile to the French, to work the miracle on pain of seeing his church cannonaded out of exist-ence; after many protests on the part of the prelate, the miracle took place.

177 : 4.—*Lombard Crown.* The famous iron crown of Italy, one of the four crowns with which the Emperors of the Holy Roman Empire were crowned. See Bryce's *Holy Roman Empire*, chap. xii. The crown is of gold and is decorated with many precious stones; it gets its name from a fillet or narrow band of iron, running round the inside, and said to have been made of a nail used in the Crucifixion. With this crown Napoleon crowned himself at Milan in 1805; the last two Austrian Emperors have also been crowned with it.

178.—*Gurta and Juba.* The last two selections are given to illustrate Newman's portrayal of the supernatural. If his con-ception of life and of religion is to be understood, the intensity of his belief in the spiritual world must be thoroughly apprehended. Cf. *Notes* **85 : 2.** Common life is for Newman enveloped at every point in a circumambient atmosphere of mystery, which at any mo-ment may part for the revelation of supernatural forces. It is diffi- cult to realize the intensity of this conviction of Newman's when we read those of his discussions in which he grasps comprehensively the phenomena of the actual world,—facts and ideas,—and arranges them unerringly in their proper relations in due subordi-nation to their determining principles. In such passages he seems anything but a mystic, and his clear apprehension of facts and rigorous application of principles seem quite out of keeping with a mystical habit of mind. Yet the orderly world of science that Newman's logic gives him, is only a part of his truth. The system of nature is one system; the system of the supernatural is another system, even more real than the natural, and infinitely more important in its issues for good and for ill. At any moment, the white light of infinite bliss may rain down on our common life, or our ordinary, every-day paths may suddenly open beneath our feet into black gulfs of infinite woe.

178 : 1.—*In the bosom of the woods.* Newman's *Callista, a Tale of the Third Century*, published in 1855, was written to illustrate the relations between Christians and heathen during the earliest days of the Church. Callista is a Greek maiden, a modeller of images, who, losing her first *naïve* delight in life and her sense of untroubled youth, grows more and more restless and distraught, until one day a priest of the new religion puts before her in simple words the story of God's love to man and his promises of eternal life to those who do his will. The world-weary girl finds here an escape from her despair, becomes a Christian, and almost at once proves her sincerity by joyfully welcoming martyrdom. Two other characters in the story are the youths Agellius and Juba, the former a Christian, the latter a scoffer at all religions. Agellius is in love with Callista but never wins more than a word from her. He is faithful, however, in his remote adoration, and is the leader of the small band of Christians, who, after her martyrdom, bear off her body for Christian burial. His step-mother, and Juba's, is Gurta, a Numidian woman, who has the reputation of a sorceress. The scene in the chapters given in the text is laid at her hut, and the time is just after the mob of the neighboring city have made a fierce onslaught on Christians. In the tumult Callista has been captured and imprisoned on suspicion.

193 : 1.—*O wisdom of the world.* Callista is in prison. She has been baptised by a Christian priest, and has received the Eucharist. An imperial rescript has just arrived commanding her torture and execution on the morrow.

August, 1898.

English Readings for Students.

English masterpieces in editions at once competently edited and inexpensive. The aim will be to fill vacancies now existing because of subject, treatment, or price. Prices given below are NET, *postage eight per cent. additional.* 16mo. *Cloth.*

Arnold (Matthew): Prose Selections.
Edited by Lewis E. Gates, Asst. Professor in Harvard. xci + 348 pp. 90c.

Includes The Function of Criticism, First Lecture on Translating Homer, Literature and Science, Culture and Anarchy, Sweetness and Light, Compulsory Education, "Life a Dream," Emerson, and twelve shorter selections, including America.

Bliss Perry, *Professor in Princeton :—*' The selections seem to me most happy, and the introduction is even better if possible than his introduction to the Newman volume. Indeed I have read no criticism of Arnold's prose which appears to me as luminous and just, and expressed with such literary charm."

Browning: Selected Lyrical and Dramatic Poems.
With the essay on Browning from E. C. Stedman's "Victorian Poets." Edited by Edward T. Mason. 275 pp. 60c.

Burke: Selections.
Edited by Bliss Perry. Professor in Princeton. xxvi + 298 pp. 60c.

Contents. Speeches at Arrival at Bristol, at Conclusion of the Poll ; Letters to the Marquis of Rockingham, to the Sheriffs of Bristol, and to a Noble Lord; Address to the King ; Selections from The Sublime and the Beautiful, from Thoughts on the Present Discontents, from Speech on the Nabob of Arcot's Debts, from Impeachment of Hastings (2), from Reflections on the Revolution in France (7, including Fiat Money).

Edward Dowden, *the Author and Critic:—*"They seem to me admirably chosen and arranged, and the introduction brings various aspects of Burke's mind truly and vividly before the reader."

Coleridge : Prose Extracts.
Edited by Henry A. Beers, Professor in Yale College. xix+148 pp. 50c.

The selections, varying in length from a paragraph to ten or twenty pages, are mainly from *Table Talk* and *Biographia Literaria*, but also from *Notes on Shakespeare* etc.

De Quincey: Joan of Arc; The Mail Coach.

Edited by James Morgan Hart, Professor in Cornell University.
xxvi + 138 pp. 50c.

The introduction sketches De Quincey's life and style.
Allusions and other difficult points are explained in the notes.
This volume and the Essays on *Boswell's Johnson* (see under
Macaulay) are used at Cornell for elementary rhetorical study.

Dryden: Essays on the Drama.

Edited by Wm. Strunk, Jr., Instructor in Cornell University. xxxviii +
180 pp. 50c.

This volume contains *The Essay of Dramatic Poesy* and,
among the critical prefaces, *Of Heroic Plays* and *The Grounds
of Criticism in Tragedy.* These are not only excellent specimens of classical English, but also have a high reputation for
the value of their literary opinions. The introduction, besides
treating of Dryden's life and prose style, sets forth clearly
how he used the theories of the drama which he found in
Aristotle, Horace, and Corneille.

Ford: The Broken Heart.

A Spartan Tragedy in verse. Edited by Clinton Scollard, Professor
in Hamilton College. xvi + 132 pp. 50c. (Buckram, 70c.)

A play notable for its repressed emotion and psychological
interest. Charles Lamb wrote: " I do not know where to find
in any play a catastrophe so grand, so solemn, and so surprising as this" [of *The Broken Heart*].

Johnson: Rasselas.

Edited by Oliver Farrar Emerson, Professor in Adelbert College.
lvi + 179 pp. 50c. (Buckram, 70c.)

The introduction treats of Johnson's style, the circumstances
under which *Rasselas* was written, and its place in the history
of fiction. The notes explain allusions and trace the sources
of some of Johnson's materials.

Lyly: Endimion.

Edited by George P. Baker, Professor in Harvard College. cxcvi + 109
pp. 85c. (Buckram, $1.25.)
The Academy, London :—" It is refreshing to come upon such a piece
of sterling work; . . . the most complete and satisfactory account of
Lyly that has yet appeared.

Macaulay and Carlyle: Essays on Samuel Johnson.

Edited by WILLIAM STRUNK, Jr., Instructor in Cornell University. xl+191 pp. 50c.

These two essays present a constant contrast in intellectual and moral methods of criticism, and offer an excellent introduction to the study of the literary history of Johnson's times.

Marlowe: Edward II. With the best passages from TAMBURLAINE THE GREAT, and from his POEMS

Edited by the late EDWARD T. McLAUGHLIN, Professor in Yale College. xxi+180 pp. 50c. (Buckram, 70c.)

Edward II., besides being Marlowe's most important play, is of great interest in connection with Shakespere. The earlier chronicle drama was in Shakespere's memory as he was writing *Richard II.*, as various passages prove, and a comparison of the two plays (sketched in the introduction) affords basis for a study in the development of the Elizabethan drama.

Newman : Prose Selections.

Edited by LEWIS E. GATES, Professor in Harvard College. lxii+228 pp. 50c. (Buckram, 90c.)

The selections lead the reader through some of the more picturesque and concrete passages of Newman's prose, to his impeachment of the liberal and irreligious tendencies of the age, his insistence on the powerlessness of science to make men moral, his defense of supernaturalism, his ridicule of English prejudice against Catholics, his statement of the Catholic position, and finally to two powerful imaginative pictures of supernatural interferences in the natural world-order.

Tennyson: The Princess.

Edited by L. A. SHERMAN, Professor in the University of Nebraska. [*In preparation.*]

Postage 8 per cent. additional.

HENRY HOLT & CO., 29 W. 23d St., New York.

Specimens of Prose Composition.

16*mo.* *Cloth.* *Per volume*, 50*c.*, NET.

Prose Narration.

Edited by WILLIAM T. BREWSTER, Tutor in Columbia College. xxxviii +209 pp.

Includes Selections from Scott, Thackeray, Hawthorne, Jane Austen, George Eliot, Stevenson, and Henry James. Part I. Elements of Narrative—Plot, Character, Setting, and Purpose. Part II. Combination of the Elements of Narration. Part III. Various Kinds of Narrative. Part IV. Technique of Good Narrative.

Prose Description.

Edited by CHARLES SEARS BALDWIN, Ph.D., Instructor in Yale College. xlviii+145 pp.

Includes: Ancient Athens (Newman) ; Paris Before the Second Empire (du Maurier); Bees (Burroughs); Byzantium (Gibbon); Geneva (Ruskin); The Storming of the Bastille (Carlyle); La Gioconda, etc. (Pater); Blois (Henry James); Spring in a Side Street (Brander Matthews); A Night Among the Pines, etc. (Stevenson).

Exposition.

Edited by HAMMOND LAMONT, Professor in Brown University. xxiv+ 180 pp.

Includes : Development of a Brief ; G. C. V. Holmes on the Steam-engine; Huxley on the Physical Basis of Life; Bryce on the U. S. Constitution ; "The Nation" on the Unemployed; Wm. Archer on Albery's "Apple Blossoms"; Matthew Arnold on Wordsworth ; etc.

Argumentation. MODERN.

Edited by GEORGE P. BAKER, Professor in Harvard College. 16mo. 186 pp.

Lord Chatham's speech on the withdrawal of troops from Boston, Lord Mansfield's argument in the Evans case, the first letter of Junius, the first of Huxley's American addresses on evolution, Erskine's defence of Lord George Gordon, an address by Beecher in Liverpool during the cotton riots, and specimen brief.

Postage 8 per cent. additional.

HENRY HOLT & CO., 29 W. 23d St., New York.

.

www.ingramcontent.com/pod-product-compliance
Lightning Source LLC
Chambersburg PA
CBHW020506270326
41926CB00008B/754